BAKER LIBRARY
MPL 4602
CASTLE AFB, CA 95342

959.704

D0607524

THE CERTAIN
TRUMPET

Other Books by Douglas Kinnard

The Secretary of Defense

The War Managers

President Eisenhower and Strategy Management:
A Study in Defense Politics

Ike 1890–1990: A Pictorial History

THE CERTAIN TRUMPET

MAXWELL TAYLOR & THE
AMERICAN EXPERIENCE IN VIETNAM

DOUGLAS KINNARD

WEST HILLS COLLEGE
LEMOORE LIBRARY/LRC

BRASSEY'S (US), Inc.
A Division of Maxwell Macmillan, Inc.

Washington • New York • London • Oxford • Beijing
Frankfurt • São Paulo • Sydney • Tokyo • Toronto

Copyright © 1991 by Brassey's (US), Inc.

All rights reserved. No part of this book may be reproduced, stored in a retrieval system, or transmitted in any form or by any means—electronic, electrostatic, magnetic tape, mechanical, photocopying, recording, or otherwise—without permission in writing from the publisher.

Brassey's (US), Inc.

Editorial Offices	*Order Department*
Brassey's (US), Inc.	Brassey's Book Orders
8000 Westpark Drive	% Macmillan Publishing Co.
First Floor	Front and Brown Streets
McLean, Virginia 22102	Riverside, New Jersey 08075

Brassey's (US), Inc., books are available at special discounts for bulk purchases for sales promotions, premiums, fund-raising, or educational use through the Special Sales Director, Macmillan Publishing Company, 866 Third Avenue, New York, New York 10022.

Library of Congress Cataloging-in-Publication Data

Kinnard, Douglas.
    The certain trumpet : Maxwell Taylor & the American experience in
Vietnam / Douglas Kinnard.
        p.   cm.
    Includes bibliographical references and index.
    ISBN 0-08-040581-9 (hardcover)
    1. Vietnamese Conflict, 1961–1975—United States.   2. Taylor,
Maxwell D. (Maxwell Davenport) 1901–1987.   I. Title.
    DS558.K56   1991
    959.704'3373—dc20   90-21405
                                                                CIP

British Library Cataloguing in Publication Data
Kinnard, Douglas
The certain trumpet : Maxwell Taylor & the American
experience in Vietnam.
1. Vietnamese wars. Policies of United States government.
Decision making 1961–1975
I. Title
959.70432

ISBN 0-08-040581-9

10   9   8   7   6   5   4   3   2   1

PUBLISHED IN THE UNITED STATES OF AMERICA

"PROPERTY U.S. AIR FORCE"
"BAKER LIBRARY"
"CASTLE AFB"

To Those Whose Names
Are Inscribed on the Wall

An AUSA Book

The Association of the United States Army, or AUSA, was founded in 1950 as a not-for-profit organization dedicated to education concerning the role of the U.S. Army, to providing material for military professional development, and to the promotion of proper recognition and appreciation of the profession of arms. Its constituencies include those who serve in the Army today, including Army National Guard, Army Reserve, and Army civilians, and the retirees and veterans who have served in the past, and all their families. A large number of public-minded citizens and business leaders are also an important constituency. The Association seeks to educate the public, elected and appointed officials, and leaders of defense industry on crucial issues involving the adequacy of our national defense, particularly those issues affecting land warfare.

In 1988 AUSA established within its existing organization a new entity known as the Institute of Land Warfare. Its purpose is to extend the educational work of AUSA by sponsoring scholarly publications, to include books, monographs, and essays on key defense issues, as well as workshops and symposia. Among the volumes chosen for designation as "An AUSA Institute of Land Warfare Book" are both new texts and reprints of titles of enduring value that are no longer in print. Topics include history, policy issues, strategy, and tactics. Publication as an AUSA book does not indicate that the Association of the United States Army and the publisher agree with everything in the book, but does suggest that the AUSA and the publisher believe this book will stimulate the thinking of AUSA members and others concerned about important issues.

Contents

PART II

VIETNAM

Preface

This book concerns the American experience in Vietnam in the 1960s, focusing on one of its key figures: Maxwell Davenport Taylor. As a four-star general he served as Army chief of staff, then in John Kennedy's administration, and ultimately in the Pentagon as chairman of the Joint Chiefs of Staff (JCS). Subsequently, as a civilian, he was in Saigon as ambassador to Vietnam; finally, he came back to the White House as a special consultant to President Lyndon Johnson.

Because soldier-statesman Taylor was obviously in the very top echelon of Vietnam movers and shakers, one may well ask what role this one individual actually played; what was his real influence on Vietnam policy decisions made by Presidents Kennedy and Johnson? This is the basic question confronted in this book. Perhaps it is unanswerable, but that is something readers must judge for themselves.

In doing the research for the book I was fortunate to have not only General Taylor's cooperation but also access to his personal papers in the National Defense University Library, comprising some thirty-three linear feet. Besides conducting twelve interviews with Taylor himself, I interviewed about forty others, including George Ball, McGeorge Bundy, William P. Bundy, U. Alexis Johnson, Ethel Kennedy, Robert McNamara, Walt Rostow, and Paul Warnke. The book also contains excerpts from official documents of White House meetings, as well as letters from principals. I have further benefitted from the writings of those who have examined the events and personalities of the Vietnam War; they are cited in the notes and sources. I myself have studied and written about this war, in which I was a participant.

Above all—which is perhaps what makes this book unique— Maxwell Taylor was a real person to me. As a young officer I worked for him when he was Army chief of staff during those difficult years for the Army in the Eisenhower administration. Once, in proposing a toast at a dinner he gave for me many years later, he said, "I don't know whether Doug is a wolf in sheep's clothing or a sheep in wolf's clothing." (One could say the same for Taylor!)

Readers should realize that this book is not a biography of Taylor. Rather, he is used as a prism to tell the story of high-level decision making in the 1960s and its consequences in Vietnam. The book is addressed to the general audience interested in that war as well as to students of recent American history.

To understand Taylor's role in the Vietnam period, one needs first to look briefly at the forces shaping the man and his career. This is the function of the Prologue and Chapter 1. These formative experiences were primarily the interwar Army of the 1920s and 1930s; the heady days of World War II, when he served as an Airborne general; and his tour as commander of the Eighth Army in the Korean War. Then came the frustrating but critical years as Army chief of staff.

Chapter 2 contains the gathering clouds of Vietnam over "Camelot," the Kennedy White House, where Maxwell Taylor was installed in an advisory job created especially for him. Then, beginning with necessary Indochina background, the book is given entirely to the Vietnam era and its aftermath, all of which is interwoven with Taylor's involvement.

Vietnam weighed heavily on Taylor, even in his reminiscences. In his 1972 autobiography, *Swords and Plowshares*, he devotes some fourteen of the thirty-five chapters wholly or partially to that subject. His perspective is set forth in the introduction: "I have necessarily been concerned during most of my career with the use of military power as a means to assure our national security and to advance our national interests." This is shaped by the need to examine the "relationships between military and nonmilitary forms of power and between the requirements of national security and those of the domestic welfare."

His own conclusions about the Vietnam failure relate less to the decision-making process itself and more to the impact of certain decisions on the outcome. Specifically, three matters are central to his analysis of our errors in the Vietnam involvement:

- the Kennedy administration's complicity in the overthrow of Diem,
- the lack of conviction with which the United States carried out the bombing of North Vietnam, and
- the absence of a formal declaration of war with which to unite the American people.

That Taylor was one of the key advisers to Presidents Kennedy and Johnson on Vietnam is not in doubt. General Earle Wheeler put it well for the Kennedy period (and the same was true in the Johnson administration): "Taylor had an influence with President Kennedy that went far beyond military matters; [Kennedy] regarded him as a man of broad knowledge, quick intelligence, and sound judgment."

The real question is what, in fact, was Taylor's influence on presidential decision making in the 1960s concerning Vietnam as military representative of the president (1961–62), chairman of the JCS (1962–64), ambassador to Vietnam (1964–65), and presidential consultant on Vietnam (1965–68)?

Others have commented on this question; for example, Jerome Slater, writing in 1977, had this to say:

> The Pentagon Papers, memoirs of government officials, and scholarly studies have established that at least since 1961 the recommendations of the military leadership, most definitely including Maxwell Taylor, the very model of the modern soldier-statesman, were almost invariably on the side of military commitment and escalation.

The most important critique of Taylor regarding Vietnam comes from Bernard Brodie in Brodie's final work, *War and Politics,* in 1973.

> General Maxwell Taylor, Chairman of the Joint Chiefs until 1964, Ambassador to Saigon during the critical period when President Johnson was making his crucial decisions to shift to a combat role, and thereafter informal advisor to the latter and to his successor bears as much responsibility as any other military man for the sad story of our commitment to Vietnam. (p. 191)
>
> Some people are more inflexible than others, regardless of

their years, and those who held important policy-making
posts in the Eisenhower, Kennedy, and Johnson Administra-
tions were all children of the cold war. Some of them, especially Rusk and Taylor, . . . were also extraordinarily rigid.
(p. 120)

The President was of course primarily responsible. But he
could have been helped, if not by the commander in Saigon
then at least by the Joint Chiefs at home. . . . Generals Maxwell Taylor and Earle Wheeler did everything in their power
to induce the President not to moderate the intensity of the
American participation in the war. . . . A wiser President
would have ignored their advice; more strategically minded
generals would have given better advice. (p. 440)

Some readers may agree with Slater's and Brodie's conclusions
about Taylor, the one person who served longer and in more diverse
ways than any other in the civil-military interface of the Vietnam
period. Other readers, especially as they recall the climate in which
cold warriors operated, may come up with different insights. What is
important—and is an underlying purpose of this book—is that whatever wisdom is gained by considering this part of our past should
apply in the future to other times and places. Never again another
Vietnam.

This book has been under preparation for such a long period and
in so many geographical locations that listing all who provided help
and support would be difficult and would involve inadvertent and
inevitable omissions. There are some, however, who must be acknowledged.

In Vermont there were Carl Blumberg, a former student at the
University of Vermont, and Mary Mitiguy, now a free-lance editor.
In Washington there was the late George Stansfield of the National
Defense University, who organized the Taylor papers deposited there
and helped me find my way through them. At West Point was my
former Princeton colleague, Paul L. Miles, Jr., and, whenever I needed
his help, Bruce Palmer, Jr., soldier, scholar, and author.

The book was completed at the Naval War College, Newport,
Rhode Island, where I was fortunate enough to spend a year as a
Secretary of the Navy Senior Research Fellow through the efforts of
my colleague Professor Alvin Bernstein, then chairman of the Strat-

egy Department at the college. Also at Newport, Barbara Atkins provided invaluable support throughout in the preparation of the manuscript. Finally, as in the past, major support came from my wife, Wade Tyree, who took time from her own research and writing to lend a hand whenever and wherever it was needed.

Prologue: The Soldier

THE WORLD OUTSIDE DAVENPORT'S FARM

Milton Davenport had only one arm. He still farmed on the spread he kept with his wife, Mary Eliza, between Keytesville and Dalton, Missouri, sixty or so miles east-northeast of Kansas City. A four-year veteran of the Civil War, he rose to sergeant's rank in the Confederate Cavalry, fighting in Missouri and Arkansas under Generals Price and Shelby. But after his horse died, Davenport explained to his grandson, he fought the rest of the war on foot, in the infantry.

The grandson visited the Davenports' farm during school vacations. Grandfather and young Max worked in the fields during daylight hours, and after supper they sometimes listened to the phonograph. Usually, however, Davenport regaled the boy with stories from the war. "He did not glorify the war or try to make it appear other than what it had been—a bitter, exhausting ordeal for soldiers and civilians alike—but his eyes would light up as he told about the 'boys' in action," the grandson wrote years later.

> Since becoming a veteran myself and recognizing privately the loss of historical accuracy and the gain in dramatic quality of my own stories with the passage of time, I sometimes wonder now whether Grandpa's "boys" were quite the heroes he depicted. But his tales had a gripping quality in describing how shared hardships bind men together in the camaraderie of arms.[1]

Varnished or not, the stories excited him. By his own later account, the future architect of U.S. policy in Vietnam sketched his earliest

1

designs for a military career with an ambitious youthful imagination fired by Milton Davenport's Civil War yarns. He was hooked. He eagerly awaited summer vacations when he could rejoin Grandpa and hear more stories: "I thought Grandpa Davenport was about the greatest man in the world."

Davenport told the boy about West Point, where Robert E. Lee and Stonewall Jackson, the grandfather's heroes, learned their earliest lessons, applied in the war with Mexico and the Civil War, and the grandson resolved to someday study there himself. Now he read more history, too. By sixth grade, he listed his future profession: major general. "I had the good fortune of knowing what I wanted to be—a great advantage to any young man," he wrote later. The grandfather, too, gave the boy his first shaky lessons in firearms with "a long-barrel, single-shot weapon called a horse pistol, because its length and weight mandated that it be rested on a horse's neck to be fired." Perhaps the boy did not know the truth about Davenport's injury—a sawmill accident. Perhaps he did know. He chose soldiering anyway.

Maxwell Davenport Taylor was born in nearby Keytesville on August 26, 1901. He was reared and schooled in Kansas City. Despite Davenport's influence on his career choice early in life, Taylor gave due credit to his parents. John E. M. Taylor, the father, had been admitted to the bar after reading law for several years. A member of a Kansas City firm, John Taylor strained to develop a legal practice sufficient to support his family: his wife, Pearle; his widowed mother; and his only child. Maxwell Taylor stressed that prosperity eluded "easy-going, cigar-smoking" John Taylor, but the attorney still hoped his son would follow in his professional footsteps. It was not to be; the law was only the second choice of career for young Maxwell Taylor.

Pearle Davenport Taylor's maternal influence was substantial. A modern family view says:

> To say that she was a doting mother is an understatement. Her possessiveness was the subject of considerable joking within the family, but the extent of her influence on her only child is not easy to assess. She was certainly instrumental in developing his interest in reading, an interest that he carried through life.

In the same account, Pearle Taylor was "strict, humorless."[2]

His mother enrolled the boy at Likens Grammar School in Kansas City, and he remained in the city school system until high school graduation. Because both his mother and Grandmother Taylor had taught him the alphabet and read to him before he entered kindergarten, he was already an advanced reader.

An early work of the youthful Maxwell Taylor, an essay (or perhaps a translation from Latin) on the Carthaginian general Hannibal, survives, written in a highly stylized Palmer-method script. It is an example of his high school academic background, overwhelmingly weighted toward the classical languages, history, English, and Spanish. After high school graduation, his zeal undiminished to attend West Point, he enrolled in 1917 at a junior college, Kansas City Polytechnic Institute, to bone up on mathematics and physics, which were ignored in high school, and to improve his Spanish. He also worked as a gas company meter reader in Kansas City's zone of ill repute. Then came 1917, with the United States embroiled in World War I. Taylor was disgusted with himself—many of his contemporaries had enlisted or were drafted into the military, and here he was, a college student living at home! He lied about his age and obtained a draft card. "In that war," he wrote, "the possession of a draft card was the next best thing to wearing a uniform if a young man wanted the respect of his associates." Taylor would see that attitude reversed in his lifetime.

John Taylor reportedly was not unhappy with his only child's stretching the truth, but immediately sought his son's appointment to West Point. Their congressman, William P. Borland, had vacancies that year for both service academies, so the elder Taylor secured a place for his boy at both the West Point and Annapolis competitive examinations. The fib about his age was pragmatically recycled: Maxwell Taylor's West Point application lists his date of birth as August 26, 1900, not 1901 as it actually was. It is no typo, no misstruck typewriter key. The entire application was filled out in longhand, neat Palmer-method script.

The separate examinations for Annapolis and West Point differed in one respect only: the Army exam tested historical knowledge, whereas the Naval Academy test included a section on geography—which Taylor failed. That settled the matter and sent Maxwell Taylor toward his longtime goal: West Point.

At that time the U.S. Military Academy (USMA) had already cut a cadet's normal four-year program to less than one. The Army anticipated a demand for more infantry shavetails for the planned 1919 victory drive in Europe; therefore, West Point had to increase production. When Taylor entered, early in November 1918, he expected his graduation and commissioning the following June. But nine days after his arrival, the Central Powers surrendered. "Fortunately for all parties, as we say at class reunions, the Kaiser and Hindenburg heard of this new threat to the armies of the Fatherland forming on the banks of the Hudson and decided to accept an armistice on November 11."[3] He was now a member of a regular four-year class, the class of 1922.

The plebes' uniforms of the period at "Beast Barracks"—West Point basic training—were not the traditional dress gray; as an accommodation to wartime, they were ordinary enlisted men's khakis, distinguished only by a wide yellow ribbon circling the crown of the campaign hat. The yellow hatband occasioned a nickname, the "Oriole" class, for Taylor and his fellow sufferers. Recent USMA graduates, newly commissioned second lieutenants, trained the newcomers, who were subjected to endless drills on the parade ground. Taylor spent November 11 marching with his class; nobody announced the war's end for a few days. Then a barracks policeman (janitor) passed on the news.

Taylor wrote later that he had arrived well prepared for the rigid academics, the equivalent, more or less, of general engineering study. Few course options existed; only advanced courses were available to those cadets already grounded in the subject. Taylor kept up his Spanish with an instructor named Matthew Ridgway and added French to his linguistic skills. Taylor remembered that he "had ample leisure" to sequester himself in the "small but well-stocked" cadet library and "continued to indulge myself in reading widely, if not deeply, in the fields of philosophy and military history."

But Taylor would witness a change in both the manner of living and the history of "The Point." In 1919, when Taylor had finished his plebe year, the Army's youngest general, Douglas MacArthur, thirty-nine, became West Point's superintendent. The cadets were already familiar with the MacArthur legend, cultivated as it was by its subject. Now he arrived at West Point with clear ideas about the changes he wanted.

MacArthur felt (as many observers and veterans of the process before and after him did) that the plebe system's ideal—"to lead, first follow"—was often subverted by the outright violence of hazing. It made many upperclassmen, those primary progenitors of West Point attitudes and responsibilities, into outright martinets. Thus, the friction of injury and resentment in plebes created by ambitious, overzealous student officers severely undermined the personal growth of later leaders. "Improvisation," not dogma, "will be the watchword," MacArthur's first annual report stressed. Flexibility was to replace rigidity. MacArthur wanted character, not characters.

The superintendent ordained that the motif of flexibility continue as much outside the classroom as within. He began an intramural athletic program with the slogan of "every cadet an athlete." Taylor confessed he was unexcited by varsity sports, save for tennis; he played on and later captained the academy tennis team. MacArthur believed (and Taylor later agreed) that cadets should learn and appreciate other sports (such as riding and polo, golf, and tennis) to continue throughout their active lives. Physical conditioning was essential for any professional soldier, at no matter what stage in his career.

For some time as a cadet, Maxwell Taylor smoked, relishing the joy of covert cigarettes. Smoking had been prohibited, but many violated the sanction routinely. Knowing that fact, MacArthur ordered it allowed only in cadet rooms, never outside barracks. For Cadet Taylor, the repeal of the prohibition meant the loss of the heady sensations of secret pleasures. He never smoked again.

Members of the class of 1922 got their first furlough on December 23, 1919. Their yearbook tells that they regrouped in New York on December 31, for a "Christmas leave banquet," where, "just to show Congress that we were behind them to a man, we endeavored to enforce the Volstead Act by making New York dry."[4] Patriotism and loyalty take many forms. Whether Max Taylor joined the party in such typical undergraduate doings of the day is uncertain. During his much later first return to West Point as an instructor, Taylor showed some disdain for the Volstead Act. He and his wife occupied an apartment above a garage in neighboring Highland Falls. There, in those Prohibition days, Taylor and another instructor, Albert Gruenther, became skilled at a recipe for bathtub gin.

"He is without a doubt one of the most learned scholars of the class," the 1922 USMA yearbook, *Howitzer,* declared of Max Taylor.

Does he give [any] outward sign of the workings of such a great mind, you ask? Rather. He can't keep his eyelids still when under any mental strain. (Real or assumed) Those eyebrows are as necessary [to] "Max" while explaining some intricate subject or while reciting in the section room, as hands [are to a] salesman of second-hand clothes.

His salesmanship thus extolled, backhandedly, Taylor was complimented for other contributions during his cadet career.

> The literary abilities of this youthful prodigy were brought to light in the spring of our yearling year when he filled the position of editor-in-chief of the Furlo Book very creditably. Since then his services as a writer have been in great demand for all our publications.

His accomplishments at tennis were also noted.[5]

Taylor's demerit sheet listed only six acquired "to August 27, 1921," but he transgressed other times in the eyes of his tactical officer, Maj. Simon Bolivar Buckner. The last incident, recounted by Taylor, happened shortly before his June 1922 graduation. One day he walked arm in arm with Lydia ("Diddy") Happer, a young Washingtonian he was seeing frequently, out of the shade of a "barrack's sally-port . . . into the sunlight."

Shortly after, the couple was interrupted by a cadet guard officer who told Taylor that Major Buckner required his presence. Taylor was by then well aware of the severity of his offense, a clear violation of the sanction against "showing affection to a young lady in public." True to Buckner's knife-edge reputation, the tactical officer proceeded to chew out the cadet. Considering the seriousness of the infraction, should Taylor be permitted to graduate in two days? Taylor hoped so "in none too confident tones." For the next forty-eight hours Taylor lived insecurely until June 13, when Douglas MacArthur handed him his diploma with a "Well done, Mr. Taylor." The affectionate incident with Lydia Happer was never entered on the demerit sheet, although Taylor himself told the story in his autobiography. (Simon Bolivar Buckner himself rose to lieutenant general in World War II before he was killed as Tenth Army commander by the Japanese defenders of Okinawa.)

STUDENT AND TEACHER

The Army Corps of Engineers usually had first pick and invariably took the cream off the top new West Point graduates. For 2d Lt. Maxwell D. Taylor, who had graduated fourth in a class of 102, this situation was ideal. For two reasons his first choice was the Engineers. First, his grandfather's hero, Robert E. Lee, had also become his own, and Lee had started his Army career in the Engineers after West Point. Second, Lydia Happer, his partner in the promenade that nearly cost him his graduation, lived in Washington, D.C.; his training as a student engineer officer would be at nearby Camp Humphreys, Virginia (now Fort Belvoir). However, Taylor would be unexcited by the reality of peacetime military engineering, which was to fall far short of his immature ideal of it.

After completing the engineering course, he was posted to the 3d Engineers at Schofield Barracks, Hawaii. In 1924, when Lieutenant Taylor was supervising the blasting out of a tunnel, there was no flagman's warning of an explosion. As a result, he suffered a partial loss of hearing for the rest of his life.[6]

Granted leave from Schofield in early 1925, he rushed back to Washington—as fast as ships and trains would take him—to marry Lydia Happer. He had left Engineer School with conditional approval from her father, a Washington Realtor, if he would first build up a bank account. This he did through scrimping for two years. The couple sailed on Army transport to Hawaii, where the bridegroom went to work as "Assistant, G-3," to Maj. James M. Moore, an assistant chief of staff, Hawaiian Division.

In May 1925 Major Moore authored Taylor's fitness report. He believed his assistant to be an "average" officer, and the overall report was mediocre. Taylor was rated "below average" in "attention to duty" and "administrative and executive duties" and merely "average" in all other categories, save for one. Moore checked "above average" in "military bearing and neatness." Moore wrote further that he had observed Taylor for one year and that the lieutenant was "of agreeable personality [but] careless and inaccurate in his work, unless rigidly supervised." In a later entry, Moore wrote that he had pointed out these deficiencies to Taylor; however, he noted no improvements.

Lest anyone think that Maj. James Moore was able to damn the Corps of Engineers career of Lt. Maxwell Taylor with faint praise, once again, as happened with his arm-in-arm stroll, greater forces seemed to be watching over him. Major Gen. William R. Smith, commanding the Hawaiian Division at Schofield, reviewed it, wrote the First Indorsement, and substantially overruled Moore's assessment. Taylor's overall rating should have been "above average," wrote the general, and his report should have read: "Of agreeable personality and good presence, is slightly deaf and . . . care must be taken to see that he hears what is said. His work is all that a man of his years and experience might be expected to give."[7]

Taylor's morale was down. But such was the case with many of his peers, for this was not prime time to be undertaking a career in the U.S. Army, in any branch. One reason went back to World War I, when 200,000 men held temporary Army officers' commissions. Afterward, 14,565 of this group applied for Regular Army status under the requirements of the National Defense Act of 1920, and 5,229 were accepted. The legislation anticipated a serving army of 280,000 enlisted men under 17,717 officers. But the fiscal support to maintain these manpower levels was not actually appropriated by Congress until June 30, 1941. The Army had, however, managed to keep an officer corps close to double its strength in pre–World War I days.

Of more immediate concern to young lieutenants like Taylor was the seniority list (the ranked order of potential promotion by longevity of service). It had ballooned at its middle by the sheer numbers of captains and majors commissioned during the war and afterward permitted to remain on active duty; this bulge was known as the hump. Many of Taylor's contemporaries at West Point who began their careers as "second looeys" low on the seniority list came to believe that the Army of the Roaring Twenties was the wrong place to begin a life's work; they departed for civilian careers posthaste.

Taylor stayed but transferred to the Field Artillery in 1926 to serve at Camp Lewis, Washington. The technology of cannonry had, for some reason, caught his imagination where military engineering had not. By now a first lieutenant, he was more enthusiastic about his work and more mature. He certainly worked better with his commanding officer, as shown in his fitness report: "[Taylor was] one of the higher types of officer and gentlemen [Captain Bibb, his superior] has ever known, particularly qualified as an instructor. A very pleasing personality." After knowing Taylor "very well" slightly less than a year, Bibb felt "a very bright future is predicted for this officer."[8]

After his service at Camp Lewis, he began, in 1927, five years at West Point, where he taught Spanish and French. Max and Diddy's first child, John, was born there in 1930. From West Point he was moved to the "Battery Officers' Course, the Field Artillery School" at Fort Sill, Oklahoma, where he snagged a "superior" efficiency report, signed by Lt. Col. Lesley McNair, for his advanced artillery education between August 1932 and May 1933.

Douglas MacArthur, by this time Army chief of staff, was well aware of the low morale among his officer corps that had been brought about by reductions during the Great Depression and the hump of delayed promotions. To provide some incentive, MacArthur ordered the Command and General Staff School, Fort Leavenworth,

Kansas, to admit a few senior lieutenants to the two-year course that had been open only to captains and higher.

Taylor entered directly from Fort Sill in 1933. His would be an illustrious class; of the 119 officers enrolled, 62 later became generals. They included Taylor's own West Point Spanish instructor Matthew Ridgway, Mark Clark, Walter Bedell Smith, and George Stratemeyer. In daily map problems and terrain exercises, students role-played senior commanders and provided tactical solutions. Competition was fierce; an officer's grades determined not only his class standing but also whether he would ever attend the War College in Washington, D.C., and therefore attain more senior promotion.

One concept dominated the students' intellectual activities. World War I had shown that all-out frontal assault was not tactically effective. Replacing this doctrine at Leavenworth in the 1930s was the buzz term "wide envelopment." It was a variation on the classic maneuver "turning movement" around an antagonist's flanks to execute sharp strikes at key points in the enemy's rearward positions.

Taylor later paid all the requisite obeisances to Leavenworth for producing, in his words, "well-trained potential commanders and general staff officers, all speaking the same professional language, following the same staff procedures, schooled in the same military doctrine, and ready to work together in any theatre of war." The result was that field commanders and staff were indoctrinated in the same thinking. They talked the same talk and saw themselves as team players. They agreed that warfare should eliminate enemy resistance by destroying its fighting forces through offensive firepower and flexible maneuver. Taylor said, "Although many of us thought the school carried the wide envelopment to extremes, it certainly encouraged bold maneuver and . . . had a wholesome effect on the development of our tactical thinking."[9]

The Leavenworth doctrine certainly seemed to work in World War II, when it was successfully tried out in battle by its acolytes. But was it a blindfold later? Did the doctrine and its initial successes bewilder these well-trained officers when the warfare they faced was transformed? How effective was an intricately plotted wide envelopment around an enemy position *when the enemy wasn't there to be subdued?*

Meanwhile, another approach was making inroads into other armies. An ancient intellectual concept of warfare was gaining popularity. It had been introduced to Soviet officers, but its greatest proponents were Asian. It was underpinning the attitudes of both

Japanese officers in the 1930s and one of their adversaries, Mao
Tse-tung, a rising force in China. Its existence predated Christ by five
hundred years.

> Now an army may be likened to water, for just as flowing
> water avoids the heights and hastens to the lowlands, so an
> army avoids strength and strikes weakness. . . . And as water
> shapes its flow in accordance with the ground, so an army
> manages its victory in accordance with the situation of the
> enemy . . . and as water has no constant form, there are in
> war no constant conditions.[10]

The writer was Sun-Tzu. After World War II his theory permeated
the thinking of many of the opponents of the United States, but the
American officers at Leavenworth with "the same professional language" and "the same military doctrine" did not have enough opportunity in the 1930s to appreciate it and to adjust their own
conception of warfare accordingly.

When Maxwell Taylor graduated from Leavenworth in June 1935,
his rating, as usual by then, was generally "excellent." Afterward,
though, he was nearly condemned to a translator's desk at the school
library. He had received kudos as a staff school student for his trans-
lations of French, Spanish, and Italian military articles and treatises,
but his skill proved a mixed blessing. Taylor was told by the librar-
ian, Maj. Charles Willoughby, that he would be retained at Leavenworth as Willoughby's assistant to continue translating. It would
have been a career purgatory.

But Taylor was lucky, thanks to the Army's traditional secret
weapon, the filing cabinet. Earlier he had discovered that the Army
routinely sent two officers annually to Japan and China for language
study. His application in 1923 had been rebuffed; Corps of Engineers
officers, he was told, were too valuably specialized for such non-
technical work and therefore were ineligible. When Taylor transferred to the Field Artillery, his application remained in a file. There,
twelve years later, it was exhumed by some anonymous Army angel,
who wrote to him to ask if his interest remained. Taylor quickly said
yes, and so the peregrinations of the family (now including a second
son, Thomas, born at Leavenworth) continued; the four Taylors
arrived in Japan in October 1935 to begin the four-year assignment.
Captain Taylor hastened to his studies, and three Japanese domestics
helped Diddy cope with the new household in Tokyo.

Taylor's Japanese language program was supervised by the U.S. Embassy, whose officers semiannually evaluated each Army, Navy, and State Department participant. Each service's requirements were taken into account; the Army course normally took two years before the student was assigned to a Japanese regiment as an observer. But Taylor learned the language quickly. Within eighteen months, he wrote later, he felt he was reasonably competent to discuss the issues of daily life, to listen to the radio, and to understand an ordinary newspaper and the four thousand basic ideograms called *kanji*.[11] In fact, his progress was so rapid that he received his authorization to observe a Japanese regiment six months ahead of schedule.

Taylor was placed with the Imperial Guards Artillery Regiment, where he observed, among other things, the austerity of field life for an army unit: "When meal time came, an officer went to a nearby tree, broke off a couple of twigs . . . as chopsticks, washed out his helmet . . . to serve as his plate, and went through the mess line." He wrote that he was observed as much as he was observing; diplomatic niceties only superficially clouded the mutual espionage agreeably referred to as "observation." He also drew high praise from his hosts for his sake-drinking capacity at parties.[12]

Then his assignment with the Imperial Guards Artillery ended suddenly. In July 1937 the Japanese invaded northern China and moved southward. As their forces approached the capital, Peking, the U.S. Embassy evacuated most of its staff to Chungking. The embassy military attaché, Col. Joseph W. Stilwell, remained to observe the war. Taylor was detached and ordered to report to Stilwell in Peking to serve as his Japanese translator. Entraining northbound in Korea, Taylor lost his trunk, thanks to local customs officers, when he crossed into Manchuria. He arrived with nothing but the linen suit he wore and his briefcase. He later remembered his gratitude to Stilwell for meeting him at the station.[13]

As the Japanese continued their southward push toward the Yellow River, Washington asked the two officers to identify the Japanese units involved. Although Taylor and Stilwell sallied into the field wherever permitted, they observed only parts of the Japanese logistical system. Washington kept up the pressure for forces identification, but the Japanese were not cooperating; unit patches and equipment markings had all been removed. Then, visiting the Summer Palace outside Peking one day, Taylor accidentally discovered some graffiti on the back of the Great Buddha. Some Japanese soldiers had written their names and units, unwittingly providing the American officer with his major intelligence coup in the unlikeliest of places.

Taylor later wrote cautiously when he assessed the controversial Colonel Stilwell: "I found 'Vinegar Joe' a genial travel companion full of Chinese lore and glad to talk about the country and people to an interested listener. He had a deep affection for the Chinese." The two of them journeyed all over northern China by any available means, improvised billets at night, and generally found ways to observe. Taylor chronically suffered from Chinese *turistas* (stomach problems); Stilwell habitually grabbed fruit at open-air markets, cursorily dusted it "with a sweaty sleeve," and ate it. Taylor felt he had no choice but to imitate his superior's example.

In his report on Taylor, Stilwell rated his translator "superior" and commented, "one of the best officers I have met in the service. I should especially desire to have him serve under my command." Oddly, Stilwell checked "unknown" for his assessment of Taylor's "physical endurance" on the efficiency report after three months of quick-marching the captain all over northern China.[14] Pessimistic about his own chances for advancement then, Stilwell told Taylor that the younger man's promotions might be jeopardized by the association.

Taylor returned to Tokyo in time to spend Christmas with his family and to begin summarizing his experiences of the past three years in a report called "Tactical Doctrine of the Japanese Army." His final 1939 report, sixty-one pages long, contained some telling conclusions: "The continuous offensive is the basis of Japanese tactical and spiritual training." And there is an echo of ancient martial doctrine in this finding:

> The Japanese appreciate the importance of secrecy and deception. No maneuver is ever attempted without including in the plan some device to deceive the enemy and conceal the true intention of the commander.[15]

It evoked Sun-Tzu's initial assumption, "All warfare is based on deception." Was it a direct reference indicating Taylor's awareness of Sun-Tzu, or was it merely an allusion to what he had learned from observing the Japanese martial way? The classical Chinese theorist goes unmentioned in Taylor's conclusions, although, according to Samuel Griffith, Sun-Tzu was frequently commented upon and applied in contemporary Japanese military treatises. After the report was filed, Taylor's transfer home was speeded to permit his enrollment at the Army War College, Washington, D.C., in early September 1939. Since 1927 he had been either a teacher or a student.

ON THE WAY

General George Marshall spoke impressively on the opening day at the War College. Taylor remembered his first look at the new chief of staff for his dominance, not for what he said. His sheer presence left its mark.

The mission of the prewar Army War College was to emphasize strategy, not the nuts-and-bolts mechanics of the earlier Leavenworth Staff School's tactical simulations and wide envelopments. Leavenworth had been hypercompetitive; the War College was not, instead stressing lectures by government leaders, experienced officers, and academics that were followed by student brainstorming on the problems presented. It would be the last class for some time, as in 1940 the school shut down for the duration of World War II.

When Taylor's name was read at graduation the following spring, he was long distant. The length and breadth of his foreign language experience made him a rarity, as both Army and Navy suffered a serious shortage of officer-linguists. Lieutenant Col. Matthew Ridgway—his former West Point Spanish teacher and Staff School classmate—was then commanding an Army department desk charged with determining Latin American national needs for warding off potential Nazi threats. He yanked Taylor out of the Army's "doctorate in warfare" program in the early spring of 1940 for a less cloistered education.[16]

Taylor was sent first to Central America and later to Peru, Bolivia, and Chile. He and his fellow military came as Santa Clauses, picking up the dollars-and-materiel wish lists of numerous Latin American high commands. The program's prospective beneficiaries caught on like six-year-olds with an F.A.O. Schwarz toy store catalog; Bolivian authorities solicited Taylor for a military aid package worth more than $200 million. The landlocked Bolivians even petitioned for a small navy to patrol the strategic sea-lanes of Lake Titicaca. Were they anticipating Nazi submarines prowling 12,500 feet up in the towering Andes? Taylor said he wasn't guessing why; he only carried the mail.

After Taylor carried that mail back to the United States, he was ordered to San Antonio to soldier again after a thirteen-year interval. Commanding an artillery battalion in the 2d Infantry Division, "a newly promoted, overschooled major" relearned the mundane facts of Army life with the aid of a patient sergeant major, Harry Robertson. Field maneuvers, not barracks duty, dominated the subsequent year: "[It] was a most useful tune-up for the responsibilities which lay ahead."[17] But he was back in Washington in July 1941, ordered to take a desk in the outer office of Army Chief of Staff George C. Marshall. The major Army decisions of the day ultimately voyaged through the chief's office in the form of position papers awaiting approval or disapproval, especially when two deputy chiefs of staff could not agree. For assistant secretaries like Taylor, the job meant marshaling all the arguments and presenting succinct oral analyses to Marshall himself.

The process began with the chosen assistant secretary entering Marshall's office armed with the documents and considerable understanding of their contents. The officer then dissected the issues, pro and con, if there were internal divergences. Rarely reading the papers himself, the chief relied on the oral presentations and the quality of the assistant secretary's answers to his penetrating questions on the issues involved.

Taylor prepped hard for his first time in action in Marshall's office by rehearsing the issues the evening before with his wife as stand-in for the chief. He went to work the next morning with his typical self-assurance, but he had left his flank open. The first item—upon which two assistant chiefs of staff disagreed—was a plan to add two companies to the Alaska National Guard. Taylor delicately listed the pros and cons and then was taken aback by Marshall's question, "What do you think about it, Taylor?" Taylor wrote later, "He looked at me with cold appraising eyes," waiting for the assistant secretary to fumble an answer. Taylor was just a lowly major, and here was the imposing Army chief of staff demanding his opinion. The lesson was not lost; Taylor wrote that never again did he go to Marshall or to any other superior with a paper without first deciding on the issue for himself and preparing his own answer.[18]

Another assistant secretary was on duty Sunday, December 7, 1941. Maxwell Taylor was at home with his family; General Marshall was riding his horse along the Potomac. When Marshall got to the War Department, he set about to make some sense of the rumors, conflicting stories, and incomplete information about the Japanese attack on Pearl Harbor. All U.S. forces had been alerted by that time, and Marshall called for a stenographer to whom he could dictate a situation report for the president.

The sole available stenographer was Aileen Morgan, a young woman noticed for her endowments but unproven in her stenographic ability. She took the dictation and returned outside to type it. Major Taylor, having heard of the attack, had rushed to his office, and Marshall paged him to get the typed letter from Morgan. Taylor continually asked her for progress reports; she always assured him it was progressing. But Taylor was suspicious. Knowing of Marshall's growing impatience, he asked, "Now, Miss Morgan, *really* how are you doing?" This key player in post–Pearl Harbor communications "looked at me," according to Taylor, "with those beautiful brown eyes filled with tears, and she said, 'Major, I didn't get a word of what the Chief said.' " Taylor entered Marshall's office with more bad news. The already tired chief of staff again stated the situation for the stenographer, and she returned to her typewriter, under Taylor's supervision. Then he carried back to Marshall's office a "dog-eared, untidy sheet" for the chief's signature and hand-delivered it himself to General Watson, President Roosevelt's military aide. When Taylor finally went home, he probably wondered if he had been properly educated for war.[19]

With the nation officially at war, Taylor grew increasingly fidgety about his duties at the Secretariat. Wartime meant faster advancement, commands, and combat, all of which were difficult to achieve while commanding a desk in the Munitions Building. His superior in China, General Stilwell, came to Washington early in 1942 and, over a seafood lunch in a Maine Avenue restaurant, asked Taylor to join his staff. (Taylor was by then a colonel, thanks to rapid wartime promotions—two ranks in less than six weeks.) He put Taylor's name on his staff list for his new Far East command, but the chief of staff approved every name on the list except Colonel Taylor's. A few weeks later, Taylor's name appeared on another list: Gen. Matthew Ridgway had submitted six names of candidates for divisional chief of staff for his new command, the 82d Infantry Division. This time Marshall approved Taylor's transfer to what would become a significant new approach to warfare—airborne operations.[20]

Despite a colorful later history as a military concept and its equally dramatic unit personifications, the airborne idea was not the exclusive property of the U.S. Army. The Germans had been using paratroopers effectively, most notably at British-held Crete in 1941. Marshall and the U.S. Army were impressed, but the cost at Crete was too great for the führer. Hitler probably pounded a map table as a period for his death sentence for future mass airborne attacks, but the Allies had no information on German casualties at Crete and Hitler's subsequent proscription. German airborne units maintained high training levels for the duration of the war but were never again dropped, glided, or flown en masse. On Hitler's orders they were kept strictly as reserves for regular ground troops.[21]

After Pearl Harbor, General Marshall approved the creation of parachute infantry regiments. Soon, larger units were envisioned, and Ridgway and Taylor's 82d Infantry was converted to the faith. Soon the 82d was joined by a temporary paper entity, the 101st Airborne Division. To take it into realization, Ridgway had to select a cadre of "experienced" jumpers in a meeting with Bill Lee, the 101st's first commander. They agreed Ridgway would keep his top staff officers including his chief of staff, Col. Maxwell Taylor. The rest of the apportionment was decided by coin toss.[22]

Ridgway, Taylor's composite commander, professor, mentor, classmate, and *compañero*, was miffed with him. The news of this was confined to memories and avoided filing cabinets. A contemporary of both officers described Chief of Staff Taylor as

> an intellectual, a thinker. He was fascinated by the intellectual side of things. He liked to see what he could do with his mind—how far he could push it. And he had an excellent mind. He could walk around things, look at them. He may have gotten emotionally involved, but he didn't show it. He was outwardly very, very cool.[23]

However, Ridgway needed no intellectual in the chief of staff slot. He did need a decisive paper-pusher. Taylor effused boredom with his assigned duties. By that time in his life, Taylor knew himself well enough to know that he functioned well at both extremes in the thought-action dichotomy. He could take a difficult problem, examine it from all angles, and draw his own conclusions, and he also adapted equally well to the other extreme, action. However, the middle ground, the tedious mundanities of daily military administration, held no fascination for the Maxwell Taylor who habitually embraced challenges, cerebral or physical. Ralph P. Eaton said Taylor was "smarter than hell," but as an artilleryman Taylor wanted to shoot. Eaton went on: "His idea of being chief of staff was to come in in the morning, spend fifteen to thirty minutes signing papers, then go down and spend most of the day with the Field Artillery and late in the afternoon, come back to the office and sign some more papers." Letters accumulated along with phone messages. Eaton had to cover for Taylor in the office on top of discharging his own duties.[24]

Fortunately for Taylor, Joseph Swing, the 82d's artillery chief, was transferred to command the newly created 11th Airborne Division. Taylor became Swing's successor at the 82d and escaped his hated paperwork. It brought him a promotion to brigadier general too. A few weeks before Christmas 1942, Taylor wrote his obligatory letter to General Marshall:

> Having received orders to assume command of the Field Artillery of the 82nd Airborne Division, I wish to express my appreciation for this promotion which you have allowed me. I pledge my efforts to merit this fine command and to apply to the best of my ability the methods of distinguished leadership which I was privileged to observe while serving in your office.[25]

In the Airborne cosmology, there was no tacit legitimacy about any officer who wasn't jump-rated. Jump-happiness infected everyone, from generals down to the lowliest, greenest shavetail. The pathogenic madness struck Taylor too, but it was not the chronic condition it was for nearly everyone else. He watched a full morning's training one day for parachute school recruits and told the school commander that he wanted to make his own first jump after lunch. The commander showed no enthusiasm for Taylor's idea. A veteran jumper, a master sergeant–parachute instructor, was standing nearby. Taylor enlisted his support for the idea, asking if all the basic training was required to make a safe jump. "Hell no," said the sergeant. "Just get out of the door and hope to Christ you hit easy." Taylor climbed aboard the C-47. It took off and circled Fort Benning while the jump-master, Capt. Julian Ewell, made some final suggestions to the novice paratrooper. Taylor got his Airborne cap patch that day, but a medic had to put a large bandage on his chin afterwards.[26]

Taylor was reportedly no fan of jumping generally. Some doubt remains as to the actual number of jumps Taylor eventually made. He made that one jump at Fort Benning, missed the later Sicily combat jump, and jumped at Normandy on D-Day and later in the Arnhem operation. Whether he jumped at other occasions cannot be determined.

THE PARATROOPER

Early in March 1943 Ridgway made a preliminary visit to North Africa to discuss how the 82d would be used in its first combat later that year in Sicily. Eisenhower was too concerned with what was happening on the Tunisian front to discuss Sicily but suggested that Ridgway spend a week touring the American sector and headquarters. Because Ridgway felt that he must have a service representative from the 82d present, he cabled Taylor to proceed as soon as possible to North Africa.[27]

When three transport ships carrying the 82d arrived in Casablanca on May 10, Taylor met them on the dock. Shortly, the division moved by truck and train 400 miles east to Oujda near the Algerian border.

On the night of July 9, the 82d participated in its first combat operation, a night drop on Sicily. It turned out to be a disaster. The pilots' inexperience at nighttime overwater navigation led them to miss their navigational landmark, the island of Malta. With 35 mph northeasterly winds blowing at them, many pilots assumed that they had been shifted off course; several planes broke formation as their pilots grew fearful of the position. As the heavy winds buffeted their aircraft, the paratroopers grew more and more airsick in the unpressurized cabins. Finally, when Sicily came into view, few sticks of paratroopers jumped at their correct drop zones (DZs); 82d troopers landed all over southeastern Sicily.

Two days later, on a subsequent drop for the 82d, disaster really struck. Almost half of the C-47s were severely shot up by "friendly fire" from antiaircraft crews.

Taylor and the bulk of his artillery did not begin combat until the second week of the battle. The 82d Division artillery was reinforced by a 155mm howitzer battalion from the 9th Division. Taylor wrote later that he was very impressed by the performance of the battalion commander, whom he had not met before—Lt. Col. W. C. Westmoreland.[28]

On August 5, 1943, Matthew Ridgway wrote the adjutant general to recommend that Maxwell Taylor be promoted temporarily to major general. Although Ridgway assessed Taylor's performance as his artillery commander to be outstanding, George Patton, then commanding the Seventh Army, disapproved it in the First Indorsement on September 3. "There is nothing that appears in General Taylor's record," he wrote, "that makes his promotion take priority over other Brigadier Generals in the 7th Army who have long and continuous battle experience."[29] Patton had his own fish to sauté; he could not permit Ridgway to feather the paratrooper nest and dispense political largesse while other colonels and brigadiers who had ridden under Patton all the way across North Africa and through Sicily were ignored. Compared to these men, Maxwell Taylor had faced little combat.

However, Taylor would get his chance to shine a scant few days after Patton had vetoed his promotion. The opportunity would be as dangerous, or more so, than combat itself.

"These risks he ran were greater than I asked any other agent or emissary to undertake during the war—he carried weighty responsibilities and discharged them with unerring judgment, and every minute was in imminent danger of discovery and death."[30] The subject was Brig. Gen. Maxwell Taylor; the context, Taylor's 1943 mission to Rome; and the writer, Gen. Dwight Eisenhower in his 1948 wartime memoir, *Crusade in Europe*.

On August 2 Taylor had gone from Sicily to Algiers to report for duty with Gen. Mark Clark, Fifth Army commander, who would lead the American amphibious landing south of Naples at Salerno. Joined by several 82d officers, Taylor opened a planning headquarters for airborne operations jointly with the Fifth Army staff. Throughout the succeeding month, Taylor and his staff proposed five separate plans for employing the 82d as a whole or in part to support the larger Salerno attack (called Avalanche). The planners foresaw an operations area from Salerno north to Naples and on to Rome.

An Italian armistice seemed contingent upon Allied aid in defending Rome against the Germans. For this task Eisenhower delegated the 82d for an airborne drop. There were, however, too many loose ends, and Ridgway considered the concept "harebrained." If all roads led to Rome and a possible divisional jump into the Eternal City, more intelligence was needed. It was, therefore, agreed that an Allied officer should go to Rome to look into the feasibility of the plan. Taylor got the assignment after volunteering in company with Col. William T. Gardiner, the senior intelligence officer of the 51st Troop Carrier Wing.[31]

Taylor and Gardiner left Palermo on a British PT boat at 2:00 A.M. on September 7. Because this mission required considerable deception, the two Allied emissaries wore no badges of rank on their American uniforms. They were acting, publicly at least, as two captured U.S. airmen retrieved from the sea. Fifty miles northeast of

Palermo in the Tyrrhenian Sea, the PT boat met an Italian corvette at daybreak and flashed the recognition signal. The two officers went aboard, headed for the port of Gaeta.

After the corvette docked, Gardiner, Taylor, and their Italian escorts all played their parts in the faked drama. A crowd gathered to watch the Italian officers goad their two "prisoners" down the gangplank with appropriate words from the script. Escorted to a waiting car, they were then chauffeured to a back road outside Gaeta and there transferred to an ambulance. The ambulance brought its passengers to the Palazzo Caprara across the street from the Italian War Office on the Via Firenze in Rome.

General Carboni, commanding the Italian army corps defending Rome, eventually appeared. Taylor and Gardiner learned that General Ambrosio, armed forces chief of staff, whom they expected to meet immediately, was in Turin on an emergency.

Carboni was depressed. He told the Americans that the Germans had added substantial reinforcements, largely airborne units, to their Rome defense. Twelve thousand paratroopers were supplemented by one hundred artillery pieces and the Panzer Grenadier Division of 24,000 troops with 50 light and 150 heavy tanks. The Germans had also pinched off supplies to the Italian units on which an invading 82d Airborne would depend for transport and replenishment. Carboni also protested that an Italian armistice would prompt an out-and-out German occupation of Rome, unstoppable by the Italians if the 82d dropped into the city. He could not even promise secure airfields for drop zones. Rome's salvation, he said, depended on not going after the Germans there; instead, the Italians wanted to wait for Allied invaders to sweep up from the south. On hearing this, Taylor and Gardiner demanded to see Marshal Badoglio at once.[32]

Hampered by the usual roadblocks, the three of them reached Badoglio's villa outside Rome shortly after midnight. The pajama-clad premier huddled with Carboni for fifteen minutes and then welcomed the Americans. He punctuated the entire discussion with proclamations of Allied friendship and ambitions for Allied cooperation. Taylor explained that the grave reasons for the late visit required Badoglio's immediate decision. Did the prime minister agree with the cancellation of an American airborne drop? Badoglio, aged and tired looking, said in French that he agreed with Carboni; Taylor wrote later that the prime minister's arguments were far too similar to Carboni's earlier ones. Finally, Taylor demanded a public announcement of armistice at the end of that day, September 8.

For security, Badoglio and the other Italian conspirators had been kept ignorant of the actual date of the planned invasion, and this fact may have explained their apparent lack of organization. They assumed that any invasion would be coming in several days, not in a matter of hours. When Taylor corrected the Italian misconception, Badoglio was upset.

At 1:20 A.M. Taylor's message to Allied headquarters warned that any airborne invasion would be impossible because of German strength and Italian inability to carry out their part of the plan. Eisenhower's headquarters ordered the two officers to return home. Again they rode across Rome in the ambulance, this time to an airfield, and climbed aboard an Italian bomber that would carry them to Tunisia. This was the most nerve-racking phase of the mission, even though the Italians had told Taylor that the bomber's flight path would be free of interference by either Italian or Allied air forces. Near the North African coast a U.S. fighter buzzed them but never fired.[33]

One of the lasting questions about the Taylor-Gardiner mission to Rome is whether Taylor choked on the situation and called off the operation himself. A close observer-participant of that time, Sir Kenneth Strong, Allied intelligence chief, nearly damns Taylor with faint praise. Strong wrote: "We briefed Taylor thoroughly on the situation before he left and placed a large sum of money in lire at his disposal. On his return he gave it all back to me except for twenty lire; I have since regarded Maxwell Taylor as a very careful and scrupulous man." But Strong's own continuing postmortem on the mission dangles too many question marks about Taylor's call from the field, even while Strong faults Badoglio for a lack of will. In short, Strong disagrees with Taylor's call.[34]

Another diplomatic chore for Taylor came when he was preparing to rejoin the 82nd for the Salerno invasion. On the same day that he and Gardiner left Rome, the king of Italy, Marshal Badoglio, and their retainers escaped to the Adriatic port of Pescara and sailed on another Italian corvette to Brindisi. The much-traveled secret radio traveled with the fugitives, who transmitted a request to Eisenhower for Allied help in forming an Italian government in exile. In response, Eisenhower sent them a group of luminaries: Robert Murphy, political adviser at Allied headquarters; Harold Macmillan, the British headquarters' political adviser; Sir Noel Mason-MacFarlane, military governor of Gibraltar; and Maxwell Taylor.

Taylor's wish for more military duties—he was impatient with this political job—was soon realized. "I became the beneficiary of a stroke of good fortune with a most unfortunate cause," Taylor wrote much later.[35] General William Lee, the father of American parachute operations and commander of the 101st Airborne Division, suffered a heart attack in February 1944 and was sent stateside, his active Army career ended. Ridgway's "search" for a replacement—Maxwell Taylor—was duly endorsed by Eisenhower and Gen. Omar Bradley. The Screaming Eagles of the 101st were skeptical. After all, Taylor had no roots in the division; he had jumped only once and was therefore still more suspect; and, above all, he had precious little combat experience, with scarcely the right to tuck his trousers in his boots. They were understandably wary as Taylor joined the 101st in England on March 8, 1944, and formally took command on March 14.[36]

Remembering the tragic and frustrating lessons of the Sicily jump, both the 82d and 101st divisions trained strenuously for the Normandy invasion. On May 10 Taylor's 101st began a training exercise called Eagle. The Eagle screamed: 75 percent of the troopers dropped landed on the planned DZ or acceptably close to it; 80 percent of the related glider force landed at their correct landing zones (LZs). "The final phase of the exercise was the assembly of our men in the darkness and their movement toward terrain objectives similar to those in France," Taylor wrote. Plans called for 6,600 101st jumpers to be dropped near Carentan, southeast of Utah Beach, and charged with blocking any reaction by the German 6th Parachute Regiment centered there. Only after the 101st was locked into departure points did each man hear the complete story of the forthcoming mission. As they looked at sand tables and maps, the jumpers were briefed not only on the 101st's responsibility but also on the missions of contiguous units, all commanded by Taylor.

There was, of course, the famous cancellation that left everyone gasping for breath. Finally, in the early evening of June 5, the supreme commander himself arrived with several aides to dine at the 101st headquarters. Eisenhower and Taylor then drove to several airfields, where the Allied commander visited assembly areas and aircraft already loaded to bid good luck to the troopers, "many in Indian warpaint and with freakish haircuts," before they flew off.

The 101st was advised to yell "Bill Lee!" instead of "Geronimo!" when jumping, in tribute to its indisposed founding father. Maxwell Taylor, Lee's successor, jumped seventh out of Plane No. 1 to land in one piece; it was only his second jump. Curious cows surrounded the

first Allied general to invade Normandy. He was in a pasture near
Pouppeville, approximately 3 kilometers east of the planned drop
zone. As he struggled with his harness, trying to snap off the chute,
Taylor heard a German Schmeisser machine pistol firing in the distance like "a ripping seat of pants." This inspired him to slice off the
parachute rigging with his knife. Lightening his load more, he cast off
his "leg-bag"—and a contraband bottle of scotch it contained.[37]

Maxwell Taylor had thus come finally to his own command in
combat. Eyewitness reports abound. The death in action at Normandy of Assistant Division Commander Don Pratt meant the promotion of Chief of Staff Gerald Higgins, already a Taylor admirer,
who came to respect his commanding officer even more. When Taylor took over the division, Higgins, figuring that Taylor would require his own men in the top jobs, offered to go elsewhere. But, in
Higgins's own words, "He looked at me for a moment, smiled, and
said: 'Jerry, if you were good enough for Bill Lee, you're good enough
for me!' During Normandy, Higgins witnessed Taylor poring over a
map one morning; suddenly and inexplicably, Taylor ordered Higgins to shift the division reserve to a new point. A few hours later, the
Germans attacked it in force. The advance battalion of the 101st was
ordered to fall back; the Germans followed into a trap. To Higgins,
Taylor's decision revealed the quality of anticipation, what modern
military behaviorists call SA—situational awareness.[38]

Higgins wrote long afterward of "an incident that I am firmly
convinced was unique in a commander under the circumstances that
obtained." At 8:00 P.M. on D-Day, Taylor and Higgins finally found
their prearranged command post in a big French farmhouse and
immediately set to clarifying the division's situation. However, the
two generals were worn out by the fatigue of the previous days'
planning and rescheduling, the momentous excitement of the drop
itself, and the subsequent ambiguity of the 101st's field organization.
An hour after their arrival, Taylor stood up and announced, "Jerry,
I am going upstairs to get some sleep. I will be down about daylight."
Higgins was aghast; plenty of pressing items still loaded the divisional agenda that evening. He started to protest, "What if . . . ?"
Taylor cut him off, saying, "You know the plans as well as I do. Your
decision will be my decision." Without another word, he climbed the
stairs to his bunk. Throughout the night Higgins agonized over wak-
ing Taylor to deliver field intelligence that kept filtering in, but he
followed his superior's advice. Shortly before dawn, Taylor re-
emerged to a briefing on the progress made that night, Higgins's own

initiatives, and whatever developments were germane to the situation. He assented, then ordered, "Upstairs with you—and get some sleep. I'll wake you when I need you."[39]

But Higgins, who served with Taylor intimately throughout the European campaign and later at West Point, writes, too, of a certain mystery, something of a strangeness about his commander:

> Did I know him personally? Yes, and no. For some reason or other he did not make "close" friends in that sense. I think I was probably closest to him personally, and that was because I was Chief of Staff of the Division when he came in and apparently he relied on me to keep him abreast of developments of *all* kinds.[40]

Despite Maxwell Taylor's competence and charm, he also had this shadowy side, that ever so delicate psychological distance he maintained.

Slightly more than a month after the Normandy invasion, the 101st returned to its old quarters in England to rest and train for more airborne operations while regular ground forces chased Germans across northern France. Plans for drops near Paris and the Belgian cities of Tournai and Liège were quickly forgotten as armor and infantry overran German defenses there nearly as fast as the plans emerged.

Maxwell Taylor made his second combat jump (and third overall) in Operation Market Garden, combining his 101st, the 82d, and the British 1st Airborne (with a Polish brigade) in an epic drop into Holland. On September 17, 1944, 20,000 paratroopers—carried by 1,500 transports and 500 gliders screened by 1,000 fighters—jumped into action in the largest airborne operation of the war (and in history). This time airborne commanders ordered a daylight drop to eliminate the nighttime problems that had shown up in the Sicily and Normandy drops. The 82d went to Nijmegen, the British-Polish 1st to Arnhem, and Taylor's 101st to the Eindhoven-Veghel area. Allied planners had gambled heavily that the operation would clear a path for the British Second Army. The British would push ahead from the Albert Canal in Belgium and swing around the eastern end of the Siegfried Line to cross the Rhine River from Arnhem into Germany. But that plan did not work.

Taylor won a Purple Heart when a piece of Lt. Henry Shrapnel's invention, German-manufactured, was delivered directly into his posterior. He was transported back to France, along with the 101st—he, to recover; they, to rest and regroup.

On December 5 Taylor and an aide left on orders to return to Washington to discuss planning for the airborne concept's future. The bureaucratic business went smoothly—General Marshall approved experienced combat commanders' wish lists—and Taylor was soon free to visit training areas for new airborne troops, as well as factories that were researching and developing new weaponry and equipment. He was aware of, but at first unexcited by, news reporting a German attack in the Belgian Ardennes woods. He had assumed, based on recent experience, a low quality of German resistance.[41]

The news grew more serious; on December 21 officials announced that the German offensive was heavy, and Taylor scurried back to Washington. The situation map showed the 101st in Bastogne, surrounded by hostile forces. Taylor learned that the German threat was judged so serious to Gen. Troy Middleton's VII Corps that both U.S. airborne divisions had been shaken from their rest and speedily transported by truck to Belgium on December 18 to face the German advance the following day. The Screaming Eagles, temporarily commanded by Brig. Gen. Anthony McAuliffe in Taylor's absence, had been ordered to restrict the Germans' western advance by holding the major highway intersection at Bastogne. By the time of Taylor's return to Washington, McAuliffe had his wagons in a circle. After quickly summarizing his stateside inspections for General Marshall, Taylor requested the chief of staff's approval for immediate return to his unit. Marshall gave his blessing, but Taylor was forced to wait three days for acceptable weather before he could fly to the Battle of the Bulge.

The division was big news now, attention accelerated by McAuliffe's impish and succinct answer to the German surrender demand: "Nuts!" Taylor was back at the division by December 27, but the remainder of the war was fairly routine for him and for the division.

When the war in Europe ended in May 1945, the 101st was stuck with housekeeping responsibilities in Berchtesgaden, Nazism's holy city and Hitler's favorite hideaway; prominent prisoners and Nazi treasure had to be guarded. In mid-July the division was moved fifty miles from Berchtesgaden south to Badgastein. After inspecting all the hotels in the resort city, the officers chose the best one for their new residence but found it occupied with staff evacuated from the Japanese Embassy in Berlin. Taylor and Higgins went over to evict them. The Japanese functionary who manned the front desk spoke perfect English and called upstairs to announce the American visitors. Sometime later, impatient with the delay, Taylor asked the deskman for the reason. The reply was that the ambassador was dressing, but then the deskman made an aside to another embassy staffer in Japanese, something like "let the American general cool his heels." Overhearing it, Taylor started chewing out the deskman in the appropriate Japanese idiom, ordering the ambassador's immediate presence or else. The lobby was filled with Japanese who stood transfixed by the sight and sound of a U.S. general lambasting the deskman in their own language.[42]

From late May to late June, when home on R and R, Taylor had learned that the 101st would be shifted to the war in the Pacific. On rejoining the division, he toured individual units to muster support for the move. He ended one speech with: "We've licked the best that Hitler had in France and Holland and Germany. Now where do we want to go?" It inspired the only mass incident of insubordination, although jocular, faced by Maxwell Taylor as a commander. His beloved Screaming Eagles screamed, "Home!"—no doubt punctuated by a few catcalls and Bronx cheers.[43]

FROM THE HUDSON TO THE KUMSONG

He went back along the banks of the Hudson; for the third time his life would be centered around West Point. While still in Europe, he found out that he would have every two-star's dream job: the superintendency of the United States Military Academy. He took over in September 1945, the fortieth man in the job since the academy's founding in 1802 and the second youngest—at forty-four—behind MacArthur himself. But if his presence at West Point was dramatic, his changes were not. Taylor saw little need for fundamental shifts in direction for educating future officers; he wrote long afterward, "Don't undertake to change the Military Academy on your own. It has been there a long time. It has a justified reason . . . for the things it does."[44] He did little to influence the academy's administration or its Long Gray Line of the Corps of Cadets. The academic side of West Point was no sacred cow to him, however.

Taylor urged the secretary of war to import "a board of consultants, headed by Dr. Karl Compton," Massachusetts Institute of Technology (MIT) president, to grade the new cadet curriculum. The consultants gave it good marks but had criticisms both of "inadequate leisure afforded the cadets and of the weight of the curriculum which should be lightened."[45] Much of this new academic load had been developed under his predecessor, Francis B. Wilby, but Taylor ramrodded into reality a new course on military leadership. It echoed some of MacArthur's admonitions on assuming the superintendency during Taylor's cadet years: leadership in uniform meant an appreciation for the psychology of command, not the brutal screaming of orders.

Raiding the ranks of the 101st Airborne Division for his West Point staff, Taylor made his old chief of staff, Gerald J. Higgins, the USMA commandant. Higgins was put to work planning the new leadership course, which emphasized the officer as humanist rather than the old officer as engineer. (Brainstorming during wartime, the two men agreed that the academy had everything else except formal lessons in leadership.) In his planning for the course, Higgins learned that the powerful Academic Board was, to a man, thoroughly opposed to the idea. To begin with, no academic department would concede a few classroom hours. When doing his homework, however, Higgins found that some departmental curricula were going on unchanged—and probably unchallenged—even though eclipsed by military technology. When Higgins brought the course proposal to a special meeting of the Academic Board in May 1946, Taylor was there but abstained from voting. Commandant Higgins's vote was the only one in favor of the proposal. The opposition leader (a department head whose name is lost to posterity) cheered the result: "That settles it!" Then Taylor, who seemed to be sitting back patiently, dropped his bomb: "The course on leadership will be instituted in the fall." Everyone was taken aback. One man stood to state: "General Taylor, the Academic Board directs the curriculum, and the vote was decisive."

Surrounded like McAuliffe at Bastogne, the superintendent resisted the temptation to repeat the monosyllable uttered by his former artillery commander. Instead, he announced: "The Superintendent thanks the members of the board for their *advice*—the decision as to whether the course will be instituted is the *decision* of the Superintendent." The Academic Board had just learned that boardroom barbed wire does not necessarily guarantee a successful defense. Taylor had shown neither cockiness nor chutzpah, merely an edge that nobody had foreseen, and he could reassure himself that even Army Chief of Staff Eisenhower saw the need for leadership training at

USMA.[46] Still, one of the board members researched precedents and told Higgins later "that never before had the Superintendent acted against the report of the Board."[47]

Taylor had plenty else to do. Going beyond what was actually required, he found more than enough to occupy his time. He also maintained visibility. One visitor during June Week 1946 wrote to the ailing Gen. John T. Pershing:

> I am very much impressed by the new Superintendent, General Maxwell D. Taylor. He is a Major General, tall, slim, very erect, and very good looking. . . . He also has some definite ideas about West Point with the emphasis on developing leadership. He had, for example, abolished the requirement for every Cadet to learn to fly. I predict he will be recognized as the ablest Superintendent West Point has had since W. C. Connor.[48]

West Point's closeness to New York City permitted the Taylors frequent opportunities to enjoy the city's culture. Mrs. Taylor had always been interested in music and theater; her husband took to opera. (Was he attracted only to opera's pageantry, or did he enjoy its music as well?) During one intermission the superintendent received a summons to meet Mrs. Vanderbilt. When he returned to his seat, Mrs. Taylor asked her husband what Mrs. Vanderbilt wanted. "She wanted to give me her private number," said the general.[49]

If any dominant theme emerged from his tenure as superintendent, it was Taylor's growing appreciation for public relations. Between September 1945 and January 1949, he logged 119 speaking engagements and public policy statements around the United States and even as far away as Sandhurst and the Imperial Defence College in England.[50] A 1948 invitation may have affected his fate later on: John F. Kennedy, a first-term congressman, asked him to address the Joseph P. Kennedy, Jr., Veterans of Foreign Wars (VFW) Post in Boston.[51]

While Taylor was superintendent, Gen. Robert Richardson, a former commandant himself, warned that the first five years after any wartime was "generally the most complex and frustrating that the Academy's authorities had to deal with." Some cadets had used West Point as a safe haven from conscription; by the time World War II ended and Taylor arrived, many of them sought to escape the Long Gray Line. By June 1946, Taylor's first year as superintendent, 185 cadets would leave the academy; a year later 172 more left. By 1948, 105 exited, but in 1949 only 67 did so. This problem did not bother

Taylor, and he would not speculate whether the fault was with the individual cadets or with overprotective parents. In his view neither the service nor USMA was responsible.[52] Moreover, this weeding out of types unsuitable for commissions was, perhaps, better for all.

But Richardson's warning applied to a new historical dimension as well. Maxwell Taylor was leading the academy at a very crucial moment in Army history. The proof of air power in World War II had expanded exponentially with the use of atomic weapons at Hiroshima and Nagasaki; there were new pressures on the Army's historical roles of cavalryman and groundpounder. Other kinds of growing pains were also evident in a changing U.S. Army and its West Point. Superintendent Taylor had to deal, for example, with racial problems, which mirrored the growing impatience of black Americans with the social status quo. Whether he acted wisely and justly is still debated.[53] He also, at Eisenhower's suggestion, made the academy's honor system more flexible and maintained it as an exemplar in the formulation of cadets' values.[54]

Less military and more public matters took his attention, too. The football rivalry between the University of Notre Dame and the USMA had grown so out of proportion that Taylor and Father Cavanaugh, the Notre Dame president, agreed to suspend their schools' annual gridiron clash. Other more traditional rivalries lessened somewhat during Taylor's tenure: on August 19, 1946, Secretary of the Navy James Forrestal witnessed "the joint landing assault exercises by Annapolis midshipmen and West Point cadets at Little Creek, Virginia, an early effort at unification in military education."[55] Presumably the truce lasted until the November kickoff.

Becoming superintendent in September 1945, Maxwell Taylor had thus "entered" West Point with the cadets of the class of 1949. Sentimentally, he hoped to see them graduate. Once again, however, the Army finger of fate, now wielded by new Chief of Staff Omar Bradley, tapped Taylor on the shoulder. On January 28, 1949, he drove down the Hudson to begin traveling to a new post.[56]

Taylor was returning to Germany as deputy chief of staff of the U.S. Army European Command, Heidelberg. "It was a very desirable post which carried with it a beautiful house overlooking the valley of the Neckar."[57] Both the job and the living quarters failed to assuage completely his longing for an Asian assignment. While packing at West Point, he had received a letter from Gen. Walton H. Walker in Japan with the invitation to become Eighth Army chief of staff. Nevertheless, the orders to Germany had come first.[58]

On May 12, 1949, the first overt act of the cold war ceased: the Berlin blockade ended. General Lucius Clay, U.S. commander and military governor, retired; and John J. McCloy became U.S. high commissioner, headquartered in Frankfurt. The tripartite civilian High Commission of the United Kingdom, France, and the United States took over the governance of West Germany. Change brought an equally shaky peace; there may have been no further need for the dramatic airlift to Berlin, yet tensions still ran high. McCloy requested Taylor's reassignment as senior U.S. representative in Berlin at headquarters U.S. Commander, Berlin (USCOB).

Taylor's work was now with three opposite numbers—one French, one British, and one Russian—at the kommandatura, the central administration for both ideological parts of the divided city. (The Russians, in fact, had withdrawn from the cooperative effort when they had begun the blockade in 1948.) One hundred miles inside the iron curtain, Taylor saw to the defenses of West Berlin and helped along the training of his forces more as police than as soldiers. With West Berlin's economy in shambles from the recent war and from subsequent diplomatic intransigence, Taylor also supervised its recovering industrial production and, equally important, its morale.[59]

Relations with the Soviets remained delicate. As provocations became regular occurrences, Taylor found himself tendering more and more diplomatic protests to his Soviet Army counterpart, General Kotikov. During one visit Taylor ostentatiously admired a large sculpture of an elephant on the Russian's desk. The opportunity for a lesson in cold war brinkmanship seemed too good to pass up. "In my country," Taylor pointed out, "the elephant is the symbol of our most reactionary party, the one regarded as impeccably hostile to the working class." Taylor's use of Marxist dialectic was so effective that the elephant mysteriously disappeared before his next visit to Kotikov.[60]

In February 1951 he was ordered back to Washington for his second tour of duty there. He departed Berlin for his Potomacside assignment with some sadness, although he realized that the battle to preserve West Berlin was not one that he could win in a predictable time period. He served first as assistant chief of staff, G-3 (operations and training), under the new chief, Gen. J. Lawton Collins, Taylor's former Normandy corps commander. By August Lieutenant General Taylor jumped to deputy chief of staff for operations and training. Both positions gave him ample opportunity to watch Korean War developments. In the first job he managed an inspection trip to Korea in May 1951. It was his first visit there since 1937, when he had passed through on the way to his translator's job for "Vinegar Joe" Stilwell in China.

His orders were to inspect the Republic of Korea's (ROK) Army and to evaluate its capabilities and weaknesses for the skeptical Pentagon brass. The ROK had an undistinguished record in the year since the war began; American field commanders perceived their indigenous allies as ineffective, even cowardly. President Syngman Rhee's efforts to expand the native force only created more doubt in MacArthur, unsure as he was of South Korean Army leadership. The U.S. Army itself had become embittered when the logistical support it gave to ROK units ended up abandoned to the enemy; the North Koreans then inflicted substantial casualties on American units with American-made weapons.[61]

Before Taylor could arrive on his inspection tour, President Harry S Truman had removed MacArthur from the United Nations command. His replacement was Matthew Ridgway, seconded by James Van Fleet as commander of the Eighth Army.[62] MacArthur might have wanted to "just fade away" in public, but privately, because of his twenty-year investment in Asia, he just would not let go. A wide-ranging 1954 interview with the iconoclastic general of the Army (finally published a decade later) reveals some of MacArthur's prejudices.

> General MacArthur expressed pity—tinged with contempt—for Gens. John E. Hull and Maxwell Taylor, successors of [Mark] Clark. He described Taylor as "one of the most promising cadets at the academy when I was superintendent. . . . I foresaw a great future for him even then." But he said Taylor is a "careful and extremely ambitious young man with the peak of his career still ahead of him and will never do anything to jeopardize his career. . . . He will never make a move without contacting higher echelons," General MacArthur said. "Such a man has a definite value. Certainly, he is just what they want in Korea now [1954]. But when such a man is finally cornered and forced to make his own decisions—as such men inevitably are—they sometimes come up with some weird ones."[63]

In summary then, the embittered "Dugout Doug" saw Maxwell Taylor as little more than a high-level gofer, never doing any more than he was told. MacArthur rated Ridgway "at the bottom" of his generals there, called him "a chameleon" to boot, and venerated the martyred Walton Walker with the "highest" rating after the Eighth Army commander died in a Korean traffic accident in December 1959.[64]

The Korean War by then had more than military problems, however. Taylor had returned from Germany to see declining support for the war at home—a foreshadowing of public attitudes toward much later events. The popular support that President Truman had enjoyed when the war began in 1950 continued during the Pusan perimeter fighting and actually increased with the Inchon invasion. Then, with retreats from the Yalu River and Chosin Reservoir, public sentiment dived. By the end of 1951 there was less broad confidence for Truman himself than for the war. Sensing an opportunity, the Republican party in Congress, led by Sen. Robert Taft, made life miserable for the president by questioning his handling of the military in Korea.

Meanwhile, North Korea and China had attacked in a major new offensive in the spring of 1951; it bogged down when the Eighth Army pushed them back to the 38th parallel. In July came armistice negotiations and the beginning of a long military stalemate. Throughout, Taylor was the Pentagon staff man watching developments in the South Korean Army. On the home front, parties changed in the White House when the 1952 presidential elections brought in Republican Dwight Eisenhower.

Believing that the United Nations (UN) commander, Gen. Mark Clark, was hobbling him from displaying initiative, the unhappy General Van Fleet declared that he wanted to retire. Maxwell Taylor later claimed surprise when he learned that he would take Van Fleet's job, "even though the defensive strategy to which the Eighth Army was condemned was no more appealing to me than it had been to Van Fleet."[65]

Taylor's defense to MacArthur's criticism was that the policy was set in stone "and it was too late to change." In his later view the policy was erroneous, but by then the resources to move north simply were not available and any U.S. offensive action would be costly. "I was quite prepared to live with a defensive strategy and not kick against the pricks," he wrote of his assurances to President Eisenhower and Defense Secretary Charles E. Wilson before he embarked for Korea. He admitted some surprise, too, at the contrast between the administration's passivity about the Korean situation and the saber rattling of Secretary of State John Foster Dulles regarding "the containment of Red China." Nobody else in the executive branch displayed such vehemence.[66]

The Eighth Army was in its last stages of combat when Taylor arrived and soon faced one remaining defensive battle—the Kumsong Salient in July 1953. The armistice agreement was signed on July 27, 1953, and became effective that day. After the armistice Taylor, now a four-star general, set about keeping his forces at a respectable level of preparation.

Rather than have UN forces inactive, Taylor sought to keep them busy; he began Armed Forces Aid to Korea (AFAK), helping Korean reconstruction with Eighth Army resources. Endemic corruption was a problem, but, according to his son, "Taylor tightened procedures where he could, but he regarded the situation he faced in Korea as normal for a war-devastated Confucian society."[67]

Even a peacetime job had its dangers. In February 1954 Taylor was visiting an ROK headquarters for a briefing when Maj. Kin Ki-oh, a believer in the popular nationalistic March North movement, entered the conference and brandished a pistol at the U.S. Eighth Army commander. Jumping on the would-be assassin, a Korean general restrained him.

In April 1954 Gen. John E. Hull (the other on MacArthur's least-liked list) retired as commander, Far East. Ridgway, now Army chief of staff, was in hot water with both Eisenhower and Secretary of Defense Wilson, and the rumor mills had been pushing Taylor as the likeliest successor for his old Latin American and Airborne mentor. Meanwhile, Taylor was to succeed Hull. In February 1955, he was called to Washington as buzzing increased about Ridgway's impending retirement. On successive days, February 23 and 24, Taylor met with Wilson and then with President Eisenhower. Both men asked bluntly if Taylor would cooperate if indeed he became Ridgway's successor. Ike wanted him to remain Far East commander a little longer before taking the Washington job. Back again with Wilson after meeting with the president, the defense secretary tried to suggest some names for vice chief of staff. When Taylor said that he would not take the job as number one without naming his own number two, Wilson backed down. The path was clear for Maxwell Taylor to become Army chief of staff.

PART I

THE CERTAIN TRUMPET

*"If the trumpet give an uncertain sound,
who shall prepare himself to the battle?"*

— I CORINTHIANS 14:8

CHAPTER I

The General and the President

Waiting to meet Maxwell Taylor at Andrews Air Force Base the morning of June 23, 1955, were outgoing Army Chief of Staff Matthew Ridgway and Army Secretary Robert Stevens, also a lame duck. Stevens had impaled himself during the Army-McCarthy hearings the previous spring and was soon to be replaced by Wilber Brucker, a World War I veteran and former governor of Michigan. On June 29 Taylor got a welcome from the president, who asked for "teamwork," and on June 30 he took the oath as twentieth chief of staff of the Army.

Max and Diddy settled comfortably into Quarters One at Fort Myer, which had a proud Army history. Once a noted cavalry post, it was also the site for developments in Army aviation, with Orville Wright himself circling the drill field. In 1908 its Quarters One became the official residence of the Army's chief of staff; some distinguished occupants preceding Maxwell Taylor included Douglas MacArthur, George Marshall, Dwight Eisenhower, and Omar Bradley. There, with the help of a large staff, the Taylors would host the social activities that were part of the job. Always an exponent of physical fitness, Max kept up his tennis routine, again with a tennis-playing aide right in his entourage.

When in Washington (like other chiefs, he would travel frequently, especially to Army activities at home and abroad), Taylor followed a very precise routine. After walking briskly from Quarters One through nearby Arlington Cemetery, he would be picked up by his driver and whisked to the Pentagon, arriving at his office at precisely 8:00 A.M.

But, ruffles and flourishes aside, this was not a propitious time to be chief of staff. Across the Potomac the role of the Army in this postwar era was being diminished. The Battle of the Bulge was history, and everybody shuddered at the thought of another Korea. The battle of the budget did not yield much glory, and it sometimes seemed to the Army that its onetime chief of staff, General of the Army Eisenhower, was bending over backward not to favor his former service. Ike was intent on being president.

What does a chief of staff do? Asking and answering this question in his memoirs, Taylor reminds us that the chief does not command the Army. "His direct boss is the Secretary of Army," with whom he spends much time, both in advising and in making sure that the secretarial orders are carried out. But the real boss of the secretary of the Army is the secretary of defense. Another important role that Taylor describes is that of Army representative on the Joint Chiefs of Staff (JCS).

> In this capacity, he is independent of the control of the Sec-
> retary of the Army and serves as a member of a committee
> inserted between the Secretary of Defense and . . . the gener-
> als and admirals who command the field forces which fight
> our wars overseas and defend our shores and continental
> airspace.[1]

The group met routinely in a secured room known as the "tank." Before going into Taylor's part in the strategy debates there, we need, first, to understand the milieu of the Eisenhower era.

THE SITUATION FACING TAYLOR

When Maxwell Taylor became Army chief of staff, Eisenhower—already president for two and one-half years—had established his own ideas on the budget, strategy, and national security. Ike had campaigned on two major premises: to end the Korean War and to reduce the budget. The two were related because ending the war was a necessary prelude to reducing the budget, but he needed to do more. His goal—to cut the overall budget from $74 billion for the fiscal year in which he took office to $70 billion the following year—meant a further paring of the defense budget. This, in turn, called for a close look at the kind of strategy the United States was going to pursue in the post–Korean War period.

Eisenhower's conservative economic views dominated his thinking on all issues, including national security. These views were genuine and long-standing. His strategic concepts on assuming office he set forth in his memoirs: to rely on deterrence and to rule out preventive war; to stress the role of nuclear technology and reduce reliance on U.S. conventional forces; to maintain allied land forces around the Soviet periphery; to stress economic strength, especially through reduced defense budgets; and to prepare for a continued struggle with the USSR over decades. To amalgamate these ideas and sell them to Americans and allies, the president used organizational means, careful selection of key appointees,[2] his own large experience in handling bureaucracies, and his great rapport with the American people.

At the apex of the defense and foreign policy process, Eisenhower refurbished the loosely structured National Security Council (NSC). Besides dealing formally with this restructured NSC, Eisenhower also depended on informal meetings about defense-related matters. The number of such meetings was substantial. One well-placed observer who was present at nearly all NSC meetings during the second administration believed that the informal office meetings were much more important than the council sessions.[3]

By July 1953—almost two years before Taylor's appointment—Eisenhower had concluded that the newly appointed service chiefs should reexamine U.S. strategic policy. Because the Korean armistice was about to be signed, the president wished to develop a long-range defense posture. He wanted the new chiefs, before they were caught up in their office duties, to evaluate overall defense policy. Their report was the first step in what subsequently became known as the "New Look," which the president later defined in his memoirs as

> first a reallocation of resources among the forces and second the placing of greater emphasis than formerly on the deterrent and destructive power of improved nuclear weapons, better means of delivery, and effective air-defense units.

The chiefs of staff agreed on a basic paper of strategic premises and guidelines. But how should they translate these generalities into the specifics for the fiscal year 1955 defense budget? They concluded that they could make no substantial changes in the defense budget of $42 billion. They reasoned that no changes in the perceived threat or alliance commitments had occurred and that there was no new guidance on employing nuclear weapons.

Defense Secretary Wilson put this problem on the NSC table October 13, 1953. The reaction of Treasury Secretary George Humphrey (who expected a defense budget of $36 billion) and of Budget Director Joseph M. Dodge was what one source called "horrified." It fell to JCS Chairman Arthur W. Radford to defend the Joint Chiefs' premises. The admiral felt that presidential guidance for employing nuclear weapons was at the heart of the matter and what he said had very significant results. He argued that if the administration accepted the use of nuclear weapons from the outset of a conflict, then it could economize on its forces. This premise led to an NSC session on October 29 at which the president approved NSC 162/2, the policy basis of the New Look. Picking up Radford's suggestion of October 13, the paper placed maximum reliance on nuclear weapons from the outset of a conflict.

However, Radford's talk of October 13 had been entirely his own; that is, neither the Army nor the Navy agreed with the new NSC policy on nuclear war. Secretary of Defense Wilson, with Radford's help, somehow got Army Chief Ridgway and Navy Chief Carney to go along, if reluctantly, with the new policy. Thus, the defense budget came down to a level acceptable to Eisenhower and Humphrey.[4]

Members of Congress examined the New Look during the hearings of the fiscal year 1955 defense budget, but they offered no challenge to the concept and almost none to the particulars. Floor debate was more active in the Senate than in the House, but in neither case was it systematic or informed. With the clearing of the defense appropriations, Eisenhower had gained his strategic policy.

By early 1955, as mentioned in the Prologue, Gen. Maxwell Taylor was to enter the picture. Because of Ridgway's misgivings about the Eisenhower strategy, Ike had decided to replace him that summer. In February, Taylor, a leading candidate for the job, was summoned from his post in the Far East to discuss his prospective appointment with the president and Secretary of Defense Wilson.

At the February 24 meeting, Eisenhower issued two demands. The new chief of staff would have to "wholeheartedly accept that his primary responsibility related to his joint duties," and he must "hold views as to doctrine, basic principles, and relationships which are in accord with those of the President. Loyalty in spirit as well as in letter is essential." Taylor's reply "indicated complete understanding and acceptance of these views of the President."[5]

Now that Taylor was Army chief of staff, he and the other chiefs were to hear more on the subject from the president. They subsequently requested through Gen. Andrew Goodpaster of the White House staff some explanation of Eisenhower's concept of the Joint Chiefs. They were told:

> While each is the head of his own service, his main task is—or should be—as one of the Joint Chiefs of Staff. The President does not consider them as advocates for the Army, Navy, etc. Though each has a particular service background, they should think and act as a body. . . . He thought great harm had been done on past occasions when the Chiefs of Staff were called upon to speak out on individual policy views without regard to announced Administration policy. . . . He would agree that there are, of course, great service pressures on the individual Chiefs of Staff, even more in peacetime than in war. Subordinates in the services may advance service interests very strongly. The Chief of Staff will be acutely aware of these pressures and sensitive to them, but he must shape them into the larger purpose.[6]

TAYLOR'S CHALLENGE TO THE NEW LOOK

In his first year as Army chief, Taylor ran headlong into strategic issues that eventually brought him into conflict with the president. While awaiting his return to Washington during the spring of 1955, Taylor received a copy of the administration's 1955 Basic National Security Policy (BNSP) paper. In examining the document, he was "struck by the breadth of its language and the degree of departure from the dogma of Massive Retaliation." Accordingly, he decided to develop his own "National Military Program" more in keeping with the Army viewpoint and yet, as he saw it, following BNSP guidance. The National Military Program went through several refinements during Taylor's early months in Washington and was the basis of what eventually became his proposed strategy of flexible response.

Taylor's program stressed deterring and defeating local aggression besides deterring general war, as emphasized in Eisenhower's New Look strategy. It would use resources to build up conventional forces. Moreover, as Taylor saw it, these forces needed to be able to employ tactical atomic weapons, even though no one was yet certain how they would work out.

By late winter of 1956 Secretary Wilson thought that it was time to assemble the military chiefs and to reexamine the basic strategic issues. He set up a meeting for them in Puerto Rico and joined them at its conclusion. Taylor thought it was a good opportunity to introduce the National Military Program into the Joint Chiefs arena, but, as he relates in *Trumpet,* "My colleagues read this Army study politely and then quietly put it to one side."[7] This reaction was not surprising, for Taylor's program would mean more money for the Army, presumably at the expense of the other services if Eisenhower was to hold the lid on the budget. As a result of the meeting, the Joint Chiefs called for a bigger budget than the earlier target of $34 billion by 1960—but without changing the New Look strategy.

Ike was bothered. "The JCS memorandum seemed to say that the U.S. military position had worsened in the last three years." With that he would not agree. Specifically, the president could not understand why, given America's technological superiority, manpower could not be cut. Secretary Wilson agreed and opined that more military strength over the past three years "would not have bettered us in our international position." Taylor's new program was off to a bad start.

In the same month, March 1956, the Joint Chiefs' draft of the new Joint Strategic Objectives Plan (JSOP) presented Taylor another occasion for questioning a basic premise of Eisenhower's strategy. His first opponent, Chairman Radford, had his eye on costs. The admiral began waving his cutlass at conventional forces, which were mostly Army. His justification was the early use of atomic weapons, but then Taylor proposed that the new JSOP limit the use of atomics during the early stages of combat with the USSR. Radford and the other chiefs were, though, still wearing the New Look; their standoff with Taylor required many gatherings that spring between the president and his military advisers.

In late March Radford brought the Joint Chiefs to the White House. He opened the meeting with the president by saying "that unless brought under control, a situation may develop in which the Services are involved in increasing public disagreement among themselves. Also, in the last four or five months, quite a large number of 'split' issues had to be taken up to Secretary Wilson." The most troublesome concerned the use of atomic weapons. The president agreed that the subject was one that "required great care in discussion"; however, he was clear in his own mind that "in any war with the Soviets we would use them." While he had the Joint Chiefs there, Ike went on to tell them that he wanted it understood "that any of them who wished could always come along with Radford to see him."[8]

Two months later Taylor accepted the president's offer. He and Radford appeared at Eisenhower's office to discuss the use of atomics, again in the context of the JSOP, which was by now before the Joint Chiefs for decision. On the one hand, the chairman and the Air Force and Navy chiefs took the view, said Taylor, that all strategic planning revolved around using atomic weapons. Taylor, on the other hand, argued that, given the concept of nuclear deterrence, the United States would more likely be fighting small wars not requiring atomic weapons.

The president disagreed; the USSR would use atomic weapons "at once," should it decide to go to war. Further, U.S. thinking should be based on such use. It was, he said, "fatuous to think that the US and USSR would be locked into a life and death struggle without using such weapons." On the question of local wars, the president declared that "the tactical use of atomic weapons against military targets would be no more likely to trigger off a big war than the use of twenty-ton block busters." All in all, the first year was frustrating for the new Army chief of staff and his National Military Program.[9]

Taylor was really under fire at this point, both as strategist and chief of service. If the bridge was out in Washington, however, he could try to build one elsewhere. He granted interview after interview to magazines, journals, and newspapers. Not surprisingly, he especially liked to address audiences outside Washington. One speech, "A National Military Program," was given off the record to the New York Council on Foreign Relations in May 1956. Hamilton Fish Armstrong, editor of its journal, *Foreign Affairs,* was so impressed that he invited Taylor to write an article. Taylor was happy to accept because many influential people in the private sector who read the journal were interested in foreign policy and security issues. But the article, "Security Through Deterrence," ran into clearance problems in the Departments of Defense and State as well as with the JCS chairman; the Defense Department declined clearance. Taylor's views, they argued, conflicted with approved policy, and the disagreement should not be carried into the public forum. The article was never published.

If atomics were what the Army needed in its budget battle, then Taylor would come up with an atomic idea. He could still hold his conviction that the United States needed additional conventional forces. In the summer of 1956 he projected the image of an army equipped with the most modern weapons and willing to experiment. Taking no time for extensive analysis, the Army undertook the program with zeal under Taylor's prodding. Under the rubric of PENTANA (pentagonal atomic-nonatomic army), the Army staff developed the Pentomic Division, a small division designed to fight in either atomic or conventional war.

In October, Taylor marched into the White House with his Pentana Plan to brief the president, Secretary Wilson, and Army Secretary Brucker. After explaining the "why" of the new organization, Taylor pointed out that it would need new kinds of equipment still being developed. In essence, Taylor was trying to establish the groundwork for future expansion of the Army budget.

An interested president listened, but countered with some points of his own. Sensitive to the services' appeals to the media to support their budget efforts, Eisenhower opposed a publicity campaign for the new division. The Army, said the president, should regard it simply as experimental. He hoped, too, that it would cut down on manpower. Taylor spoke for the Army that a tactical nuclear battlefield required more, not fewer, people, but no one was listening.[10]

Late in 1956 Eisenhower turned to the fiscal year 1958 defense budget. He summoned all the principals, including Taylor and the other chiefs, in his office on December 19 to discuss the new budget. In spending money for defense, he noted, one approached a point of "lessening returns or even of net loss." In the end, he said, this could "weaken the country's overall position." Whereas he realized that some members of the Joint Chiefs might doubt the wisdom of the defense budget, in the end it was a matter of presidential decision.[11]

Ten days later, in the Pentagon, an unusual meeting followed through on the December 19 meeting. Taylor was not present; the chiefs were not players on this made-up team. Jerry Persons, Andrew Goodpaster, and Bryce Harlow came over from the White House; Secretary Wilson and Admiral Radford were the principals from the Defense Department. They talked about those absent, however. The question was, how committed were the chiefs to Eisenhower's defense budget? Wilson and Radford declared that the chiefs went along with the president's program, but Goodpaster pointed out that the group had not intended this when they met with the president. Radford responded that the chiefs had not spoken up in that session. One of the defense officials present observed that at least one of the services was organizing an "end run" to Congress and seemed determined not to let "the President get in the way."[12] Nothing much came of this threat, for Secretary of the Treasury Humphrey held a news conference on January 15, 1957, in which he predicted a "depression that will curl your hair." This statement stimulated Congress to join the president in holding down the defense budget for fiscal 1958. Again, everything boiled down to dollars and cents.

TAYLOR'S FINAL BATTLES AND DEPARTURE

By the summer of 1957 Maxwell Taylor had completed two frustrating years as Army chief of staff. Even though the 1956 crises in Suez and Hungary seemed to prove his point about conventional wars, his National Military Program had made little headway. Rather, the fiscal year 1959 defense budget was threatening Army manpower. The Defense Department planned to reduce Army strength from 900,000 to 700,000 over several years, with an initial drop of 50,000 as part of the new budget. Although the Army leadership did not become aware of this planned cut until July 22, Taylor met it head-on at a meeting of the National Security Council on July 25.

After the Defense Department had explained the manpower cuts, Taylor showed how the cuts could be deep, dangerous wounds. He listed the varieties of possible wars (as set forth in current strategic appraisals): cold war, conflicts short of general war, and general war, with little likelihood of that occurring by surprise. Taylor stressed that the new manpower goals were based on *the least likely war possibility*. He concluded that

> the constant downward trend in certain types of forces may lead to the abandonment of a forward strategy . . . we will lose still further the ability to react swiftly and effectively to the most likely form of military challenge—limited war—and run the hazard of . . . backing into the general war we are seeking to avoid.[13]

Taylor's logic may not have persuaded the others at the NSC meeting, but, ironically, he got outside help—from the Soviets. When the Soviets launched their satellite *Sputnik* in the fall of 1957, one reaction was a small increase in the Army budget for fiscal year 1959. This change meant a smaller cut in Army manpower than the Defense Department had programmed.

The president, however, was not one to overreact to *Sputnik*, especially when it came to defense spending. On October 30 he told the new secretary of defense, Neil McElroy, "If the budget is too high, inflation occurs, which in effect cuts down the value of the dollar, so nothing is gained and the process is self defeating." Ike still intended to cut manpower, and the Army's Pentomic Division would help him do that. This development was not exactly what Taylor had in mind when he had approved the new division for the atomic battlefield.

When McElroy sought the president's guidance on the fiscal 1959 defense budget, Ike maintained that the services needed to cut down on their wish lists. He reminded McElroy that "the individual chiefs tend to be caught up in demands for more for each separate service and are unable to review the matter in terms of their responsibility." McElroy suggested that he bring the Joint Chiefs in to obtain the president's views. Eisenhower countered with a proposal to invite them to a stag dinner.[14]

After dinner Taylor heard the president say that during three meetings that day several people expressed concern over the rivalry among the military services. The Joint Chiefs "must be above narrow service considerations." Each chief "should try to approach problems from a national standpoint. . . . It is wrong," he continued, "to stress or simply to press for Army, Navy, and other service interests. Perhaps the members of the JCS should turn over the executive direction of their service to their deputy and concentrate on their joint responsibilities."

Disagreeing with certain aspects of the president's proposal, Chief of Naval Operations (CNO) Adm. Arleigh Burke felt that diverse views were desirable, reflecting individual backgrounds. Taylor observed that the problem was really budgetary and, further, that the president's proposal concerning the vice chiefs would require an organizational overhaul. Deputy Defense Secretary Donald Quarles was for a single defense appropriation that the department could in turn apportion out to the services. In closing the session, Eisenhower said it was "essential that the group stay close together. They must stand firmly behind the budget. . . . Once they agreed to it, although it may not meet their individual desires, they should say this is what we believe."[15]

Thwarted in his direct efforts to get more resources, Taylor was always on the lookout for a strategic approach to increase the Army's budget. He saw an opening in an article by John Foster Dulles in the October 1957 issue of *Foreign Affairs:* the secretary of state hoped that in the decade ahead low-yield atomic weapons would permit less reliance on the country's "vast retaliatory power." In April 1958 this comment was the subject at an extraordinary meeting in McElroy's office. Secretary Dulles was present, along with the deputy secretary of defense, the service secretaries, the Joint Chiefs of Staff, and others. McElroy said that the president had requested this conference to consider an important matter Dulles had raised with him a few days earlier—national strategy.

Dulles explained that for some years he had supported the massive retaliation concept. Now he wondered whether tactical atomic weapons made more sense for U.S. strategic policy. Others began to inject their own thoughts. According to Chairman Nathan Twining, the smaller weapons being developed could not stop a large-scale attack. Taylor pointed out that tactical nuclear weapons had the advantage of strategic flexibility but that not enough were in the inventory. Deputy Defense Secretary Quarles said that the country could not escape relying on massive retaliation. And so it went, an interesting and inconclusive session; still, Taylor could assume that Dulles would side with him when the matter arose again.[16]

Several months later the question of strategy came before the NSC. At issue was the 1958 revision of the BNSP. This time the Navy and Marines backed up Taylor in making the Army's point: they needed to pump iron into the forces that would fight in limited wars. Acting as the spokesman for those who favored this view, Taylor made a strong presentation. He expected support from Dulles, but the secretary remained silent.[17] However, this forum differed from that in McElroy's office in one important respect: Eisenhower, architect and still proponent of a nuclear-heavy strategy, was present. After hearing the Air Force position—that is, to retain the status quo—the president decided that the BNSP would not be revised that year.

To Taylor, the status quo stance meant that the 1960 defense budget would be as frail as the previous budget had been. He was right. Eisenhower was determined to have a balanced budget in fiscal year 1960. As he tells in his memoirs,

> I planned to let the Congress know that if it materially added to the budget I would respond with a veto. . . . In preparing the budget, the giant military demands gave us, as usual, the gigantic headaches. No major item budgeted in each of the Armed Services was approved for inclusion unless the question "why" was answered to my satisfaction.

In November 1958, when the 1960 defense budget was almost ready, the president met with his civilian defense advisers and the chairman of the Joint Chiefs. In the Defense Department presentation, McElroy pointed out that he had reduced the service estimates by almost a billion dollars, but Director of the Budget Maurice Stans called for more cuts—in the vicinity of three to four billion—and Ike concurred. Meanwhile, Eisenhower thought it wise to have a stag dinner, to include the Joint Chiefs, prior to a formal NSC meeting on the reworked Defense Department budget.

Taylor described the session as follows:

> We Chiefs had been given to understand that the purpose of the meeting was to allow us to discuss the problems of the new budget with the President. However, it turned out to be quite otherwise. . . . After receiving something in the nature of a "pep talk," the Chiefs were allowed to respond.[18]

The White House record of the meeting stated that President Eisenhower asked each chief to express his views in light of the "vital necessity of maintaining both an adequate defense and a national economy not impaired by inflation, loss of confidence, or run on the dollar." The paragraph summarizing Taylor's reply to the president and the latter's rejoinder is instructive:

> General Taylor, who spoke first, questioned the division of Defense funds among the services, indicating that the decision to carry forward the same percentage division this year as existed in previous years was arbitrary and failed to take into account the completing of the Air Force reequipment phase and the rising need for Army modernization. As to the broad point concerning consideration of a sound economy, he said that he as a military man respected this consideration but felt that it lay outside his responsibility. The President contested this view, pointing out that at our military colleges a major subject of inquiry is the economy and industrial base of popular adversaries; if these considerations have military

significance for our adversaries, they have military significance for ourselves.[19]

A few days later McElroy pressed the chiefs for written endorsement of the new budget, although they had not had much time to
consider the document. Finally, on January 19, 1959, the Joint Chiefs
gave the budget what Taylor called "rather tepid support"; nonetheless, McElroy presented it to Congress. What bothered the chiefs was
not the overall dollar amount of the defense budget so much as the
way their individual services were funded.[20]

By 1959 the climate was right for Congress to intervene in defense
matters. Technology was in a state of flux, raising many technical
and strategic questions; few people seemed certain of the answers.
Because the services were far apart in their objectives, Congress could
readily see them swiping at one another or at the administration.
Finally, there was the intrusion of politics: the Democratic sweep in
the 1958 congressional elections and the upcoming presidential election encouraged Congress to challenge the administration.

Committees in the House and Senate asked the usual questions
about hardware and strategy—and the more unusual question about
who had played what part in developing the defense budget, including its guidelines. In these hearings the senior military spelled out
publicly how they disagreed on the particulars of the defense budget.
Still, the most spectacular hearings that spring were not those related
directly to the appropriations process; rather, those conducted by
Senator Lyndon Johnson's Preparedness Subcommittee wanted to
know exactly how the Eisenhower defense budget had been developed.

The memorandum of support for the budget solicited by McElroy
from the chiefs spurred the Johnson subcommittee hearings. The
chairman summoned the Joint Chiefs to express their views under
oath and subsequently to file written statements concerning their
reservations on the budget. These hearings showed the break between the administration and the chiefs, especially Taylor, on both
strategic and budgetary issues. Taylor summed up his own view of
the importance of these hearings as follows:

> This open testimony of the Chiefs of Staff before the Johnson
> Subcommittee had a country-wide impact. Along with their
> testimony released from closed hearings before other Con-
> gressional committees, it revealed for the first time the extent
> of the schism within the Joint Chiefs of Staff and the division

in their views on Massive Retaliation and related matters of strategy. This revelation profoundly disturbed many members of Congress as well as thoughtful citizens generally.[21]

The *New York Times* of March 9, 1959, carried the story of the chiefs' testimony before Johnson's subcommittee, as well as the texts of their memorandums to the committee. Meeting that same morning with JCS Chairman Twining, an irked President Eisenhower instructed Twining "to caution the Joint Chiefs that the military in this country is a tool and not a policy-making body; the Joint Chiefs are not responsible for high-level political decisions." As the meeting came to a close, "the President philosophized briefly on the difficulties of a democracy running a military establishment in peacetime."[22]

The hearings, politically embarrassing to the administration, were undoubtedly so designed. They were, in effect, setting the stage for the defense debate of the 1960 campaign. Although they had little effect on either the Eisenhower strategy or defense budget, they did mark the final milestone in Taylor's Army career. The *Times* article of March 9 noted that in his testimony Taylor was among all the chiefs the "most vehement" in his comments concerning the administration's defense policies. On that same day an Army announcement stated that General Maxwell Taylor would be retiring at the end of June.

Apparently Taylor would have been interested in being chairman JCS, but that was not in the cards. Earlier in the month Secretary McElroy had discussed with him the possibility of succeeding Gen. Lauris Norstad, supreme allied commander Europe (SACEUR), after a year of understudying him as deputy. Taylor advised the secretary that he was not interested, and McElroy so advised the president.[23]

From early March until the end of his term, Taylor gave some thirteen speeches touching on his disagreements with the administration. The best known was that before the National Press Club five days before his retirement. There he declared that frustration in his efforts to modernize the Army had led to his decision to retire an "obsolescent general from inventory." He had, of course, completed the full four-year tour as chief of staff.

His more important permanent contribution came by way of a book, *The Uncertain Trumpet*, published by Harper. He worked on the book during the last couple of months of his tour while leaving day-to-day Army affairs to his vice chief and successor-to-be, Gen. Lyman Lemnitzer. With the aid of selected Army staff officers, mainly from his immediate office, he assembled the supporting materials and drafted the book, a trenchant critique of Eisenhower's defense strategy.[24]

Reviewing *The Uncertain Trumpet* in the *New York Times*, Jack Raymond pointed out that Taylor timed the book to coincide with the opening of Congress on January 6, 1960, "in hope that it might trip off a great debate on national security in the final year of the Eisenhower Administration." It did that and more, turning out to be the basis for the defense program set forth by John Fitzgerald Kennedy (JFK) in his successful 1960 campaign against Richard Nixon. It also led to Kennedy's appointment of Taylor to high positions in his administration, positions that were to lead to the most important decade of Taylor's career—the 1960s, the decade of Vietnam.

But in June 1959 Taylor's bags were packed, the uniforms ready for storage. After retiring, he went for a while to Mexico City as chairman of the board of the Mexican Light and Power Company. It was a long way from reading meters in Kansas City, but it was also a long way from Milton Davenport's exciting tales of battle. At the end of 1960, when there was a management change in the company, he became a New Yorker. The Lincoln Center for the Performing Arts was being constructed, and Maxwell Taylor was to be its president. The curtain seemed to have closed on his Army career—but it was signaling only an intermission.

CHAPTER 2

A Soldier in Camelot

On January 20, 1961, when John F. Kennedy set forth his vision for the United States in his inaugural address, Maxwell Taylor, the new president of the Lincoln Center for the Performing Arts, was comfortably settled in a New York apartment, the first home the Taylors had ever owned. As he listened to the president's activist phrases—"Let every nation know, whether it wishes us well or ill, that we shall pay any price, bear any burden, meet any hardship . . . to secure the success of liberty"—Taylor could not know that the president's first attempt to put these principles into action would lead to Taylor's own return to government service.

Taylor had not lost interest in national security problems—quite the contrary. *Foreign Affairs* had just published his article "Security Will Not Wait," presumably directed to the new administration. "The military trend is running against us," he wrote, "and decisive measures are needed to reverse it." His basic theme was the same as that in *The Uncertain Trumpet:* the United States needed a flexible military strategy designed to deter small or large wars and to assist in winning the cold war. Actually, the new president was already familiar with these views, having used Taylor's book as a basis for criticizing Eisenhower's defense policies. Perhaps Taylor had aimed the article at the fledgling administration—a reminder both about strategy and about himself.

In any event, Taylor did return to government in what was to be the most influential decade of his life. It all began with the infamous Bay of Pigs fiasco that Camelot got itself into only a few months after the president's militant phrases had rung out to the world. To understand how the situation came about, we should look back at the Eisenhower administration's Cuban policy.

Fidel Castro took over in Havana in January 1959 with much popular support in the United States for his government. But as communist involvement in the Castro coalition increased, Castro began to portray the United States as the enemy of his revolution. By March 1960, Ike, fed up, approved a Central Intelligence Agency (CIA) recommendation: to form a force of Cuban exiles for possible military use against Castro.[1]

How the force would act was not clear, but the first idea involved guerrilla operations. By the time of the U.S. elections in November, it had evolved into an invasion plan, with a military force of sorts being trained "secretly" in Guatemala. As with all contingency plans, its producers might not put the show on the road, but, if they did, they had many ways of doing so and many choices to present to the new president. And, as always, when a military force is created for a specific purpose, the creation began to take on a life of its own.

The situation in Cuba continued to deteriorate until, in one of his last diplomatic initiatives, Ike severed relations with the Castro government in early 1961. Thus, Eisenhower's Cuban legacy to the new administration was, in the words of Kennedy insider Arthur Schlesinger, "a force of Cuban exiles under American training in Guatemala, a committee of Cuban politicians under American control in Florida," and a CIA plan to use these exiles for invading Cuba and for installing the committee as the provisional government of Cuba.[2]

President-elect Kennedy first learned of the Cuban plan in mid-November 1960. Throughout the early days of his administration, he considered various options and questions: Should the force be landed? If so, where? Would such a landing provoke an uprising against Castro? How could the force be dispersed if not used? One thing was clear: he never had any intention of employing U.S. troops.

In a decision that he later called "stupid," the new president finally gave the go-ahead to Operation Zapata, an invasion of Cuba by the exiles. It began on Monday, April 17, 1961, and ended two days later as a complete disaster, all the invaders killed or captured.

In New York, Taylor read about the event in the newspapers but, like any other reader, had no inside information. Then on April 21, everything changed. He received a call from President Kennedy, whom he did not know personally, asking him to come to Washington immediately to discuss the disaster.

THE CUBA STUDY GROUP

The following day Kennedy briefed Taylor privately on the origins and purpose of the Cuban operation. Wanting to find out why it had failed, he asked Taylor to work out of the White House as chairman of a study group consisting of Attorney General Robert Kennedy and two involved officials, CIA head Allen Dulles and CNO Adm. Arleigh Burke.

The charter of the Cuba Study Group was set forth in JFK's letter to Taylor that same day, April 22. Interestingly enough, the letter made only passing mention of the main purpose of the group—to discern the lessons of the Bay of Pigs. Instead, it emphasized determining what the role of the United States should be in guerrilla and antiguerrilla activities. Taylor would obviously be the most objective member of the group. Robert Kennedy would be looking after his brother's interests; Dulles and Burke, those of the CIA and Joint Chiefs of Staff, respectively. This group was Taylor's first acquaintance with Bobby Kennedy, who impressed him favorably. Their activities together in the group led to a warm friendship, although years later they would differ over the Vietnam War.

All in all, the group met with some fifty witnesses in twenty-one sessions. The final report, which Taylor sent to the president on June 13, consisted of four separate memorandums: a narrative of the operations, the causes of failure, the conclusions of the group, and their recommendations.[3] We will return to the report shortly after looking at an interesting incident that occurred in the course of the investigation. It revealed to Taylor the president's concerns about the Joint Chiefs.

What bothered the president about the Operation Zapata decision was whether the Joint Chiefs had fulfilled their responsibilities in advising him. They, of course, felt that they had; after all, this was a CIA undertaking, with their role one of only comment and support. Their doubts about certain aspects of the plan—particularly the choice of landing areas—apparently never came through clearly to JFK. One of the Joint Chiefs, Lyman Lemnitzer, later told me that communicating with the new president was harder than with Eisenhower because Kennedy did not seem to grasp military matters.[4] In any case, whatever the justification, Kennedy felt that the Joint Chiefs had let him down; from then on, relations between the chief executive and his senior military advisers were strained.

This was the prevailing atmosphere when Taylor ran into JFK outside the Oval Office in late May. Kennedy said that he would be going over to the Pentagon to talk to the chiefs and asked for suggestions. As Taylor tells it, he had by chance developed a working paper on the subject of the chiefs' responsibilities to the president. Taylor's ideas apparently coincided with the president's because Kennedy took the paper to incorporate into his own at the Pentagon meeting. The president's remarks about the Cuban affair included these:

> I must say frankly that I do not think that the JCS gave me the support to which the President is entitled. While the CIA was in charge of it, I would say that you should have been continuously scrutinizing the military soundness of their plan and advising them and me as to your views. The record as I know it does not show this kind of watchfulness.
>
> [Regarding the role of the JCS] the advice you owe me as Commander-in-Chief . . . should come to me directly. I imagine that there will be times when the Secretary of Defense will not agree with your advice to me, in which case I would naturally expect him to tell me so and why.[5]

Kennedy further indicated that the chairman would normally represent the chiefs in meetings with the president but that the chiefs should work out their own procedures to have the chairman express their views, corporate or otherwise. He hoped, though, that they could agree among themselves on proposed courses of action.

On June 13, 1961, Taylor forwarded to the president the results of the Cuba Study Group. After describing the operation and its failures, the report went on to the group's conclusions; two, in particular, are pertinent: (1) the Joint Chiefs had not adequately reviewed the plan, and (2) the United States must in the future be prepared to conduct such operations.

The final part of the report was the group's recommendations, which stressed matters of organization. Maxwell Taylor had always inclined to address political problems with organizational innovations. In this case, the principal recommendation was to establish a strategic resources group. Headed by a presidentially appointed chairman, the group's high-level membership would include the undersecretary of state, deputy secretary of defense, director of the CIA, and chairman of the JCS. Its purpose would be to serve the president as a staff for cold war operations. Naturally, Secretary of State Dean Rusk was less than enthusiastic, but the president eventually approved a Special Group Counterinsurgency. Although its powers were somewhat less than envisioned in the recommendation, it did serve to instigate high-level interest in counterinsurgency for a time.

MILITARY REPRESENTATIVE OF THE PRESIDENT

The president had wanted Taylor in the administration in some capacity from the outset, and others had suggested him. In reporting Taylor's appointment as president of the Lincoln Center in October 1960, the *New York Times* had opined that, should Kennedy win the election, he might try to bring the general into his administration. In fact, a few days after his inauguration Kennedy had Secretary of State Rusk telephone Taylor to offer him the ambassadorship to France; Taylor, having just signed a five-year contract with the Lincoln Center, declined.

Now that Taylor was in the White House for the Cuban study, Robert Kennedy approached him about a nonspecific job with the administration; toward the end of the study, this became an offer of director of the Central Intelligence Agency to replace the bureaucratically wounded Allen Dulles. In turning down this position, Taylor did say he would accept a job that called on his military background. Incidentally, the people in the Kennedy White House believed erroneously that Taylor had resigned as Army chief of staff in protest over the Eisenhower nuclear-heavy strategy. He had, in fact, served his full four years and retired.

There was talk with JFK of reactivating the position of chief of staff to the commander in chief as a spot for Taylor. Roosevelt had created the position in World War II. Admiral William Leahy, who held the wartime position, also acted as chairman of the Joint Chiefs of Staff. At that time, however, the Joint Chiefs were nonstatutory, and there was no JCS chairman. When the National Security Act of 1947 established the Joint Chiefs and its 1949 amendment created a statutory chairman, however, naming another de facto chairman was probably illegal.

The solution was to create a new position within the White House known as the military representative of the president and to recall

Taylor to active service to fill that position. Word of the possible appointment was leaked to *New York Times* columnist James Reston and other reporters and made the papers on June 20 to test reaction to the appointment.

In making the appointment, Kennedy wrote a fairly specific letter as to what he expected of Taylor. He was first of all to be a staff officer, without command authority, and with interests in primarily the military and intelligence fields. He was not to be interposed between the president and any of his statutory advisers such as the secretary of defense or the Joint Chiefs of Staff.[6] In the intelligence field he was to work closely with the president's Foreign Intelligence Advisory Board (of which he had been a member from May 4 until his new appointment) and to ascertain that the government's intelligence apparatus was meeting the president's needs.

Two tasks the president did assign to Taylor are of specific interest and are worth quoting:

> Review the planning being done on Berlin and submit to me your comments and recommendations.
>
> Review the planning on Vietnam and give me your views on how to respond to President Diem's request for a 100,000-man increase in his army.[7]

Copies of this letter went to Rusk, Secretary of Defense Robert McNamara, Dean Acheson (then providing advice to Kennedy on Berlin), McGeorge Bundy, and Allen Dulles. To avoid misunderstandings and to cement his own role, Taylor suggested a meeting, which the president promptly scheduled, with JFK, Rusk, McNamara, and himself.

Having settled Taylor's role and the immediate problems on which he wanted help, the president sent a memorandum to the Joint Chiefs two days later. Still smarting from the Bay of Pigs fiasco, JFK told them the relationship he expected of them in cold war operations. Some excerpts: "I expect your advice to come to me direct and unfiltered. . . . I look to the chiefs to contribute dynamic and imaginative leadership. . . . I expect them to be more than military men . . . [and] to combine all assets in a unified, effective pattern."[8]

The chiefs feared that the new military representative of the president would wall them off from Kennedy. Although Taylor's intent was always not to do so, but rather to assist them in getting through to the president, and the chiefs' fear turned out to be unfounded, it had some basis. In *The Uncertain Trumpet* Taylor had written, "I would dissolve the JCS as it now exists and replace it by a single Defense Chief of Staff" (p. 176). Is that what he would do—and become—now? Outside the government some others were also a bit skeptical about Taylor and his new role. Wrote military historian "Slam" Marshall of the *Detroit Times* in one of the flurry of articles about the new appointee, "Taylor is the wrong man for this job. . . . He's actively interested in the exercise of power for his own sake."[9]

Still, Taylor kept reasonably close liaison with the chiefs, although they never really trusted him, and serious problems never developed. Kennedy had considered firing Chairman Lemnitzer, whom he considered likeable but "dim," and replacing him with Taylor. Rather than create a furor in the Pentagon and on Capitol Hill, however, he decided to bide his time.

More delicate relationships that Taylor had to work out were those within Camelot itself. Kennedy had, at least for the time, dismantled the NSC apparatus. In its place he had surrounded himself with individual advisers of varying degrees of brilliance and experience. Thus developed almost a contest among equals, not all in the White House, for the president's ear. (Later we will look at how Taylor fared in the bureaucratic politics of this environment.) In effect, Kennedy had established a little NSC of his own, including Taylor, Secretary of State Rusk, Secretary of Defense McNamara, Special Assistant for National Security Affairs McGeorge Bundy, and his brother Bobby. Looking at the background and personality of each is interesting.

Dean Rusk was a Georgian, born in 1909. He graduated from Davidson College in 1931, became a Rhodes scholar, and joined the faculty of Mills College in California. He was associate professor of government and dean of the faculty there when he went on active duty in the Army in 1940. World War II eventually took him to the headquarters of the China-Burma-India Theater in New Delhi. Here, the quality of his cables brought him to the attention of officials in General Marshall's command post, the Operations Division of the War Department, to which he found himself ordered in 1944.

He became a particular favorite of Marshall's, displaying the same qualities that people ascribed to him later as secretary of state: hardworking, steady, loyal, and diplomatic. Eventually, his association with Marshall and other officials led him to the State Department; by 1950 he was its assistant secretary for Far Eastern affairs. In 1952 he became president of the Rockefeller Foundation, a prestigious and powerful post. During his eight years with the foundation he became fairly well known in the Democratic establishment and, not by co-incidence, published an article in the April 1960 *Foreign Affairs* concerning the president and foreign policy. Shortly after the 1960 election, the Georgian shot a letter off to the Yankee president-elect on the need to heal racial scars. He was campaigning hard but cautiously for the job of secretary of state.

Recommendations supporting Rusk came to JFK, including one by the influential and aging Robert Lovett, whom Kennedy had offered the post of either secretary of state or defense. Only McGeorge Bundy of Kennedy's advisers had doubts, sensing perhaps something second-rate in the enigmatic Rusk. Still, Rusk had a lot going for him; in particular, it was obvious that he would not be a strong secretary, which suited Kennedy, who wanted to be his own secretary of state. He appointed Rusk, but there was never any intimacy between the two. Rusk found it hard to communicate with JFK and to adjust to the deliberately freewheeling style of the Kennedy White House.

Lovett had also recommended Robert McNamara for defense secretary. Comparatively unknown, McNamara had been president of Ford Motor Company for about a month when asked about his interest in the job, first by Bobby Kennedy and then by Sargent Shriver.

The president's attitudes toward the State and Defense departments had an important difference. Although Kennedy was determined to be the de facto chief of Foggy Bottom, he was willing to let the Pentagon head run his own department. This difference was evident in the pre-appointment interview, when McNamara insisted on choosing his own assistants and Kennedy agreed.

Born in San Francisco in 1916, McNamara graduated from Berkeley in 1937 and received an MBA at Harvard in 1939. He subsequently served on the faculty there, specializing in the application of statistical analysis to management problems. He spent World War II working in statistical control in the Army Air Corps and was for a time under Curtis LeMay. After the war he and nine other statistical control experts hired themselves out to the Ford Motor Company as a group. McNamara rose rapidly in the firm; when elected its president in late 1960, he was the first nonmember of the Ford family to hold that office.

Bob McNamara was a relentlessly driving automobile executive, but in his spare time he relaxed with discussions, reading, and classical music. These avocations put him in good stead in Kennedy's Camelot.

Almost everyone agrees about McNamara's personal characteristics: intelligent, competent, decisive, analytical, hard working, and most comfortable when dealing with figures. The rimless glasses and "Stacomb" (slicked back) hair gave him a formidable look, but on social occasions he could be engaging. Other characteristics were less desirable: his inability to compromise was a serious disadvantage for a political appointee; although not evident until much later, his temperament was highly emotional underneath his stern exterior, perhaps too much so for a person who would later direct America's only lost war. His greatest problem, however, was his lack of a sophisticated world view, an asset not usually provided to motor company executives. Still, this did not slow him down or concern him at the moment, activist that he was.

How did this relentless executive with an accountant's mind-set work out a relationship with Rusk, the benign Rhodes scholar at State? In fact, the two had a close rapport, although, as the 1960s wore on, some question arose as to which one was really making foreign policy. McNamara was always ready with a definite position for the president, even if the military chiefs had not agreed on it. The Rusk team, by contrast, often raised diverse opinions in discussions with the president, which JFK liked because he then had a greater hand in foreign affairs.

Before looking at McGeorge Bundy, we should understand what Kennedy had in mind for him as his special assistant for national security affairs. Previously, the NSC was staffed chiefly by career officials from various government departments. The special assistant, a position Eisenhower had created as a presidential appointee, was to be the linkage between these members of the NSC staff and the president. Both the special assistant and the staff were primarily concerned with planning rather than operational questions. What Kennedy wanted, however, was a personal staff in which the distinction between planning and operations was intentionally blurred. Further, the special assistant was to work on a daily basis with the president, and many of the members of the staff were to be recruited from outside the government. As it developed, with certain exceptions, the staff concentrated on foreign policy rather than on defense issues, again in keeping with the president's interests.

McGeorge Bundy was by any standard a brilliant student as a young man. Born in 1919, he attended Groton and Yale, where he was class orator in 1940. He then went to Harvard as a junior fellow; when World War II came, he served in the Army as a captain on the staff of Adm. Alan Kirk, who was involved in the D-Day landings on Normandy. Bundy spend the 1950s at Harvard, first as a lecturer in government and later as a most effective dean of arts and science.

Although nominally a Republican, Bundy developed a close relationship with Sen. John F. Kennedy in the late 1950s. When Kennedy became president-elect, the academic community, and others such as Walter Lippmann, promoted Bundy for a high position in the administration.

Bundy's characteristics were a forceful personality, a relentless drive for power, a sharp mind, a cold warrior mentality, and an unusual insight into others, particularly their motives. On the more mundane side, he was a good administrator and memo writer; although cool and austere, he could, like McNamara, be charming on social occasions. In addition, he had the kind of style associated with those descended from the Lowells.

Some critics claimed that he lacked depth and tended to be programmatic when it came to understanding the side effects of problems. In this regard, the critics said, he overestimated his ability to handle complex issues. Notwithstanding, he quickly became indispensable to the president in foreign affairs; he moved rapidly into the vacuum at State created by Rusk, with the assistance of his small but highly talented staff.

Our final characterization is of Robert F. Kennedy. His was a special position in the administration, apart from the fact that he was attorney general of the United States. He had really wanted to be at Defense, but understandably McNamara had passed on that suggestion.

Born in 1925, he served in the Navy in World War II and graduated from Harvard in 1948 and then from the University of Virginia Law School. In the 1950s he served briefly on the staff of the McCarthy committee and then for many years as chief counsel of the Senate Rackets Committee.

He was most active in securing his brother's nomination, especially at the 1960 Democratic convention. After JFK assumed office, Bobby became the ramrod of the administration and played a fairly significant role in foreign affairs. He was primarily responsible for the great, almost juvenile, emphasis that the administration put on counterinsurgency in its early days. He enjoyed, of course, total confidence in his relationship with his brother. Accordingly, he displayed a toughness and assurance in the inner circles of the White House that no one else could quite assume.

Especially interesting was his relationship with Maxwell Taylor.

All the officials just mentioned were impressed by Taylor's intelligence, competence, and effectiveness, but Bobby Kennedy and Taylor had a close personal relationship. Particularly taken with Taylor's war record and with the image he projected as a military intellectual, Bobby was a major force in promoting Taylor with the president. Ethel Kennedy told me that Bobby "worshipped Taylor" and considered him a Renaissance man. In any case, the hardness and relentlessness Robert Kennedy displayed with others was absent in Taylor's case. Taylor could handle Bobby.

An amusing incident illustrated this relationship. At a meeting of the Counterinsurgency Group, Bobby argued for adding Secretary of Labor Arthur Goldberg to the forum. When the others turned thumbs down, Bobby became belligerent and threatening. Everyone at the table, including Edward R. Murrow, folded before his onslaught, that is, everyone except Taylor, who said, "No, Bobby, it would not be right to add him to the group." At this point Bobby pushed back his chair and banged down his briefing book; before stalking out and slamming the door, he said, "Shit, the second most important man in the world just lost another one."

These, then, are the circumstances, the charter, and the major personae of Camelot surrounding Taylor as he assumed the role of military representative of the president in the summer of 1961—pretty heady stuff after the four frustrating years in the Pentagon dealing with the Eisenhower administration!

Let us turn now to one of the issues that Kennedy's letter of appointment had asked Taylor to tackle as an immediate task: Berlin.

BERLIN

Taylor knew the problems of Berlin. From September 1949 to February 1951 he was the first U.S. commandant of Berlin, and during Nikita Khrushchev's ultimatum of 1958–59 he was chief of staff. By the time he became military representative of the president (MIL-REP), the Berlin crisis had gained a life of its own. It was difficult for Taylor, a newcomer, to have a major influence on events, but he did play a part.

When Kennedy took office, the people in his administration acknowledged that Berlin would present problems. The city had been a test of East-West relations since the end of World War II; tensions anywhere between the United States and the Soviet Union would surface as problems in and around Berlin.

At the end of the war, Berlin was an enclave in East Germany, more than a hundred miles from the border with West Germany. It had been divided into four zones of occupation: the Soviets were in the eastern part, while Britain, France, and the United States were in the western. Bickering over access to the city began as early as 1945 and peaked during the Berlin airlift of 1948–49. In November 1958 the Soviet Union sent an ultimatum to the other occupying powers that Berlin be made a free city within six months. Eisenhower rejected a military buildup proposed by some of his advisers, and the crisis ended in 1959 when Ike and Khrushchev had a summit rather than a war. One of the most vocal opponents of Eisenhower's approach was Truman's secretary of state, Dean Acheson, who argued for a large increase in Allied military strength to meet the crisis.

In the Kennedy administration two events precipitated the Berlin crisis: first, a Soviet aide-mémoire to Bonn on February 17, 1961, that stressed the need for a peace treaty that would make Berlin a free city; and, second, Kennedy's address to Congress proposing amendments to the defense budget to improve U.S. military strength. Although Kennedy's speech was not related directly to Berlin, it fueled Khrushchev's fire against the new administration. To cool things off, Kennedy agreed to a meeting with Khrushchev in Vienna on June 3 and 4.

However, all that spring Kennedy's push for improved U.S. defense put Khrushchev into a belligerent mood for the meeting. The Vienna session was brutal, curing Kennedy of any notions of summitry as a solution to East-West problems. Although they discussed other matters, their main topic was Berlin. On the second day Khrushchev astonished Kennedy with a Soviet memorandum giving the United States six months to come to terms on making Berlin a free city and ending Allied rights there. Khrushchev committed Soviet prestige to this end by making the memorandum public a week later.

At home again, a distressed Kennedy addressed the country on Berlin on June 6. The previous March he had asked Dean Acheson to prepare a scenario for dealing with potential Berlin problems within the context of the North Atlantic Treaty Organization (NATO), and he now called for those plans. Acheson, a strong man with very definite ideas on the need for firmness in the NATO areas, knew exactly what he wanted, and he was hard-nosed. He proposed some strong medicine: mobilization and a declaration of national emergency. He reasoned that Berlin was merely a pretext and that Khrushchev was really testing U.S. will. Thus, responding properly called for building up conventional and military forces.

The Acheson report could not help but draw fire from certain members of Congress and the State Department, as well as from some in the White House. For example, an NSC memorandum of early July set forth the disadvantages of mobilization. Other voices in the White House, most notably Arthur Schlesinger, argued effectively with the president to try more negotiating with the Soviets before making any drastic moves.

At this point Taylor entered the problem in his new role as MIL-REP. One of his first meetings with the president was at Hyannis Port on July 8, 1961; Rusk and McNamara were also present. At this session Kennedy made clear that military preparations were needed, but that Rusk, as secretary of state, should prepare ways of negotiating.

Sensing that the president was tending toward a diplomatic settlement, Taylor suggested spelling out the pros and cons of various courses of action. On July 13, after the NSC met, these were discussed at a smaller meeting in the president's office attended by his top officials, including Taylor and JCS Chairman Lemnitzer. They did not solve the problem, but the president began to socialize the others in the direction he wanted to move, that is, negotiation through strength, without mobilization.

At a meeting in the president's office a few days later—which included McNamara, Rusk, Bobby Kennedy, Taylor, Bundy, and speech writer Sorensen—the military approach was even more muted, and the group discussed having the president address the nation. At this point JFK appointed a steering group on Berlin, with Rusk as chairman and Taylor one of the members.

The following day the president met with the Joint Chiefs and based his comments on a paper prepared by Taylor. Kennedy began by reminding the group that their own recommendations to meet the crisis would mean about 400,000 more military personnel and some $7 billion more in the defense budget. Letting them down gently, Kennedy indicated that although he favored some military increase—for worldwide readiness rather than for Berlin alone—he was not prepared for such drastic measures and would like to avoid, if possible, declaring a national emergency.

His speech to the nation on July 25 was the climax of the post-Vienna Berlin discussions. Although Kennedy did seek $3 billion more for defense and the call-up of certain reserve units (which was to have enormous impact later on the way the Vietnam War was fought), he emphasized peace through negotiation. Even so, for some reason the press picked up on the military aspects of his rhetoric.

August brought its own problems in Berlin. Khrushchev's reply to Kennedy's speech came on August 7 but was less important than what was happening on the ground. In July, 30,000 East Germans had left for the West through Berlin, and in the first twelve days of August, 20,000 more streamed into West Berlin. On August 13, however, the East Germans halted the flow and began building the Berlin wall. This construction effectively halted the movement, because the remainder of the East-West border had been barricaded for many years.

In retrospect, the wall was probably a good thing in that it put a cap on tensions, although this result was not apparent at that time. An American protest dispatched to Moscow did not seem adequate to West Berlin Mayor Willy Brandt, who wanted more, at least for morale purposes. Thus, JFK sent Vice President Lyndon Johnson to Berlin as a high-level emissary. A symbolic gesture was also made to reinforce the American garrison in West Berlin with an infantry battle group. No one could know what the Soviet reaction would be. But there was none.

Of special interest here is that at the meeting resulting in the battle-group decision, no member of the Defense Department was present—but Taylor was. The New Frontier indeed had a loose organizational style.

The wall stopped the refugee flight, and there was no military confrontation between East and West. Negotiations of a sort went on, but in the end the crisis simply faded away. On October 17, in the course of a six-hour speech to the Twenty-second Congress of the Soviet Communist party, Khrushchev in effect called the crisis off.

What was Taylor's role in all this? He had come into the situation too late to make a strong individual impact, but he did establish his position in the highest councils of Camelot. He proved less of a hawk than he would be a year later in the Cuban missile crisis. But in 1961 he worked in the White House; in 1962 he worked in the Pentagon. He was, as always, adaptable to his situation.

BUREAUCRATIC POLITICS

Although having a staff of only twelve, McGeorge Bundy's White House group, technically under the aegis of the National Security

Council, was actually the primary foreign policy manager for President Kennedy. According to Bob Komer, a member of the staff, the group acted as the "eyes and ears" of the president, a "shadow network" that told the president what was going on before he received a formal recommendation. This type of operation could not help but outpace the slower-moving State Department. The vigor with which the group operated also posed problems for MILREP, which was primarily concerned with defense matters.

In contrast, Taylor moved cautiously, offering advice only when asked and avoiding taking on too heavy a load for his small staff. He also, in the words of one of his assistants, was very careful "not to get his hands dirty [or] to leave any bureaucratic trail" of his actions. In addition, MILREP was operating within a White House organizational process without modern precedent in informality. Kennedy had little managerial experience, and he had been taken in by Senator "Scoop" Jackson's well-known critique of the Eisenhower NSC system, which, although erroneous, became the conventional wisdom. Jackson had charged Eisenhower with having an overly formalized system based on the premise that the NSC was actually Ike's decision-making forum. In fact, as was mentioned previously, Ike made the real decisions with small groups in the Oval Office. The NSC did have an important function for Ike, but not as much as Jackson said that it did. Eisenhower saw it as a bully forum for achieving consensus and coordination, for whipping decisions into actions, and for "blessing" the more controversial ones.

Kennedy dismantled Ike's NSC apparatus and gave Bundy's office great ascribed power, but by October 1961 he was having second thoughts. He then told Bundy that he would like to have regularly scheduled NSC meetings. By wrapping himself in the sanctity of the NSC forum, the president would be off the hook.

Taylor and his group felt that Kennedy's principal NSC advisers—who had never exercised any major military responsibilities—tended to ignore the difference between theory and practice. This tendency, they felt, caused a serious problem between defense planning and execution. The solution, as Taylor saw it, was to develop a basic national security policy paper to serve as a guidepost for defense budget and defense policy development. The Eisenhower administration had had such a paper, although there is not much evidence that Ike ever paid much attention to it. Because of Kennedy's lesser experience in defense issues as compared with Ike's, however, MILREP felt that such a device would be useful. It would require the president to think through his own goals in defense rather than to react to episodic advice or situations.

In another part of the White House, some of Bundy's staff downplayed the value of such a guide. However, the Departments of State and Defense made attempts to develop such basic policy papers. One effort was a December 1961 paper by the Policy Planning Staff in State. In analyzing it, Taylor's staff felt that it was too passive, for example: "When crises erupt, we should seek to resolve them in a way which will restore equilibrium without incurring the increased costs and risks that would be required to alter the existing balance of advantage drastically in our favor." However, MILREP felt that the paper was adequate and that it would be "bucking city hall" to fight it too hard, so they went along.

When possible, MILREP did comment on such papers and scored some minor successes in being heard. Taylor was able to comment, at least, on the defense budget, but because doing so was not a particular assignment from the president, as were Berlin and Vietnam, he found making any real imprint difficult. Matters such as the defense budget, which proceeded by the calendar, were too far developed to change significantly by the time they got to the White House.

Given these crosscurrents, MILREP—an office that JFK after all invented when he lost confidence in the JCS—had to feel its way cautiously, especially with the Defense Department bureaucracy. In the fall of 1961 it did try to inject itself into the defense budget process, thus formalizing its role, but this effort was unsuccessful because of McNamara's swelling power. The attempt was based on Taylor's observation that the president was not getting adequate military advice on the defense budget. Even the Joint Chiefs' comments on McNamara's proposals had very little effect. Most of the advice coming directly to Kennedy was from professors, economists, political analysts, and cost accountants, the so-called whiz kids. As Taylor perceived the situation, McNamara's recommendations did not have to pass the reviewing stand of military officials.

By late January 1962 Taylor thought that it was time to evaluate his office's operation and to advance any ideas on changes for increasing its effectiveness. Accordingly, his executive assistant, Col. Julian J. Ewell, later of Vietnam fame, asked each of the professionals in MILREP for comments. Because of their candid nature, the replies give us an interesting backstage look at how Camelot managed its national security affairs.

Because MILREP was based on Taylor's stature and was not a permanent institution, it was not a scheduled stop in the State-Defense paper flow. Noting this, one staff member pointed out that the staff had to walk a narrow path between being ignored and being considered pushy or meddlesome.

What concerned the members most was their relation with Bundy's NSC staff. Because Taylor was not in the chain of command, his office was outside the normal channel of events and depended on various grapevines for information. He was increasingly threatened by Bundy's staff, particularly Bob Komer and Carl Kaysen, who were adept at keeping their projects away from MILREP. As time went on, Bundy's morning liaison meeting for the White House staff discussed key problems less and less. When it did, it was in a kind of shorthand known only to those directly involved. This price was what MILREP had to pay for sitting in on another agency's meetings. Although the Bundy-Taylor personal relationship was good, the lower levels of the NSC staff tended to wall off MILREP on many matters.

The outside agency most relevant to Taylor's duties was, of course, the Department of Defense. By early 1962 McNamara had established himself as the strongest secretary of defense to date. He was no longer the greenhorn of early 1961, preoccupied with counting beans and noses. His strength had built up at the expense of the JCS—setting the stage for the later Vietnam disaster. Thus, Taylor's power in the White House depended increasingly on bureaucratic maneuvering.

Bundy was an ally in keeping Taylor in the White House, for he sensed the danger of McNamara's growing power. Not only did it threaten his own influence on the president but Bundy also felt that JFK needed someone around to pass military judgment on McNamara's proposals; he knew that the present JCS was not likely to fill that role. However, the preparation of the defense budget in the fall of 1961 (as previously mentioned) had revealed McNamara's strength and Taylor's difficulty in inserting himself into this vital but protracted bureaucratic matter.

The MILREP directive from the president gave Taylor a great deal of intelligence oversight, stemming from Kennedy's loss of faith in Allen Dulles over the Bay of Pigs. Taylor did achieve a very successful liaison with the CIA, thanks to the assignment of an effective CIA officer to his staff. By 1962 some of the White House staff, Bundy in particular, began to question this broad intelligence charter for Taylor; the president's growing confidence in John McCone, Dulles's replacement, seemed to Bundy to make Taylor's oversight function unnecessary—but it was not changed during his stay in the White House.

Perhaps the most important and clear-cut instance of Taylor's being bypassed was in nuclear matters: atmospheric testing, nuclear dispersal, and the production of nuclear weapons. Keeping MILREP out of this area was, in particular, the group known as "the antinuclear wrecking crew," a coterie of personal friends dispersed in various jobs around the White House and the Departments of State and Defense. In general, they were lone wolves with a high degree of intellectual self-assurance (usually not based on knowing the subject) and a deep emotional bias against nuclear weapons. One of their techniques was to deal with an issue covertly and as rapidly as possible so as to dispose of the matter before it could be debated. They were not concerned with being thorough, only with making their end runs.

They particularly avoided touching base with Taylor because, even if they could predict his reaction, his precise and conscientious analysis would show up their fallacies. In a matter involving nuclear dispersal, for example, a senior adviser informed JFK that Taylor was abreast of the problem when he actually was not, thus preventing the president from hearing Taylor's potentially conflicting views.

Still, in spite of the White House bureaucratic jungle in which MILREP operated, Taylor always had the president's confidence; because of this, his office scored philosophical gains despite the surreptitious opposition. At a time when military influence was at a low ebb in the White House, the presence of this office demonstrated to the rest of the bureaucracy that the military voice was not entirely muted. Unfortunately, no coattail effect developed; the senior military in the Pentagon were not able to build on Taylor's influence to regain prominence on their own merits.[10]

NATO

Early in his administration, Kennedy had to deal with NATO and its member countries over intense nuclear issues. The many crosscurrents included de Gaulle's desire for a French nuclear force, combined with the skittishness of Kennedy's advisers over the entire nuclear issue; the problem of keeping Germany as a contented nonnuclear country; and the issues of who would provide the conventional forces in the move away from Eisenhower's heavy reliance on nuclear weapons. The frosting on the cake was the irritant to McNamara of Supreme Allied Commander, Europe (SACEUR) Lauris Norstad's role in pushing for a NATO medium-range ballistic missile (MRBM) force.

Norstad was a man of considerable political clout in NATO Europe. A 1930 graduate of West Point commissioned in the Air Corps, he had become a brigadier general in World War II at the age of thirty-six, and subsequently a protégé of Ike's. He had been in Europe since 1950 and a four-star general since 1952. Eisenhower nominated him to supreme command in 1956 and strongly backed him. Much to the dismay of Rusk and McNamara, Norstad saw himself as an international servant not subject to U.S. direction in the same way that a commander of U.S. forces would be. McNamara could never swallow this, although Norstad was correct.

This consideration of a NATO nuclear force had begun during the closing years of the Eisenhower period. In December 1960 at a NATO ministerial meeting, the outgoing administration proposed assigning to NATO five ballistic missile submarines if a system of control could be developed. In May 1961, four months into office, Kennedy picked up the ball. He raised the possibility of a multilateral seaborne nuclear force once NATO had developed its conventional strength. This caveat, a big one, was based on Kennedy's strategy of flexible response. It would require greater reliance on ground forces, most of which the Europeans would supply.

The concept of a multilateral force (soon called MLF) was at the heart of the nuclear control question that so concerned the New Frontier. Before it died, the concept went through two phases. First, there was the notion of submarines manned by sailors of several NATO nations—if anyone can imagine that. The next approach, also with mixed manning, was a surface force, which was more manageable technically but difficult to visualize how it would work in practice. In either case, the president of the United States would have been the one to press the nuclear button.

Because of this strategic caldron bubbling in Europe, Taylor decided to make a trip there in March 1962 "in order to be of greater value to the President." His visit included France, Germany, England, and Italy. The most controversial problems he found were the depressed state of Franco-American relations, German concerns about its defense, and the NATO attitude toward the U.S. strategy of flexible response.

Taylor's Paris meeting with U.S. and European officials included Ambassador James Gavin, Supreme Allied Commander Norstad, and the French minister of defense, as well as the French military chief of staff. The person that Taylor did not meet with was President Charles de Gaulle, although he was the one who set the tone of U.S.-French relations. De Gaulle had two goals: to restore French grandeur and to regain strategic independence from Washington. Accordingly, in 1958 he decided to build French nuclear weapons. He disliked Kennedy's flexible response policy; it appeared to him an American device for more central control of nuclear weapons. The MLF offended him for the same reason.

In Germany Taylor met with senior German and American military officials. The Federal Republic had become a member of NATO in 1955 on the understanding that it would have no nuclear weapons, although its military forces would be part of NATO and it would share as an equal in NATO decision making. In the late 1950s and early 1960s, the Germans did acquire nuclear-capable weapons, although the United States retained custody of the warheads. Kennedy's people worried that the Federal Republic might want to produce such warheads independently, following the French example. The MLF initiative was meant to nip this idea in the bud.

These were the thorny issues that Taylor described in his report to Kennedy on April 3. Taylor came down hard on the need to normalize relations with France and to include, if necessary, providing technical aid to the French nuclear program. About Germany, Taylor felt that Bonn should be reassured that a NATO strategy did indeed plan to defend Germany's border. He proposed to back up such words by developing an MLF at once from existing weapons; the force could then be modernized with the MRBM force that Norstad was proposing.

Taylor's third point was NATO ambivalence about the "new" U.S. strategy of flexible response. The gut issue was how to get the European allies to furnish more of the conventional forces needed if nuclear weapons were not to be used at the start of a conflict. What Taylor suggested was a thorough look at force requirements by NATO officials, including U.S. military professionals. This process would help to satisfy the Germans, he thought, and at the same time might help Norstad get the MRBM force he wanted.

The president quickly referred Taylor's report to Rusk and McNamara, whose responses, to put it mildly, were not supportive. State was not interested in reopening the question of nuclear aid to

France or in any comprehensive force study at the moment. The notion of an improvised multilateral force was also dismissed. At Defense, McNamara deprecated the military value of such an MLF. In the end, Taylor concluded that his trip, although educational, was a zero in terms of action. If he had not already realized it from the midyear review of his office, he knew for certain now that a presidential adviser, however prestigious, was no match for the Defense and State bureaucracies.

After looking at the Taylor report, Rusk suggested educating the NATO Council about current U.S. strategic thinking. The forum he had in mind was the Athens meeting of the foreign and defense ministers of the council scheduled for early May. The idea was to review the circumstances in which the alliance might have to use nuclear weapons. (The outcome subsequently became known as the Athens Guidelines.) The principal performance would be a speech by U.S. Secretary of Defense Robert Strange McNamara.

A "final" version of the proposed talk reached MILREP in late April. The text contained horrifying figures about casualties in a nuclear war, but it assured the Allies that the American nuclear posture was very good indeed and did not need the small independent nuclear capabilities of, say, France or Britain. McNamara then went on to damn the MRBM notion with faint praise. A section on tactical (small) nuclear weapons stated that using them would bring on a general nuclear war. Overall, MILREP found the speech too much of a made-in-the-USA product and too didactic.

In a note to McNamara, Taylor went to the heart of the matter. McNamara's paper depicting the disaster of general atomic war also showed that tactical atomic weapons would simply escalate to general war. This conclusion led to an obvious need for conventional forces that, even if the goals were met, were years away. Therefore, Taylor pointed out, the picture set forth was one in which Europe could not be defended for the present except by general nuclear war, hence by its own destruction.

Norstad, given an advance copy, thought the speech arrogant and degrading to his MRBM requirement; "but," he said to the officer courier from Washington who had brought him the copy, "what can one expect from the inexperienced people who write these papers in Washington?" McNamara did give the speech, and many NATO officials simply found it confusing. As for the "inexperienced people" in Washington, they were shortly to ease Norstad into his postmilitary career.

Following the Athens meeting was a flurry of activity about MRBMs for NATO. The Europeans, especially NATO Secretary General Dirk Stikker, began to push hard on the subject, with Norstad's loud applause from the sidelines. Basically, the American position remained: the Europeans should be rational enough to see that they had no alternative to depending on the United States for nuclear defense; therefore, they had to forget the MRBM.

Now the problem focused on Norstad, scheduled to speak about the NATO MRBM to the North Atlantic Council on July 25, 1962. Alerting Kennedy to the speech, Taylor pointed out that during the conference Norstad might state his differences with the U.S. government over this matter.

The president's reaction was quick. In a July 2 memorandum from the president to Secretaries Rusk and McNamara, JFK said:

> I am enclosing a copy of a memorandum that I have received from General Taylor. I think this matter of Norstad's testimony should be considered by us. While he is an Allied Commander of NATO he will also speak as an American citizen . . . we should do something about it. Likewise, his nose is somewhat out of joint [and] he therefore might make some statement . . . embarrassing to us.

Now McNamara played hard ball. He sent an exclusive message to Norstad, saying that it might be profitable to discuss several matters, including the MRBM question, in Washington. On the morning of July 16 they met for two hours in McNamara's office. After a discussion of the MRBM question, in which Norstad felt that he was getting nowhere with McNamara, the latter pointedly asked what Norstad's personal plans were. Norstad replied that he had enjoyed his service as SACEUR very much but that, if the feeling was that he should go, he was ready. That afternoon, at the end of a meeting with JFK, Norstad said, "I understand we have a personal question to discuss." The president looked embarrassed and annoyed, and that was where it ended.

On July 20, 1962, President Kennedy announced senior military personnel changes. General Lauris Norstad would retire as supreme allied commander on November 1 (McNamara, with his usual degree of personal sensitivity, was pushing for August 1); his replacement would be JCS Chairman Lyman Lemnitzer; and Gen. Maxwell D. Taylor would become chairman of the Joint Chiefs on October 1. The four-star general was now the premier knight of Camelot.

RETURN TO THE E RING

On August 9, 1962, the Senate Armed Services Committee conducted hearings on Taylor's confirmation as fifth chairman of the Joint Chiefs of Staff. His confirmation was not in question, but the legislative experts in the Pentagon had some advice to prepare him for the hearings. Not altogether facetiously, they recommended that he re-read his *Uncertain Trumpet*. What they had in mind in particular was his book's proposal for a single chief of staff, that traditional bête noire of Congress. The Pentagon experts felt that the senators might ask Taylor how he could reconcile accepting the chairmanship of a group in which he did not believe—presuming he had not changed his views on the matter. On strategic issues, they might ask about his opposition, also set forth in *Trumpet,* to Eisenhower's nuclear strategy. Would his appointment presage a change in U.S. attitude toward the nuclear defense of Europe?

During the hearings, both the organizational and strategic questions did come up. Taylor assured the committee that neither matter should bother them. He was not returning to the Pentagon in a crusading spirit for reorganization, he said, and he hoped that he was uninfluenced by any bias derived from his past experience. That answer disposed of the question of the single chief of staff. Regarding the strategic issue, he assured the committee that he was an advocate of a powerful nuclear strategic force; and, if an attack on Europe came, the United States had to "use whatever weapons and forces are necessary to defeat it." He was confirmed unanimously.

C.H. Sulzberger commented in the *New York Times* that Taylor had managed "to adjust his concepts to complete endorsement of the McNamara [strategic] theory." The August 25 *Nation* was less generous in its comments: "Now everyone was happy with General Taylor's views since, on the record, he was willing to fight anywhere, any time, with anything. But it would seem that when he puts the martial instrument to his lips, his pitch may be as uncertain as that of other buglers."

Before leaving the White House, Taylor had an exit visit with JFK. He was setting the stage for the next act: the interaction between the JCS chairman and his commander in chief. *Trumpet* had some implicit criticisms of Eisenhower for, in effect, trying to socialize the chiefs to his views on budgets and strategy. The book had especially cited Chairman Radford for attempting to impose Ike's strategic views on the chiefs. However, Taylor's White House experiences changed his feeling about this relationship, in particular the role of the chairman. He had "come to understand the importance of an intimate easy relationship with the President." Further, "the Chairman should be a true believer in the foreign policy and military strategy of the administration which he serves."

In this final meeting with Kennedy he also touched on military and presidential relationships in hopes that the military voice would be heard in the high councils of government. He also understood that there had been some presidential dissatisfaction with the work of the Joint Chiefs. He went on to express to JFK his hope that in the future "the military voice could be heard clearly and in time." Further, he would seek frequent appointments with the president and use the telephone when it seemed necessary to get his personal views on important matters.

Taylor was sworn in as chairman JCS by his friend Attorney General Robert F. Kennedy in the Rose Garden at noon on October 1, 1962. In returning to the Pentagon the old soldier was going to familiar territory, but in his new role he had two new sets of relationships to work out: one with the most powerful secretary of defense to date and the other with the military chiefs of service, who were somewhat apprehensive that Taylor would represent the White House point of view rather than the military's. Perhaps this concern was legitimate, given Taylor's relationship with the president for the previous eighteen months.

By the time that Taylor reported to the second-floor E Ring (the outside of the five rings—A, B, C, D, E—of the Pentagon) office, McNamara had been chief of the Pentagon for twenty-one months and was securely ensconced. As secretary of defense he was the same active spirit that he had been at Ford. To put it in his own words, the task required "active, imaginative, and decisive leadership, not simply refereeing disputes." Through this aggressive attitude he became the watershed secretary, the first one who really controlled the Pentagon and, thus, inevitably conflicted with the military.

McNamara knew that to gain control of the Pentagon he did not need additional legislation. He felt that Eisenhower's 1958 amendments to the basic law were adequate, although untapped. What he planned was to use management skills within the legal authorities of that act.

The big tools he pulled out of his box were the planning-programming-budgeting system (PPBS) and systems analysis. PPBS was installed by Charles Hitch, a civilian economist; systems analysis developed through Alain Enthoven, a civilian operations research analyst working for Hitch. PPBS assembled both an information base and a control device linking long-range planning and shorter-range budgeting. McNamara had Enthoven prepare military-economic studies that compared alternative ways of accomplishing national security objectives based on cost effectiveness. These studies were put into gear with what McNamara called "draft presidential memoranda."

There is little question that McNamara's management system permitted him to take the budgetary and strategic initiative from the military services. The draft presidential memorandums were a way of setting forth strategic assumptions and thus, for all practical purposes, of defining the solution. Undoubtedly, McNamara's system angered the military, which considered strategy their realm. One of their more frequent criticisms of McNamara's management was that it downgraded military professionalism. In effect, they alleged, strategic decisions were being made by the whiz kids without proper consultation with the professional military.

Before accepting the appointment as chairman, Taylor met with McNamara on the problem of the whiz kids. Hadn't they taken over too much of the advisory role of the JCS? Taylor pointed out that the Joint Chiefs had the statutory obligation to serve as the principal military advisers to the secretary. After listening to Taylor, McNamara agreed that, whatever decisions he made as secretary of defense, he would always listen to the military voice first, even though his decisions might not always accord with the Joint Chiefs' recommendations.

Relations with McNamara as they worked out for Taylor after reaching the Pentagon were good indeed—and well managed by Taylor. Roswell Gilpatric, McNamara's deputy, pointed out that before Taylor arrived the military were skeptical of the way McNamara operated, particularly his unwillingness to listen to their briefings. He did not like people in uniform with pointers reading charts. He wanted to ask his own questions and was not tactful in the way he handled the interaction.

Once Taylor came on board, this changed, according to Gilpatric. Taylor "sensed McNamara's greatness . . . and in many senses he emulated him. Taylor prepared all his own papers and never read from them."[11]

Fred Hoffman, the military affairs writer for the Associated Press, commented in a feature article on the "Bob" and "Max" footing that

McNamara and Taylor enjoyed; he noted that Taylor in his role as chairman purposely subordinated himself to the defense secretary.

There is no question of McNamara's high regard for Taylor. He once told me that Taylor was by all odds the "most outstanding military man of the postwar period" and that no man in uniform in his period "had such a sophisticated, insightful knowledge of the security problem."[12] Taylor reciprocated the praise, later describing McNamara as the "greatest" secretary of defense that he had worked for: "intelligent, able, decisive, industrious, and self confident." He did add that he found it best in working with McNamara "not to get things to him too fast."[13] In any case, the working relationship between the two was close. What the senior military, Taylor's other teammates, thought of all this is another matter.

Of the individuals who have served as chairman of the Joint Chiefs of Staff, undoubtedly Radford (Taylor's nemesis in the 1950s) and Taylor were the most powerful. Their power primarily derived from their rapport with the defense secretary and with the White House. But neither was popular with, or particularly trusted by, their colleagues, the service chiefs.

Writing in *Newsweek*, Gen. Thomas White, Air Force chief during Taylor's earlier tenure in the Pentagon, hoped that the new chairman would encourage his JCS colleagues to carry a serious dispute directly to the president. He added that Taylor, as Army chief, had "set the precedent by repeatedly marching with the Chairman to the White House to air his differences before the Commander in Chief."

One of Taylor's colleagues on the JCS felt that the chiefs should have accompanied him to the White House more often, as there was "an unconscious filtering process" by which Taylor "watered down" the chiefs' views. William Bundy agreed, pointing out that Taylor "was a little suspect as a White House man" but that, as time went on, he did become more of the chiefs' man.

Members of his immediate office thought he did a faithful job in representing the chiefs' views, although one felt Taylor would never recommend to the secretary "something that he knew McNamara would not approve." All seem to agree that Taylor did dominate the meetings of the Joint Chiefs and pushed the administration's ideas vigorously—some felt to the point of being subservient to McNamara. Perhaps a fairer interpretation would be that he served as a broker (a term used by one of his assistants in talking to me) between the professional military and the political appointees. If so, this role was considerably different from that of his predecessor's, Lyman

Lemnitzer, who thought of his job as representing views of the professional military.

Taylor met almost daily with McNamara and his principal assistants. In addition, McNamara and his deputy met routinely with the entire Joint Chiefs of Staff in their own meeting room, the so-called Tank. These meetings were structured, with an advance agenda; but one service chief of a later period, Harold K. Johnson, told me that he could not recall anything definite coming out of these meetings. He never came away feeling that there had been any real discussion with McNamara. The meetings seemed to him cosmetic.

Besides having a close relationship with McNamara, Taylor worked hard at keeping open his lines of communication to the White House by frequent trips across the Potomac. Because of his work load and location, however, he did not have the same personal contact as before with JFK. Taylor regretted that change, for, as he told an interviewer in 1964, he had "learned to appreciate the value of propinquity and the tremendous gain of having a direct access to the President and his thinking."

When he was leaving the White House and the question arose whether someone should replace him as MILREP, Taylor advised the president against continuing the office. He felt that it had served its purpose of overcoming the president's loss of faith in the military. Taylor's presence had given JFK a feeling of assurance, but the administration was now experienced and such a senior military presence in the White House did not seem desirable, certainly not to Taylor.

He did manage, however, to leave behind a member of MILREP, Col. Lawrence Legere, to serve on McGeorge Bundy's staff. As one might suspect, he served Taylor as an excellent liaison, keeping him informed as to how national security winds were blowing in the White House. Particularly useful were the routine memorandums recording the various issues coming up at Bundy's daily staff meeting. These topics had a wide range; for example, Bundy was upset because the draft of McNamara's budget contained too many original policy statements; another memorandum might contain details of a Hyannis Port meeting that Kennedy was having with a head of state in a few days.

Another important connection with the Kennedy White House remained: a social one with Bobby. The Taylors had become great friends of Bobby and Ethel; Max and Bob frequently competed over a tennis net.

To staff his Pentagon office, Taylor brought most of his team from the White House, along with a former aide, Col. Bernard Rogers. In addition, he created a new position—not without some opposition from the services and Congress—of assistant to the chairman, which he filled with Maj. Gen. Andrew Goodpaster, well known for his five years as Ike's personal assistant in the White House. (Both Rogers and Goodpaster in later years became the supreme allied commander in Europe.) All in all, Taylor was well established a year and a half after his return to the government.

He fell pretty much into the routine of his days as Army chief of staff: large quarters at Fort Myer overlooking Washington; a walk through the Arlington National Cemetery each morning, at the end of which a car picked him up for the Pentagon; and hard work on physical fitness, with tennis, calisthenics, diet, and a noontime nap. Arriving at work at 8 A.M., he would find the cables and intelligence reports from overnight on his desk. The workday featured briefings and meetings with McNamara, the other chiefs, and sometimes the president. Behind his desk was an autographed picture of JFK. Added to the day was the heavy but usually enjoyable social schedule that the office entailed.

THE MISSILES OF OCTOBER

The first shock wave hitting the newly installed chairman was the Cuban missile crisis of October 1962. More than any other matter during his Pentagon days, this crisis brought him into personal contact with the president and his White House advisers. The events have been so minutely described and exhaustively dissected that I need only summarize them here.[14]

As of 1990, the USSR had not yet released documents on the crisis, even though Soviet officials have commented on it. Thus, mystery still surrounds Khrushchev's extraordinary decision. Why did he decide to place offensive nuclear missiles in Cuba 90 miles from the United States? Without having all the pieces of the puzzle, we still have enough to give us a picture of the situation.

The Soviets had tried to exploit the 1957 *Sputnik* launching with claims of missile superiority over the United States. Kennedy himself had contributed to the misconception in the 1960 campaign with his missile-gap rhetoric. In reality the Soviets had not moved that far ahead, and the gap was theirs. The most important reason for the lag was that the Soviets were waiting for the maturity of their solid-fuel missile development, although they had produced many of the earlier shorter-range, liquid-fueled predecessor.

Soon after taking office, Kennedy and his assistants realized—and publicly disclosed—that there was no missile gap. The Soviets, of course, already knew this, but their allies did not. Probably to regain credibility with their allies and bring pressure on the United States in foreign policy issues, Khrushchev and his advisers decided to plant their shorter-range, liquid-fueled missiles next door to the United States. Khrushchev apparently did not understand just how strongly the Americans would react when they caught the Kremlin at its lethal game.

Castro himself was in trouble. Cuba had been pressured by the United States and the Organization of American States (OAS) since his declared allegiance to the Soviets in December 1961. To complicate matters further, he had growing problems with his own economy. To bolster his position, he wanted to develop a military force that could crush any external or internal threats to his regime. Turning to his friends in Moscow, he asked for strong defense assistance. The Soviets responded during the spring of 1962 with great quantities of conventional armaments: tanks, helicopters, high-performance aircraft, and coastal vessels. At the same time—and to meet their own ends—the Soviets proposed deploying their ballistic missiles in Cuba. Castro agreed.

Soviet missile-related equipment began arriving in late June, and about mid-July the missiles came. At this time, before anyone in Washington knew about the missiles, Kennedy was under pressure from Republicans (eyeing the off-year November elections) to do something about the conventional arms buildup in Cuba. Kennedy took the position that they were defensive arms; the Kremlin, of course, took the same position.

This, then, was the situation until Sunday, October 14, when a U-2 overflight took photographs that revealed medium- and intermediate-range ballistic missile pads under construction in western Cuba.

The following evening, Chairman Taylor, at a dinner party he was hosting, heard the news from one of his guests, the director of Defense Intelligence. Kennedy got the word early on Tuesday from McGeorge Bundy. Then a flurry of meetings with the president began, resulting in the formation of a group called the Executive Committee of the National Security Council (EXCOM). Taylor was the only military member of this group; among the others were Bobby Kennedy, Rusk, McNamara, CIA chief John McCone, Treasury Secretary C. Douglas Dillon, Bundy, Ted Sorensen, Ambassador to the Soviet Union Llewellyn Thompson, and assorted officials in State and Defense, as well as, upon occasion, UN Ambassador Adlai Stevenson. The group broke down roughly into hawks and doves of varying degrees with some members shifting between the two positions. By his own admission, Taylor was from start to finish a hawk: he favored bombing the Cuban missile sites before they could be completed. The doves, worried about Soviet retaliation elsewhere, began pushing for a limited naval blockade of Cuba as the first step. Both sides realized that escalation from either level might eventually lead to a need to invade Cuba—or worse.

As the only military member of EXCOM, Taylor had another group to contend with—the Joint Chiefs. While the huddled members of EXCOM recognized Taylor as a hawk, the chiefs suspected him of being a dove. Frequently they cross-examined him to determine how vigorously he pushed in the White House their rationale for bombing.

Finally, Taylor arranged a meeting for the chiefs with JFK. As he said later, it "made the Chiefs feel better." In fact, though, the president's mind was already made up to go the blockade route. Still, JFK waited for an EXCOM vote—eleven to six for the blockade, with five civilians joining Taylor as hawks—before making his decision final.

On the evening of Monday, October 22, after private conversations with selected members of Congress and with the support of the OAS and NATO, JFK made his famous television address breaking the news of the crisis to Americans and to the world. He announced the quarantine of offensive missile equipment to Cuba and called on Chairman Khrushchev to remove the missiles. The line most remembered in the speech was that any missile launched from Cuba would "require a full retaliatory response on the Soviet Union."

Then came the tense waiting period. Almost continuously, EXCOM met in the White House and the Joint Chiefs in the Pentagon. The blockade itself was formally under way on the morning of October 24.

McNamara's intense interest in the details of the blockade led to his famous confrontation with CNO Adm. George Anderson, who became incensed with what he regarded as civilian intrusion into operational details. At one point the admiral opined that these details were not the secretary's business and that the Navy had been conducting such operations since the days of John Paul Jones.

Taylor supported the secretary against the Navy charge of civilian overcontrol. He argued that the blockade was really not a military situation but rather a political strategy, with the pawns being military hardware. In effect, the chairman felt that this action was political chess and that the Navy ships were being directed by the master player, the president.

In any event, the blockade succeeded. Twenty-five Soviet ships strung out across the Atlantic and headed for Cuba turned back. Soviet ships carrying cargo of other types were allowed to pass; only one was boarded by the U.S. Navy.

Then came the two famous letters from Khrushchev to Kennedy. The first, on October 26, was strange and disjointed in style; it proposed that in exchange for an American pledge not to invade Cuba the USSR would remove its missiles. The next day came a more urgent but less favorable letter, tying the missile removal to American removal of its NATO missiles in Turkey. This letter raised new issues, but as work on the Cuban sites continued, Taylor and the chiefs urged the president to conduct an air strike against them in a day or two. Fortunately, cooler heads prevailed, including that of Bobby Kennedy; on their advice, JFK ignored the second letter and responded to the first.

The break came on Sunday, October 28, when Radio Moscow relayed a new message from Khrushchev. In exchange for Kennedy's promise not to invade Cuba, the USSR would remove the missiles. The whole crisis had been, as Wellington said after Waterloo, "the nearest run thing you ever saw in your life."

In his memoirs twenty years later, Taylor felt that the decision-making process during the crisis, although not tidy, was vastly better than that of the Bay of Pigs episode eighteen months before, largely because Kennedy was more experienced and was dealing with familiar advisers. In looking back at that time, in which he was a hawk all through, Taylor saw the crisis as a classic example of how military power could be used as a deterrent—its primary purpose in a nuclear world.

During his tour as chairman, Taylor participated in many strategic issues, particularly those involving NATO. None was quite as dramatic, though, as the Cuban missile crisis.

In the area of arms control, in particular, the Limited Test Ban Treaty of 1963, Taylor deserves high marks. Through his efforts the Joint Chiefs agreed to support this first major arms control agreement with the Soviet Union in August 1963. The Senate ratified this treaty only because the Joint Chiefs were "on board."

However, the major strategic issue of the 1960s turned out to be American involvement in Vietnam, and Taylor was one of its chief architects. The remainder of this book concerns America and Vietnam—America's greatest foreign and defense policy failure of this century—and in particular the role of Maxwell Davenport Taylor.

PART II

VIETNAM

*"A failure is never anything but a failure,
on the battlefield the price is blood."*

— *WEST POINT BUGLE NOTES, CIRCA 1922*

CHAPTER 3

The Inheritance and the Mission

$\mathbb{B}$efore going into Taylor's role in Vietnam—a central theme in this book—we need to look at the country's history and the American experience there prior to the Kennedy administration.

THE INHERITANCE

An ancient country, Vietnam had been independent until the French occupied it in the mid-nineteenth century, officially annexing it as a French colony in 1879. A succession of uprisings against French rule had all been unsuccessful. In 1930, however, Ho Chi Minh, a young revolutionary, unified three communist groups and established the Indochinese Communist party. Then, in World War II after the collapse of France in 1940, Japan occupied Vietnam. The occupation was strange, as, for reasons of military economy, the Japanese left the French infrastructure, both military and civilian, essentially intact. Throughout the war, Ho and his followers operated out of the Viet Bac, a wild region in northern Vietnam near the Chinese border. By early 1945 a substantial Vietminh (as Ho's group was then called) military force had been established. Foreseeing the defeat of Japan, they were prepared to seize power when the opportunity came. Accordingly, after the atomic bomb was dropped on Hiroshima, Ho and the Vietminh acted rapidly. On August 19 they entered Hanoi. On September 2, they declared Independence Day for the new Democratic Republic of Vietnam.

During World War II, President Roosevelt, although he knew little about Indochina, had definite ideas, involving a sort of trusteeship arrangement, on the future of the former French colonies of Vietnam, Cambodia, and Laos. He did little, however, to promote the concept, probably because it was not a high-priority item among the strategic questions before him. The trusteeship notion did not survive into the Truman administration. Opposition came not only from France and Great Britain but also from the U.S. bureaucracy, particularly the European-oriented officers of the State Department.

As agreed at the Potsdam Conference, the French did return to Vietnam after initial occupations by the British in the south and the Chinese in the north. The purpose of the occupation was to remove the Japanese forces. In the fall of 1945, the French occupied southern Vietnam, but reoccupying the northern part was slower going because the Vietminh's real strength lay there. Their experience in the south convinced the French that their return to Tonkin (as the northern part of the country was known) was impossible without an agreement with the Vietminh leadership. The two sides made such an agreement on March 6, 1946, with a conference to work out details to be held later. The specific Vietminh goals at this point were threefold: to remain on the defensive long enough to prepare for a long war, to win firm support from the population, and to exterminate the leadership of other nationalist groups. The French goal was less definite, but some important French circles hoped for the reestablishment of a colonial regime.

The agreement looked at first like a defeat for Ho, who had tried unsuccessfully to internationalize the Indochina problem with appeals to the United States, USSR, and the UN. In the long run, however, the agreement helped him; without it, the First Indochina War—for which the Vietminh were not yet prepared—would probably have broken out sooner.

As the months went by, relations between the Vietminh and the French steadily deteriorated. By December 1946 the First Indochina War, which was to last until the spring of 1954, was under way. Besides taking military action, the French tried to establish a Vietnamese government to counter Ho's, while conceding as little real authority as possible. The seven years of struggle witnessed a vastly changing panorama on the international scene as well as domestic changes in the two nations involved.

When the French and Vietnamese began their long battle, the American position was one of caution. American foreign policy centered around Europe, but the United States had an overwhelming position in eastern Asia as a result of World War II. The policy of nonintervention began to change in 1949 as events in China leading to the communist takeover intruded more and more on the U.S. consciousness. France's struggle with Ho and his followers came to be seen as a critical element in the containment of communism in Asia. The loss of Indochina, it was perceived, could mean a chain reaction of communist takeovers in Southeast Asia—the domino principle espoused by Acheson and later by Eisenhower. Thus, in 1950 the United States took a giant step into the muddy waters of Indochina.

In February of that year the United States recognized the Bao Dai regime, a Vietnam government under French control. Less than two weeks later came the first French request for military and economic assistance. President Harry S Truman's decision on May 1, 1950, to grant France's request must be considered the first great benchmark in the U.S. involvement in Vietnam. A few months after the Korean War began in June, a U.S. military mission approved by Truman was dispatched to Saigon as the nucleus of a military assistance advisory group (MAAG). Although the money allocated was small at first, it grew throughout the Korean War, especially after China intervened there in the fall of 1950; by 1954 it reached more than one billion dollars in a fiscal year.[1]

When Truman left office in January 1953, the American public understood little of the Vietnam situation. Certainly the precarious nature of the French and their puppet, the Bao Dai regime, was not realized by then. The threat as Truman saw it was that of international communism, and for reasons of U.S. security, the United States needed to prevent Vietnam from being taken over by that "monolithic" force. By then the military assistance program was heavy and still increasing. Eisenhower, taking office in 1953, inherited a vastly more complex foreign policy situation in Vietnam than Roosevelt's vague notion of a trusteeship arrangement for that area.

The Eisenhower administration accepted Truman's Indochina policy, that is, the notion that the Vietminh were an instrument of international communism and that the fall of Indochina would trigger the loss of all of Southeast Asia with disastrous strategic consequences for the West. Noting signs of French weariness over the seemingly endless war, the new administration made clear its intentions to keep supporting France; however, it wanted France to be more aggressive militarily and to be more explicit about the independence of the states composing Indochina.

In the spring of 1953 Lt. Gen. Henri-Eugene Navarre was selected as the French commander to conduct a more aggressive military policy. His early offensives failed to destroy the enemy's main battle force or to liquidate the guerrilla threat inside French lines. He decided then to pursue the Vietminh forces into their mountain redoubt; thus, in late November began the most famous battle of the First Indochina War—Dien Bien Phu.

The battle, however, steadily became more disastrous for the French, and by January 1954 their situation was foreboding. At this point members of the Eisenhower administration debated whether and how to aid the French and, if necessary, how to pick up the pieces. By March the desperate French sought Eisenhower's approval of U.S. air strikes. Ike felt that this action would first require congressional approval and allied action. By April, when clearly neither Congress nor the British would agree to this proposal, Eisenhower said no to the French. On May 8 Dien Bien Phu fell. The next day talks began in Geneva on the future of Indochina.[2]

The United States was a reluctant partner to the talks, and Secretary of State Dulles remained just long enough to instruct the American delegation about its role: that of an "interested nation," not a principal. In that way, whatever settlement was made, the United States would not go on record as officially approving it.

As the conference wore on, the Americans realized that probably the best they could hope for was to salvage the freedom of Laos and Cambodia and the southern part of Vietnam. Pressured by the USSR and China, the Vietminh reluctantly agreed to a temporary partition of Vietnam. On July 21, 1954, the French and Vietminh military commanders signed the Geneva Accords, providing for a cease-fire, disengagement, and a temporary division of Vietnam at the 17th parallel with the Vietminh north and the French south of the line. They postponed settling the political issues caused by the division of the country until 1956; then Vietnam was to be reunified by general elections.

Throughout the Dien Bien Phu crisis, Dulles had called for a collective security treaty for Southeast Asia. Shortly after the Geneva Accords, he saw it become a reality. The Southeast Asia Treaty Organization (SEATO) was signed in Manila in September 1954 by the United States and seven other countries. South Vietnam, Laos, and Cambodia were specifically included as "protocol states" that the signatories would support in case of armed attack or subversion, at the states' request. The members of SEATO were the United States, United Kingdom, France, Australia, New Zealand, Thailand, the Philippines, and Pakistan. From the American view, the pact gave a green light for American or allied intervention in Indochina if it became necessary.

In the immediate post-Geneva period, South Vietnam was a jungle of political factions, both religious and secular. The French were still there, and nearly a million refugees were streaming down from the north. The government in the south was essentially nonexistent, although nominally presided over by Bao Dai.

Into this mishmash the United States injected itself with the goal of stabilizing South Vietnam and thus also Southeast Asia. As Bao Dai seemed to need a prime minister, Ngo Dinh Diem was chosen. The exact circumstances surrounding his appointment in 1954 are not clear, but an American finger was in the pie. In October 1955, during a national referendum between Bao Dai and Diem, Diem (with American help) obtained a suspiciously high 98 percent of the vote. Then proclaiming Vietnam a republic, he became its first president.

Diem, born in 1901, attended the School of Law and Administration in Hanoi, a French institution for training native bureaucrats. By 1933 he was minister of interior to Bao Dai, who had just become emperor, but he soon resigned in a dispute with the French and disappeared from public life. In 1950 he left Vietnam and found his way to a Maryknoll seminary in Lakewood, New Jersey, and later to a Benedictine monastery in Belgium. Lecturing widely, he became known to many influential Americans, including Sen. John F. Kennedy and Cardinal Spellman. A compulsive talker, introverted and lacking charisma, nonetheless he was a strong Vietnamese nationalist who had had some degree of administrative experience.

In late 1954 Eisenhower committed American money to the new regime. In early 1955 additional military assistance was added, but it went directly to South Vietnam rather than through the French. The United States was now officially propping up an independent South Vietnam. This move was the second great benchmark in American involvement in Vietnam. This American support enabled Diem to foil a series of plots against his government, and by late 1955 he was its strongman. As time went on, his government became increasingly authoritarian, eventually bringing about its downfall, but during the 1950s that outcome was not clear.

A key decision by Diem—encouraged and supported by the United States—was not to hold the 1956 nationwide elections called for in the Geneva Accords. South Vietnam by now was beginning to stand on its own feet and seemed to have the makings of a valid nation; meanwhile, North Vietnam was going through a period of harsh repression and most certainly would not have permitted free elections throughout Vietnam.

In an ambitious program during the middle and late 1950s, the United States reorganized, equipped, and trained the South Vietnamese Army, based on the American model. The United States also supplied millions of dollars in foreign aid between 1955 and 1960; it held Vietnamese inflation in check by covering South Vietnam's foreign exchange deficit and by providing consumer goods in quantity. Unfortunately, the American program benefitted the urban areas more than the countryside, where the most deprivation occurred. Actually, the U.S. economic program fostered Vietnam's dependency rather than moving the country toward genuine independence.

The basic problem of Diem's government was political—its increasing authoritarianism. It manifested itself by allocating the bulk of American aid to the military and police forces and leaving only a small portion for economic development and by trying to keep all political power within Diem's own family. The result was discontent within the country, and the early fence sitters became anti-Diem. For the Viet Cong (the southern Vietminh), the war had never really ended. Feeding on the growing discontent, they resumed their struggle through guerrilla warfare in 1957 and 1958. In early 1959 North Vietnam formally approved the resumption of the struggle in the south and began sending arms and advisers to the Viet Cong. By the end of the Eisenhower administration in late 1960, the insurgents in the south joined together to establish the National Liberation Front. It aimed to overthrow the Diem regime, end American involvement, and achieve unification with the north.

SITUATION IN 1961

During the Cuban missile crisis and the subsequent problems of Berlin, Kennedy was simultaneously caught up in the long-range problems of Southeast Asia. At first the problem was Laos. When Eisenhower briefed the president-elect on trouble spots, he told JFK that Laos was America's major problem in Southeast Asia and might even lead the United States to war.

The political status of Laos was a product of the Geneva Accords of 1954. Basically, the country was divided into three factions: the communist Pathet Lao, a neutralist group under Prince Souvanna Phouma, and a right-wing group under Gen. Phoumi Nosovan. Between the accords and the beginning of the Kennedy administration, the political situation was checkered with high intrigue and maneuvering for power, both internally and externally. Considering a neutralist government dangerous, the Eisenhower administration cast its support behind Phoumi Nosovan on the right.

Early in the Kennedy administration, the crisis peaked when the neutralists and communists joined forces against the Phoumi government. The Kennedy administration considered the possibility of military intervention, which was ruled out by the almost impossible logistics of supporting American troops in that landlocked country. Instead, Kennedy opted for negotiations, which went on in Geneva from May 1961 to July 1962 and eventually formed a coalition government under a neutralist premier. The neutralist solution later proved to be a farce, as the North Vietnamese would use Laos as a base for some 80,000 troops, most supporting the Ho Chi Minh Trail in the movement of supplies and troops to the south.

When the Laos crisis dissolved, the main interest in the area shifted to the problem that would dominate the remaining years of Camelot—Vietnam. Given the lack of foreign policy successes by the administration up to this point, Vietnam looked more and more like a place to win one.

Shortly after the Bay of Pigs, Kennedy ordered a review of the Vietnam situation. What could the United States do to prevent communist domination there? The review, headed by Deputy Secretary of Defense Roswell Gilpatric, recommended a small increase in the American advisory group and a substantial increase in the South Vietnamese Army. Kennedy agreed to a 20,000-man increase in South Vietnamese forces, along with more advisers. Involving only a hundred Americans, this decision was, however, the prologue for American actions that would exceed the limits of the 1954 Geneva Accords.

A short time later, in May of 1961, Kennedy agreed to send more Americans in the form of Special Forces. He also approved increasing the forces of South Vietnam and of examining a possible U.S. troop commitment in the future.

In the midst of these May decisions, Kennedy decided to send Vice President Johnson (LBJ) to South Vietnam. This was the trip in which LBJ referred to Diem as "the Winston Churchill of Southeast Asia." During a meeting, Diem told LBJ that he had no need for American troops, at least at that time. Still, on Kennedy's behalf, Johnson asked Diem to forward a list of military needs.

It was not long—June 9, to be precise—until Diem had a letter off to Kennedy asking for no less than 100,000 troops in the South Vietnamese Army, to be financed by the United States, and for a considerable expansion of the U.S. military advisory group. This letter was important to Maxwell Taylor. From then on, he was face-to-face with the dragon of Vietnam.

As Taylor tells the story in his memoirs, he had a chance encounter with Kennedy in the White House while the president was holding Diem's letter. Asked by JFK for his comments on the missive, Taylor began, in his words, "an involvement in the Vietnam problem to which I was to commit a large part of my life during the next eight years."

Taylor responded by suggesting an interim reply approving an increase of 30,000 South Vietnamese troops. By early August—against the background of the Berlin crisis—Kennedy approved this increase.

Diem was not the only person pushing increased support for Vietnam. Even before Diem's letter, Walt Rostow, Bundy's assistant for the area and an aggressive believer in counterinsurgency, was pushing for greater support. The Joint Chiefs also thought that Diem should be requesting U.S. troops at this point. In fact, by October Kennedy had proposals coming from many directions for more American support of Vietnam: U. Alexis Johnson in the Department of State and William Bundy in the Defense Department were two of those on this bandwagon.

In May 1961, a new American ambassador to Vietnam, Frederick J. Nolting, was aboard with instructions to reduce the friction that had existed between his predecessor, Elbridge Durbrow, and Diem. Indeed, as is clear from his communiqués, he was all for backing Diem "to the hilt." He wrote, "Where we think he is wrong, we can bring about improvement." He cautioned that "the Diem government must make a 'break-through' to regain popular support. If the situation drags on in an inconclusive manner for many more months either a military coup or an open proclamation of a Communist Government and widespread civil war is likely."

In October, pressured within his administration and by media reports that American forces might be dispatched, Kennedy decided to send a mission to Vietnam to get facts on which to base his decisions. To head this mission, he chose Max Taylor, with Walt Rostow as a kind of deputy.

Walt Whitman Rostow, born in New York City in 1916, graduated from Yale and was a Rhodes scholar before receiving a Ph.D. from Yale. During World War II he served with the Office of Strategic Services (OSS) and was involved in selecting bombing targets. In the 1950s he was a professor of economic history at MIT and a prolific writer who impressed Sen. John Kennedy. As president-elect, JFK promised to place Rostow in charge of policy planning at State; but Rusk had other ideas, and Rostow ended up as McGeorge Bundy's deputy. He was hawkish on Vietnam and a definite believer in the efficacy of bombing.

In Kennedy's letter of instruction to Taylor, the goals of the mission were broad. The president wanted Taylor to discover what American medicines would help keep South Vietnam alive, but, he added, in the final analysis the responsibility rested with the South Vietnamese themselves. He stressed that political, economic, and social elements were as important as the military. Talking with Taylor just before the trip, Kennedy made clear that he hoped to avoid committing American combat troops. That was the real worry in the mind of JFK.

THE TAYLOR-ROSTOW MISSION

Because of the presidential decisions it precipitated, the Taylor-Rostow mission[3] was a benchmark of American involvement in Vietnam. It compared to Eisenhower's decision to replace the French in the south and to supply aid to the Diem government in 1954.

Accompanying the two principals to Vietnam were nine experts from various government agencies. The political-social experts were Sterling Cottrell and William Jorden; the military expert was Maj. Gen. William H. Craig. Unconventional warfare was the area of Maj. Gen. Edward Lansdale; covert activities, Joseph Smith. Rear Adm. Luther C. Heinz handled MAAG and military aid; James W. Howe, economic aid; and George W. Rathjens and William H. Godel, research and development.

Taylor made clear to all of them that he would write the report to the president, with Rostow's assistance. The other members would write reports in their areas of expertise to be appended to Taylor's document.

On October 17, 1961, the party left for Vietnam. En route, Taylor and Rostow consulted with the other members in small groups to outline work assignments. Their first stop was Honolulu, where they received extensive briefings on the Vietnam situation from Adm. Harry Felt, U.S. commander in the Pacific. He had no doubt that the situation was bad and that America had to help. He was, however, inclined to withhold American combat forces for the time while providing logistic and support units.

The issues facing the mission on arrival in Saigon can generally be grouped into four areas. First was the buildup of the Viet Cong from around 10,000 troops in early 1961 to around 17,000. Second was the question of how to bring the peasants in rural areas closer to the central government (or the daytime government, as the nighttime government in the countryside was increasingly that of the Viet Cong). Third—and the big question on President Kennedy's mind when he dispatched the mission—was whether the South Vietnamese Army could really cope with the Viet Cong without American troops. Finally, could the Diem government itself survive? If not, what were the alternatives, if any, to sticking with Diem?

In the background were two other matters of interest. On October 18, about the time the mission arrived in Saigon, Diem declared a state of national emergency. Nature complicated the situation with another emergency, not related to Diem's. The worst flood in decades ravaged the Mekong Delta, destroying crops and lifestock and leaving thousands homeless.

The mission fanned out to its areas of interest, but Taylor and Rostow's first job was to meet with Diem at the presidential palace. One member of the mission was a friend of Diem's: Air Force Gen. Ed Lansdale, the group's expert on unconventional warfare, was an old Vietnam hand who had been there from 1954 to 1956.[4] He had been invited to dinner by the president when the group arrived, and while Taylor was holding a press conference at the airport, he left for the palace. What struck Lansdale most at seeing Diem again was how his brother Nhu seemed to influence him and thus probably the whole government. This change most likely dated from an abortive coup against Diem in November of 1960, after which Diem trusted no one outside his family. Weary of the plotting against him, he had given his brother considerable power.

Present at Taylor and Rostow's meeting with President Diem the day after the group's arrival were five other Americans and one Vietnamese. The gathering turned into a four-hour dialogue between Diem and Taylor in French. It was close to a monologue—Diem talked as incessantly as he smoked—but Taylor occasionally interjected points or questions.

As the meeting ended, Taylor asked whether U.S. combat troops would be necessary. Diem replied ambiguously, although he did make the point that, if this happened, the United States should be prepared to stay the course. Diem's remark reflected his skepticism of American intentions about Vietnam in general and about his own future in particular. He was concerned about the lack of a formal U.S. commitment to South Vietnam's survival and the people's (read Diem's) fear that the United States might abandon them.

While in Saigon, Taylor also called on Maj. Gen. Duong Van Minh. Minh had the title, but not the authority, of head of the Military Field Command because Diem and his brother Nhu feared a coup if "Big Minh," as he was known, commanded troops directly. Minh was a harsh critic of the way that Diem operated and felt that the president downgraded the military command and favored Catholics at the expense of others. Two years later, Minh was to be one of the coup leaders who threw out and murdered Diem.

Taylor and Rostow visited the demilitarized zone at the 17th parallel and flew over the enormous flood in the Mekong Delta in the south. Before they left Vietnam, they made an exit call on Diem. At this meeting, Taylor set forth his initial conclusions.

Feeling that the most critical issue was likely to be the commitment of U.S. troops, he came up with a gimmick to solve the problem—the introduction of a flood-relief task force for the Mekong. It would contain some American combat troops along with other troops, such as engineers. As Taylor saw it, this presence would demonstrate U.S. resolve to stay the course while being connected with a humanitarian objective. Hence, the troops could be removed at the end of the Mekong emergency without any loss of prestige. What Taylor had in mind was a force of 6,000 to 8,000 men. Diem seemed enthusiastic about the idea.

The visiting Americans then flew to the Philippines to write their report. They worked at the summer capital of Baguio, which Taylor had visited in 1939 on the way home from his four-year language stint in Japan. The group generally agreed that as things stood, the life expectancy of the South Vietnamese government was short. It had many weaknesses: poor intelligence gathering, a defensive outlook, and overly centralized control. To correct these deficiencies and take advantage of enemy vulnerabilities, South Vietnam needed more American aid and guidance right away. The tide was running in favor of the enemy.

Taylor addressed these needs from the Philippines in two "eyes only" messages to the president to prepare JFK for the report that was coming. The twenty-five-page Taylor and Rostow report was accompanied by the numerous appendices that the other members of the mission wrote on matters of their own expertise.

In the eyes-only messages, Taylor pointed out the South Vietnamese people's doubts about both American resolve and about the ability of the Diem government to defeat the insurgency. He proposed a massive joint effort and a limited partnership with the Vietnamese government. He also went into some detail on the flood-relief task force, which was to become the most controversial aspect of his report.

He set forth the pros and cons of the troops recommendation. In effect, he felt that no other action would be as convincing about the seriousness of American intent, hence so reassuring to the people and government of South Vietnam. He did acknowledge that U.S. strategic reserves were already weak, that such action might build tensions with the Soviet bloc, and that U.S. prestige would be further engaged.

Moreover, if enough troops were not sent at first, Saigon would pressure the Americans for reinforcements. In what became a famous line in the message, he commented on the hazards involved: "The risks of backing into a major Asian war by way of SVN are present but are not impressive. NVN is extremely vulnerable to conventional bombing, a weakness that should be exploited diplomatically in convincing Hanoi to lay off SVN." Perhaps Taylor was pulled here by the old targeter, Walt Rostow, a great believer in the efficacy of bombing.

On November 3 the mission presented the full report to the president in Washington. He thanked them and said that decisions would await a full study of the report by the State and Defense departments. The following day the New York Times reported that General Taylor did not look favorably on sending troops to Vietnam. We can assume that the source of this erroneous report was someone in a high place who wanted to "test the waters."

At this time JFK had many other foreign headaches. Berlin still held a tense center stage, and there were still serious problems in the Congo as well as the ongoing negotiations about the future of Laos.

The Taylor-Rostow report set off a debate within the government. It began in a meeting at State, with Taylor present, on Saturday, November 4, the day after the mission reported to the president. Undersecretary for Economic Affairs George Ball substituted for absent Secretary Rusk. Shortly to replace Chester Bowles as undersecretary of state, Ball had worked closely with the French during the First Indochina War and observed how the Vietminh exploited Vietnamese nationalism and bogged down the French militarily. He was convinced that Americans, even without the taint of colonialism, could do no better.

McNamara and his deputy Gilpatric were at the meeting, as were many other top officials from the Departments of State and Defense, the Joint Chiefs of Staff, and the CIA. During the long, frank discussion, some were particularly dissatisfied with the flood-relief task force. Ball, who subsequently became the house dissenter on American involvement in Vietnam, was especially direct. He was appalled at the notion of an American troop commitment, which he felt would involve the United States in a long fight that was really a civil war.

Although McNamara had little sympathy for Ball's approach, he had his own concerns. Without a categorical commitment to use every American resource, sending the type of force recommended for psychological support of the Diem regime made him uneasy. He asked himself, Just what is our policy to be? Are we committing ourselves or not? When the meeting broke up inconclusively, McNamara's staff went to work on a memorandum to the president expressing the defense secretary's views.

On Monday morning, November 6, Walt Rostow briefed McGeorge Bundy's staff on the trip at the Bundy daily meeting. He portrayed a feeling of crisis in Southeast Asia in general and in South Vietnam in particular. He went on to say that, despite all this, General Taylor was somewhat more optimistic when he returned than when he left. (One wonders on what basis Taylor felt this.) He said that Taylor found Diem eventually to be receptive to ideas that he had previously resisted. For example, Diem was willing to improve a centrally directed intelligence operation and joint U.S.-Vietnamese cooperation at provincial—that is, state—level. On the same day

Taylor was meeting privately with Rusk and McNamara; when he left the meeting, he believed that the secretaries of state and defense generally agreed with his report. Shortly, however, Rusk had serious reservations about committing any American combat forces.

On the following day George Ball, meeting with the president on another subject, stayed afterward to discuss the Taylor report and to indicate his strong opposition. Referring to the French experience, Ball felt that any commitment of American troops would eventually lead to a force of 300,000. Kennedy replied with his now famous remark: "George, you're just crazier than hell. That just isn't going to happen."

Meanwhile, McNamara and the Joint Chiefs were developing their own views, which they provided to the president in a memorandum on November 8. The somewhat ambiguous memorandum indicated that McNamara and the JCS were inclined to approve a troop commitment, but, they cautioned, the United States should be prepared to send additional forces up to perhaps more than 200,000.

McNamara and Rusk, probably sensing that the president did not want to commit troops, then got together on a second memorandum dated November 11. On this day the president was to hold a meeting about how to act in Vietnam. It would be a day of climax.

Walt Rostow, knowing the nature of the forthcoming compromise memorandum, sent an advance copy of his own to the president. Noting that the memo coming from Rusk and McNamara stopped short of recommending a troop commitment at that time, Rostow commented:

> General Taylor's proposals are, in my view, conservative proposals for action on our side ... to buy time and permit negotiations to take over for an interval, under reasonably favorable circumstances. I think it unwise to inhibit ourselves ... for fear of what the enemy may do by way of reaction.

The second Rusk-McNamara memorandum called for deferring the combat force but agreed to other proposals such as significant support forces of helicopters, transport aircraft, additional U.S. advisers, and much more economic aid. All of this was set against a list of general reforms to be presented to Diem.

The memorandum also set forth a definite statement of U.S. strategic interest in not losing South Vietnam (SVN) to communism. Such a loss "would not only destroy SEATO but would undermine the credibility of American commitments elsewhere." Although the

WEST HILLS COLLEGE
LEMOORE LIBRARY/LRC

president accepted this strategic view in the end, he did not approve an all-out American commitment to prevent the loss of South Vietnam.

On November 11 the president made his decisions as follows:

    a. He rejected sending organized combat units but approved and expanded other forms of military support proposed.

    b. He approved and made more exacting the concept of American and Vietnamese partnership. Greater American military support would be contingent on Diem's acceptance of fairly drastic changes to include American "partners" at many levels.

    c. He affirmed the great strategic importance of SVN, implying that the United States might take actions and commitments later if needed.

Although there was a formal NSC meeting on the fifteenth to discuss these matters, in effect what the president decided on the eleventh was the crossing of the Rubicon.[5] On November 15 action cables went out to Ambassador Frederick Nolting that summarized the president's decisions, including the condition of Diem's acceptance of American partnership with the South Vietnamese government.

In meeting with Diem, Nolting stressed this point, as well as the need for governmental reforms. Although Diem did not get the American troop contingent he probably expected, he did get tremendous American support. He also got demands for partnership from Kennedy that he had not anticipated, demands that he no doubt interpreted as concessions of Vietnamese sovereignty.

In a few days the Diem government responded with a series of newspaper articles attacking the American position. Nolting protested to Diem, who denied government involvement. The local CIA representatives were aware, of course, that his brother Nhu had set the newspaper attack going. Vietnamese such as Minh, seeing the obvious rift with the Americans, began to prepare for a coup against Diem. But the timing was wrong, as no one was on hand to replace him, and the Kennedy administration discouraged that approach, at least for a time. Time for Diem to go came two years later, although Kennedy did not live long enough to see the results.

In the end, Diem appeared to make some concessions to Nolting— nothing that kept him from making his own decisions, to be sure— but Diem did agree to consult with U.S. advisers and to develop democratic institutions in South Vietnam. These promises satisfied Kennedy, who backed off on more exact compliance with American wishes. What else could he do? More support units were already en route, and the international consequences of another American withdrawal after Cuba and Berlin were too much to contemplate. Shortly thereafter, Diem and Kennedy exchanged letters—made public on December 15—announcing in a general way that the United States was stepping up aid to South Vietnam.

To orchestrate the new effort, two agencies emerged: a group in Washington indirectly involved and a headquarters in Vietnam, the Military Assistance Command Vietnam (MACV), later to become famous or infamous, depending on one's perspective. Both the CIA and the JCS felt that a Washington-based steering group should integrate the counterinsurgency effort. At the president's request, Taylor drew up the charter of what was called the Special Group (Counterinsurgency), and Kennedy signed it on January 18, 1962. The functions of the group included ensuring that government agencies recognized insurgency as a worldwide problem and reflected this status by developing the doctrine in training military forces and officials.

General Taylor was the first chairman of this group, which included JCS Chairman Lemnitzer, CIA Director McCone, Attorney General Kennedy, and various other high-level officials. The group's agenda was far-ranging, including Latin America, but JFK wanted the group to focus on Southeast Asia. It was very active throughout 1962; thereafter, the group supervised programs that it had initiated. Taylor remained chairman until he left the White House to replace Lemnitzer at the Pentagon later in 1962.

Through the Special Group, Kennedy propagated his strong interest in unconventional warfare. He started a governmentwide fad on the subject that reached absurd proportions. Because the president wanted counterinsurgency training to be a promotion requirement for general officer rank, a flurry of crash courses began in the war colleges and other parts of the military schooling system, most of which were "ticket-punching" items. In all, during 1962 some 50,000 officer-level military and civilian officials participated in counterinsurgency training—most of lunch-hour depth.

The second agency, the Military Assistance Command Vietnam (MACV), was created because of the need for an office in Vietnam to direct the flow of advisers and combat and logistic support units brought there by the stepped-up American effort. Therefore, MACV was established on February 8, 1962, and placed under control of the commander in chief Pacific (CINCPAC). In military jargon it was a subunified command, in other words, not a theater headquarters. Although not a problem at first, it would become so when U.S. combat forces were employed and CINCPAC was interposed between the war and Washington.

MACV had many functions. Besides advising the Saigon government, it controlled U.S. field advisers and American combat support and logistic agencies. In later years, the headquarters took charge of the American combat effort and subsequently the pacification program.

The first commander was Gen. Paul Donal Harkins. Fifty-seven and a 1929 graduate of West Point, he had been a cavalry officer and served as Patton's deputy chief of staff of the Third Army during World War II. More a staff officer than a commander, he owed his appointment and consequent four-star promotion to Maxwell Taylor. They had had a long association: Harkins was commandant of cadets during the last year of Taylor's tenure as superintendent of the Military Academy, he was chief of staff when Taylor commanded the Eighth Army in Korea, and he was on the Army General Staff the first two years that Taylor was Army chief of staff. The implications of this relationship would become apparent later as Diem's credibility worsened. Harkins's tour in MACV lasted more than two years, when he was succeeded by another Taylor protégé—William Westmoreland.

The vanguard of the new American support approved by Kennedy was not long in arriving. On December 11, 1961, the aircraft ferry, *Core*, arrived in Saigon with CH-21 helicopters and T-28 fighter-bombers, along with their pilots and ground crews. The personnel statistics show the pace and extent of the buildup. At the time of the Taylor-Rostow mission, about 900 American military were in Vietnam; two months later in January 1962, there were 2,600 and by the end of that year 11,000. When Kennedy was assassinated in November 1963, there were about 16,700. The man orchestrating the buildup for Kennedy was Robert McNamara, who became the president's action officer for Vietnam in November 1961.

In summary, the Taylor-Rostow mission occurred when South Vietnam was steadily going to pieces and when Kennedy's foreign policy count was full of strikes and fouls: the Bay of Pigs fiasco, the

Berlin stalemate, and the unpopular neutralization of Laos. The Taylor-Rostow proposals fixed Vietnam as a place where the United States could win one.

Although Kennedy did not promise to prevent South Vietnam's fall, he said no to the notion of a negotiated settlement. He vetoed the small troop commitment proposed by Taylor but left the possibility open for later. All this time, the debate on troop commitments was distracting the decision makers from what was really happening—a significant American escalation of men, supplies, and money to Diem. Moreover, once the United States had a military headquarters in Vietnam, there would be a bureaucratic demand for more resources as time went on. Having ignored the Geneva Accords of 1954, Kennedy had set in motion a chain of events whose outcome could only be further escalations; the only questions were when and how much. The Taylor-Rostow mission and its resulting presidential decisions were the third of the five great turning points in America's longest war. In one way or another, Maxwell Taylor was involved in three of them.

CHAPTER 4

View from the E Ring

Chapter 2 saw Maxwell Taylor installed in October 1962 as chairman of the Joint Chiefs of Staff, a position he held until July 1964, twenty-one months in all. This chapter focuses on Chairman Taylor's perspectives and role in making Vietnam policy during his tenure, a time when the United States had to deal with the buildup of problems in that country.[1]

Before beginning this chapter, we should take an overview of its main points:

- Just before moving to the Pentagon, Taylor made a sweep through Vietnam to assess the situation since his benchmark visit in the fall of 1961. He felt that progress was uneven, particularly in the political and social fields, and he saw Diem as still the difficult introvert. A major problem was determining just what progress was being made; in this, the American Headquarters (MACV), established after Taylor's last visit, was not of much help. General Harkins, the commander, and his staff were unsophisticated in addressing nonmilitary matters and tended to provide overly optimistic reports. More significant were the inscrutable, complex, sensitive Vietnamese themselves; above all was President Diem's insistence—probably understandable—that U.S. observers not pry into Vietnamese matters.

· During his tenure in the Pentagon, Taylor made several trips to Vietnam and Honolulu, usually with McNamara, to evaluate the situation. Two of the most notable were just before and just after the Diem assassination in the fall of 1963. These visits usually resulted in recommendations for more support to the South Vietnamese. Throughout, Taylor had his own back-channel communications to Harkins. Later this relationship was to call into question the credibility of some of Harkins's optimistic reports to Washington. In addition, by the time of the Diem coup, Harkins and American Ambassador Henry Cabot Lodge were barely on speaking terms, at least on official matters, presumably the main purpose for their presence there.

· From late spring through the fall of 1963, Diem's shaky status as president of South Vietnam preoccupied American officials. The Buddhist crisis, which began in May, brought matters to a head. Then there was the notorious cable of August 24, 1963, from the State Department to newly arrived Ambassador Lodge. Obtaining only perfunctory clearance, W. Averell Harriman, Roger Hilsman, and Michael Forrestal slipped it out of Washington on a weekend, when most senior officials were out of town. It set in motion the events leading to Diem's overthrow and assassination on November 1. Considering this cable the biggest American mistake made in the Vietnam endeavor, Taylor objected at the time but was not willing to risk his clout with the president by taking a stronger position. After Diem's overthrow, South Vietnam bled all the more, both militarily and politically. The era of coups began, and the Viet Cong insurgency became more active. South Vietnamese morale evaporated as its Army personnel began deserting in droves.

· Kennedy's assassination came three weeks after Diem's, and Lyndon Baines Johnson took over the mantle of U.S. leadership. Although LBJ generally kept to Kennedy's policies on foreign and defense affairs, his operational style was quite different. Taylor's rapport with him, although not so close as that with Kennedy, was good. When Ambassador Lodge threw his hat into the 1964 presidential primary, the United States needed a new ambassador to Saigon. Johnson considered Dean Rusk, Robert McNamara, Bobby Kennedy, and Maxwell Taylor. He selected Taylor.

THE PERIOD OF OFFICIAL OPTIMISM

By early 1962 Kennedy's approval of the Taylor-Rostow recommendations had concrete results: a sizeable number of advisers, helicopters, coastal and river craft, fixed-wing support aircraft, and other support forces went out to South Vietnam. In the eyes of the new military commander, Gen. Paul Harkins, all this assistance was beginning to pay off. Looking ahead, he felt that more American advisers—influencing all aspects of military effort—would spur the Vietnamese. The key to improvement, he reasoned, was the proper training of Vietnamese officers and noncommissioned officers. According to optimist Harkins, once the training had taken effect, the Viet Cong (VC) should be defeated in about a year.

This burgeoning American support did, in fact, pay dividends early on. The introduction of American helicopters created a whole new style of warfare. With their mobility vastly improved, the Army of Vietnam (ARVN) could surprise the Viet Cong even in their base areas. Nevertheless, although terrorized by the helicopters at first, the Viet Cong eventually developed countermeasures; instead of running, they began shooting back. More and more, they ambushed landings or moved to areas too remote for heliborne operations.

This commitment of the helicopter units in late 1961 and through 1962 was pushing the United States deeper into the war. The American manpower commitment rose from around 900 at the time of the Taylor-Rostow mission to more than 11,000 by the end of 1962. Moreover, the United States permitted the advisers and pilots to participate in actual combat against the Viet Cong. As early as 1961–62, more than thirty Americans had died as a result of enemy action. Still, it was a period of great optimism—but more so at American headquarters in Saigon than in the field. Some field advisers believed that with increased aid the ARVN could outstrip the VC units, but most doubted that the guerrilla terrorist threat to the South Vietnamese population would soon end.

If Taylor was the father of the American buildup and Harkins the cheerleader, then the ramrod, or manager, was Secretary of Defense McNamara. Looking back in late 1961, McNamara felt that he had failed in his responsibility to Vietnam earlier. Now he made up for it with a vengeance. In December 1961 he made the first of what would be some nineteen trips to Honolulu or Saigon to carry out what he saw as his Vietnam responsibilities. On seven of these trips he was accompanied by Maxwell Taylor. Known as secretary of defense conferences, these meetings occurred every month for the first four months beginning in December 1961. On the agenda were such matters as the various aspects of training, the ARVN, and the role of advisers.

As the secretary of defense himself presided at these meetings, the question of Vietnam was being handled at a much higher level in the Department of Defense than it was in the Department of State. Dean Rusk was, of course, well aware of this difference. In effect, McNamara was filling a void in Vietnam policymaking created by the secretary of state's diffidence on this subject. Going beyond the military aspects, McNamara's discussions went into pacification and other matters. As with other programs he worked on, the secretary of defense was impatient for results: he wanted quantitative constructions of what was happening.

After each trip, McNamara met with the news media for a progress report. At least in the early days, these reports always indicated his pleasure with how Vietnamese armed forces were training or taking the offensive. The reports included the usual statistical indicators (for which the war later became known) about the higher casualty rates the South Vietnamese were inflicting and the number of Viet Cong weapons captured.

McNamara, although aware of political as well as military aspects, was relatively naive about the South Vietnamese people themselves. In retrospect there is no question that he was overly optimistic with his statistics. After a May 1962 trip, he stated that "every quantitative measurement we have shows we are winning the war." Undoubtedly, quantitative measurements did point in that direction for at least a little while. But it did not occur to him then that perhaps there were no reliable measures of progress in this strange kind of war into which the United States had stumbled.

Simultaneously with the advisory and support buildup of the military, based on the Taylor-Rostow report, a development in the pacification area was the strategic hamlet program. In February 1962 the South Vietnamese government began acting on a pacification plan submitted by R. G. K. Thompson, who had worked on pacification for the British in Malaysia.

An earlier plan had called for uprooting people from their ancestral homelands to move them into more guarded or strategically secure spots. That program, much criticized, was recognized as a failure and abandoned. Thompson's program, based on his Malaysia work and the earlier plan, was less ambitious about the size of the hamlets and the extent of displacement. The hamlets would be very small, and people would not have to move great distances. The notion was one of an oil-blot pattern; gradually, the hamlets would be established in relatively secure areas. As each hamlet became stable, more would be established on its outskirts and then eventually spread outward from several central points. Controlling the program was Ngo Dinh Nhu, the brother of President Diem. Although the United States provided such boosts as building materials, barbed wire, ammunition, and guns, Nhu, along with the British Thompson, sold the idea to Diem.

When Taylor traveled to Vietnam in September 1962, the strategic hamlet program was high on the agenda, as in August the Vietnamese government had announced its national strategic hamlet plan. In the later writings about this period, the hamlet program received unmerciful criticism, some of it justified. The general charges were that too many strategic hamlets were planned too fast, that the oil-blot approach was abandoned, that the size and success of the program was exaggerated by lower-level Vietnamese to gain news admiration or approval, and that the figures were padded by Nhu. But with all its faults, the program went on until about 1963.

The best illustration of action following overoptimism during this period was the planning for U.S. withdrawal. It demonstrates how a combination of eager intentions and poor assessment of a situation can lead to a misplaced effort. Of course, events elsewhere played a part in this planning as well. Washington was worried about heightened Soviet activities in Cuba during the late spring and summer of 1962, and it was a time of change in Laos, as a fourteen-nation conference in Geneva finally produced a political-military solution on which rightist, neutralist, and communist factions could agree. In addition, an aura of confidence was coming from Saigon about the vigor and resolve of its strategic hamlet program.

Against this setting Secretary McNamara scheduled one of his Honolulu conferences for July 23, 1962, coincidentally the same day on which the Laos agreement was signed in Geneva. McNamara's session promptly embraced a number of reports portraying the South Vietnamese as marching to victory against the insurgents. Apparently convinced that these reports reinforced what he had heard before, McNamara directed preparation of a plan for further strengthening

South Vietnamese regular forces and security forces. This action would permit some phaseout of U.S. advisory training and support contingents and reduce the effort to a small mission by the end of 1965. In effect, it called for winning the war in roughly three years or, put another way, for controlling the communist insurgency long enough to enable the South Vietnamese to fend for themselves.

Maxwell Taylor made his next trip to Vietnam at the peak of all this optimism. The end of American involvement was in sight, it seemed, as a result of his recommendations to Kennedy the preceding fall—and the president's consequent action. He arrived in Saigon on September 10, 1962, so that he might "form an impression of the progress of the many programs which stemmed from my previous visit almost a year before." Actually, this trip took him to many Far Eastern countries; he called it a "refresher visit" preparatory to taking up his duties as chairman JCS.

Reflecting on the trip later, Taylor was impressed by progress in the training of the South Vietnamese armed forces. But he also noted the hostility of the media representatives toward Diem; many seemed to be committed to a full-scale vendetta against the South Vietnamese president. Overall, Taylor concluded that "we were achieving qualitative progress in the military but that the socio-political programs continued to lag."

In his memoirs Taylor prides himself on assembling junior officers without senior officers present "to assure relatively uninhibited replies" to his questions.[2] Not all the personnel in the field saw it that way, though. Lieutenant Col. John Paul Vann, adviser to the 7th ARVN Division (and later to become the most famous of American advisers) was delighted with General Harkins's invitation to join him and General Taylor for lunch at Harkins's Saigon villa on September 11, 1962. Here, as Vann saw it, was an opportunity to tell Kennedy's military representative just how bad the situation really was in spite of all the official optimism. He hoped that his information would result later in pressure on Diem and Harkins to get things moving.

Despite Vann's hopes of conveying the real story to Taylor (and Taylor's later comments that he had heard the uninhibited views of the younger officers), he did not get a chance. To put it in Vann's own words: "Luncheon lasted one hour and fifteen minutes. General tenor of conversation such that General Harkins presented views and/or overrode key points I tried to present."[3]

Just before departing two days later, Taylor gave a press conference at Tan Son Nhut air terminal.

One has to be here personally to sense the growing national character, the resistance of the Vietnamese people to the subversive insurgency threat. My overall impression is of a great national movement, assisted to some extent, of course, by Americans, but essentially a movement by Vietnamese to defend Vietnam against a dangerous and cruel enemy.

With that Taylor was off, after a stop in Indonesia, to brief the president, McNamara, and the Joint Chiefs on his observations. But not far ahead was an encounter that would wipe away American smiles—the battle of Ap Bac.

AP BAC AND ITS AFTERMATH

Far away from Taylor's E Ring Pentagon office was a place called Ap Bac in the Mekong Delta, 40 miles southeast of Saigon. On January 2, 1963, a battle there was a landmark in the American outlook on Vietnam. Involved were around 2,500 troops of South Vietnam's 7th Infantry Division. Equipped with automatic weapons and armored amphibious personnel carriers, they were supported by bombers and helicopters. Their enemy was a group of around 350 guerrillas whose Viet Cong radio transmitter had been picked up by U.S. signal intelligence personnel.

Despite all their weapons and their overwhelmingly superior forces, the South Vietnamese failed to defeat the guerrillas, who escaped almost intact after inflicting fairly severe losses and destroying five Huey gunships. Around eighty South Vietnamese were killed; over a hundred were wounded. Three Americans were killed and another eight wounded. The losses for the Viet Cong were small—perhaps under twenty killed and forty wounded. When John Paul Vann made his candid after-action assessment of what went wrong, he came into conflict with General Harkins and the American military command headquarters in Saigon. In any event, what happened that day in the Mekong Delta was to assume considerable importance well beyond the battle itself.

Ap Bac was for the American press corps the climax to the tension that had been building since the previous October between the press and the Diem government. Objecting to critical reporting, the Diem regime had tried to exert controls. The correspondents knew nothing about the battle of Ap Bac at the outset, but they were soon exposed to the critical views of the advisers, especially those of John Paul

Vann. He described the battle as a "miserable damn performance . . . like it always is." The furious correspondents turned this into a major media event. They were now the foes not only of Diem but also of the American mission, especially the military commander, Gen. Paul Harkins.[4] The U.S. mission handled itself poorly, in the process losing credibility for honest reports. Even though Harkins and his boss in Hawaii, Adm. Harry Felt, termed Ap Bac a South Vietnamese victory, everyone else knew otherwise.

One legacy of Ap Bac, then, was that it turned an important segment of the press against American officials in Vietnam. Convinced that they were being lied to, reporters became even more hostile than before. And for everything that went wrong, the media made Diem the scapegoat. Some reporters even had the goal of bringing down the regime.

Out of this debacle the communist forces gained psychologically as well. They had needed some kind of tangible victory on the battlefield to show that they could defeat American technology, especially the dreaded helicopter. Ap Bac was, in fact, a battle for which the communists had prepared very carefully; it could not have worked out better as a morale booster. Here was their proof that they were the best fighters—a fact that the American headquarters was trying to hide.

THE BUDDHIST CRISIS AND THE WASHINGTON DECISION MAKERS

Despite the Ap Bac downfall, top American officials in Saigon remained optimistic. Aid programs were moving along, while General Harkins was planning accelerated combat actions for the Vietnamese units. He also worked on additional support for the strategic hamlet program. Early in 1963 Harkins wrote to Diem that he felt we—meaning the South Vietnamese and the Americans—had taken the initiative from the enemy.

Both before and after the Ap Bac battle, Kennedy heard regularly from officials that he had sent to Vietnam. Some of these reports were not hopeful; some were mildly optimistic. All in all, though, the president had some cause to worry about American efforts. Perhaps the most disturbing report came from Sen. Mike Mansfield about his Vietnam visit in late November and early December 1962. Returning to Washington in mid-December, he gave the president a private, confidential account. Although indicating some progress, the report said, among other things, that "it would be well to face the fact that we are once again at the beginning of the beginning." It pointed out that the Vietnamese political structure in Saigon was "far more dependent on us for its existence than it was five years ago." In general, the report was not one to give the president confidence one year after his approval of the Taylor-Rostow recommendations.[5]

In early January 1963, President Kennedy dispatched Roger Hilsman of the State Department on a fact-finding trip to Vietnam, along with Michael Forrestal, who had filled the NSC staff vacancy created by Walt Rostow's departure for the State Department. In their report, which was not highly comforting to the president, Hilsman and Forrestal told of many problems but still saw reasons for hope. They pointed out that the ARVN and U.S. forces were probably winning, but a good deal more slowly than they had hoped. They criticized the coordination of the American agencies in Vietnam; the American effort was fragmented and possibly duplicative. The report included a call for some kind of an American authority there—"the right kind of general" with sufficient stature to dominate American efforts in Saigon.[6]

Following the Hilsman-Forrestal trip, JCS Chairman Taylor sent his own team to Saigon, headed by Army Chief of Staff Gen. Earle G. ("Bus") Wheeler. A 1932 West Point graduate, Wheeler had climbed to his present position because of his skills as a staff officer; his commands were only incidental. He came through as gentlemanly, urbane, and highly articulate. He did understand the Washington bureaucracy as well as any active-duty officer did at that time. He was to play—both in that role and later when succeeding Taylor as chairman—an important part in Vietnam decision making.

When Wheeler and his twelve-man JCS team returned to Washington, they presented findings to Secretary of Defense McNamara and Chairman Taylor as well as to the other Joint Chiefs of Staff and eventually to the president. Their report was somewhat more optimistic than the Hilsman-Forrestal findings and definitely more so than Senator Mansfield's. Their conclusion was that the previously desperate situation in Vietnam had been turned around: "victory is now a hopeful prospect." They felt that the South was winning slowly and had no particularly compelling reason to change the efforts. They did, however, hedge their optimism somewhat in noting that restrictions against going into Cambodia and Laos made "victory more remote." And, like the earlier report of Hilsman and Forrestal, the Wheeler report was highly critical of the way the American press was covering the war.[7]

In April, national intelligence estimates concerning Vietnam were a mixed bag: while communist progress had been blunted and the situation was improving, Diem's ability "to translate military success into political stability" was in question. In that spring of 1963, it is true, the strains on the American alliance with Diem were beginning to show. Diem had been particularly depressed by Kennedy's attempts to neutralize Laos; he certainly did not want a similar situation in South Vietnam. At that time Diem seemed to have developed some kind of siege mentality; if not rejecting U.S. suggestions, he often gave evasive responses, along with lengthy discussions on Vietnamese history to point out that Vietnam was not an American protectorate. Still, that spring he was confident of his republic's strength; he had no inkling of the crisis that was to break out in May in his native city of Hue.

The triggering event of the Buddhist crisis took place on May 8, 1963, in the streets of Hue, the long-ago capital of all Vietnam and now a center of Buddhist activity. Thousands of Vietnamese had gathered to celebrate the anniversary of Buddha's birth and simultaneously to protest a government ban on displaying religious flags. Although this ban was long-standing, Catholic flags had been prominently displayed during an anniversary for Diem's brother, Ngo Dinh Thuc, archbishop of Hue. Meanwhile, Diem had declared that the ban on Buddhist flags would be enforced.[8]

The protest got out of control. When charged by a crowd, the police fired, killing and wounding many South Vietnamese. No other issue could have been more inflammatory or more calculated to arouse a Buddhist-Catholic antagonism. There were also political implications: the Diem regime itself, which relied disproportionately on Catholics as senior officials, was being challenged. Catholics were seen as having preferred positions and educational opportunities. Although Buddhist protests in Vietnam were not new (they had occurred during the French period), the roots of this particular protest were deeper and more widespread than anyone realized.

Through May and early June, Buddhist groups pressed their demands on Diem and his brother Nhu, a de facto ruler of the government, but received little satisfaction. As the depth of their grievances became more evident, Washington instructed the acting American ambassador, William Trueheart, to get tough with Diem. At the same time the American journalists in Saigon were beating the drums.

Their articles, favoring the Buddhist side, were extremely critical of the Diem regime. These press reports, which were polarizing the overall situation, had the effect of stiffening Diem and Nhu's resistance to any American suggestions.

Then, on June 11, a well-known bonze, doused with gasoline, burned himself to death in the square of Saigon. The already biased media gave this shocking event intense worldwide coverage. As a result, Diem made some kind of agreement with the Buddhist leaders, but it did not hold up; the atmosphere became steadily more tense.

In late June, Kennedy appointed a new ambassador to Vietnam: Henry Cabot Lodge. The two men were old political adversaries, going back to 1952, when Kennedy edged him out for a Senate seat from Massachusetts. Moreover, a Nixon-Lodge Republican ticket had opposed JFK for the presidency in 1960. Now, however, the Democratic president saw the desirability of having a prominent moderate-wing Republican as a political anchor if Vietnam came up in the 1964 campaign. Up to this point, it was not a partisan issue, but in case it was by 1964 Lodge's presence should forestall a political fight.

Maxwell Taylor, chairman of the Joint Chiefs of Staff, had much in common with the new ambassador—and Taylor's later term as ambassador would be sandwiched between Lodge's two assignments in Saigon. With similar life spans (Lodge's, 1902–85; Taylor's, 1901–87), the two spent their adult years until old age in public service. Lodge's service was mainly congressional and diplomatic—including a United Nations ambassadorship—but in World War II he, like Taylor, served both in combat and liaison.

Both men, tall and straight, were athletic and scholarly; both had a flair for foreign languages—and for their own. Both were involved in Vietnam decision making at the time when to speak or not to speak was crucial. In the summer of 1963 they were on opposite sides of the globe and sometimes on opposite sides of the question.

South Vietnam was, in fact, becoming a hot issue when Kennedy and his senior advisers met, although in July 1963 the Pentagon and CIA seem not to have been nearly so involved as the State Department was. Ambassador Nolting, having returned from leave, went to Saigon instructed to persuade Diem to make peace with the Buddhists. In a series of meetings Nolting tried to put this idea across but had limited success. Senior State Department officials, particularly W. Averell Harriman and Roger Hilsman, made no bones of their intensively negative views of Diem. (In retrospect, this attitude fore-

shadowed an American policy to displace him.) The press and private reports from Washington alerted the already suspicious Nhu
and Diem that Lodge's arrival would mean changes.

Such was the situation when fateful August 1963 arrived. In making farewell calls before his August 15 departure, Nolting did manage to get Diem to promise that he would publicly repudiate some
statements about the Buddhists made by his sister-in-law and official
hostess, Madame Nhu. A favorite target of the American press, the
"Dragon Lady" received the comic-strip epithet for her not-so-comic
behavior. She was seen as a tactless virago at the center of power who
urged Diem and Nhu on to violent repressions against the Buddhists.

On the night of August 21–22 just such a repression occurred. The
Diem government sent Army units to invade the main pagodas in
Saigon. Besides inflicting much physical damage, soldiers arrested
and injured many bonzes and others. The act was calculated to destroy any hope of reconciliation with the Buddhists. Its timing presented the Americans, particularly Lodge, with a fait accompli; with
whatever force necessary, Diem and Nhu meant to rule.

Shocked Washington officials thought at first that the raid had
been the work of the regular Army. Soon, however, they learned that
the invaders belonged to Colonel Tung's Special Forces, designed for
a normal combat role but actually used by Diem and Nhu for their
security. Like other troops, they were supported by both U.S. military assistance funds and the CIA.

Shortly after arriving in Saigon, Lodge cabled Washington that the
only solution was to get rid of the Nhus in some fashion. Specifically,
he reported that Vietnam Army officers were outraged at the Army's
being identified as the pagoda raiders. They approached an American
contact to ask how the United States would react if the officers served
an ultimatum on Diem to oust the Nhus. The implication was that if
Diem refused to comply they would then take over the government in
a coup.

The reply to Lodge became one of the most notorious documents
of our Vietnam experience and has since become known as the August 24 cable. Informing Lodge that the United States could no longer
tolerate Nhu's power, it demanded that he be removed. Regarding
Diem himself, the key operative sentence was: "We must face the
possibility that Diem himself cannot be preserved."

The origins of Cable 243 are well known. Assistant Secretary of
State for Far Eastern Affairs Roger Hilsman and Under Secretary for
Political Affairs W. Averell Harriman were the real authors. August

24 was a Saturday; getting out such an important cable on a weekend, when most of the principals were out of town, was in effect an end run (as Taylor later described it). It would not have been possible without the aid of Michael Forrestal, a Kennedy White House aide.

Taylor, who knew nothing about the cable until that evening, later wrote about its highly questionable procedure:

> They drew up the cable, cleared it with Under Secretary George Ball, who was out playing golf, and got a telephone clearance with the President in Hyannis Port. It was then dispatched without concurrence of the Defense Department, the Joint Chiefs of Staff, or the CIA, all of whom had a vital interest in its contents. Yet when we all got together the following Monday morning, its authors couldn't explain what the cable actually meant."[9]

Get together they did that Monday and each day that week—in an atmosphere that was the opposite of sweetness and light. The gist and feel of these meetings come through in excerpts from the memorandum for the record taken down by Marine Maj. Gen. Victor Krulak, Taylor's special assistant.

MONDAY, AUGUST 26

The President asked General Taylor, in light of his experience in the Pentagon, what chance a plan such as outlined in State Cable 243 would have of succeeding. General Taylor replied that in Washington we would not turn over the problem of choosing a head of state to the military.

. . .

Mr. McNamara then raised the question of who Ambassador Lodge believes could replace Diem, stating that if we stand by and let a weak man get in the Presidency we will ultimately suffer. In this regard the President asked if the Foreign Minister who recently resigned might be a good candidate, to which Hilsman replied in the negative—stating that it is his view that the Generals would probably support Big Minh.

. . .

Mr. Rusk then stated that, in the broad sense, it appears that unless a major change in GVN [government of Vietnam] pol-

icy can be engineered, we must actually decide whether to
move our resources out or to move our troops in.[10]

When the president polled each participant as to whether the cable
should be rescinded, the consensus was to let it stand. Even such opponents as Taylor, McNamara, and McCone went along with the decision, evidently feeling that the damage had been done already. They
still felt, however, that the United States would do better working with
Diem than with an unknown head. That same day the CIA instructed
agencies in Vietnam to begin an ongoing discussion with ARVN generals about coup possibilities based on the August 24 cable.

In Saigon, Ambassador Lodge, strongly anti-Diem throughout,
proposed to work directly with the generals about the removal of
Nhu instead of presenting Diem with an ultimatum. The idea was to
keep the element of surprise, but rumors of American approval of a
coup were already circulating in Saigon.

TUESDAY, AUGUST 27

Following the arrival of the President, Mr. Rusk proposed
that there be frequent meetings on this subject until a break
is seen; something on the order of the Executive Committee
arrangement followed during the Cuba crisis.

. . .

The President stated that it was his view that a coup should
not be attempted if its chance of success is slim and then
asked if the list of generals we have could make a coup succeed. To this Mr. Nolting replied that he did not believe so.

. . .

The President asked if, having proceeded this far, we could
not turn back.

. . .

Mr. McNamara stated that we must ask Ambassador Lodge
and General Harkins to appraise the measure of success; if
they are not sanguine, they should caution the military leaders involved to go slowly.

. . .

The President asked directly whether General Harkins supports this coup plan, to which Hilsman said yes, and General Taylor said that Harkins has been told what to do and is complying.[11]

However, Taylor's Pentagon cable to Harkins the next day indicated that the Department of Defense had not participated in the August 24 cable and that there were now second thoughts about its directives.[12]

WEDNESDAY, AUGUST 28

Mr. Bundy asked for some form of estimate of the loyal forces in the Saigon area. General Taylor replied that the forces loyal to Diem may outnumber the coup forces by two to one; on the other hand, forces more remote from the capital are weighted heavily on the side of the generals identified with the coup. . . . He made the point that, in any case, numbers are less important than capabilities and resolutions.

. . .

Mr. Ball stated that, in his view, there is no option but to support a change which will eliminate the Nhus; that things have now gone a very long way and that the problem is how to make the action work.

Mr. McNamara stated that he was reluctant to follow this line of reasoning, but that events of the past might have undoubtedly pushed us far down the road.

. . .

Mr. McNamara stated that he believed we should make clear to Ambassador Lodge that he should not allow a coup to start if he is fearful that it would fail, because if it does, we lost South Vietnam.

. . .

Governor Harriman stated that in his view we have lost South Vietnam if we do not have a successful coup.

. . .

The President then directed that a message be sent to the Ambassador which expressed the general thought that we should not undertake this enterprise unless we believe it will succeed.

. . .

The President asked about exile for Diem and Nhu, stating that nothing should be permitted to happen to them.

Ambassador Nolting made a final statement of his position, saying that nobody can hold that fragmented country together but Diem; that there is no great possibility of getting Diem to send Nhu away but that perhaps one more attempt would be in order. To this Mr. Bundy commented that Ambassador Lodge did not agree and Governor Harriman stated that he was definitely opposed to this action.[13]

All week the wires burned between Saigon and Washington, as Lodge and Harkins were asked for opinions and advice about a coup. Lodge always wanted to support the generals; Harkins still wanted to give Diem another chance.

THURSDAY, AUGUST 29

Secretary Rusk opened the conference by stating that he had in hand responses from both Ambassador Lodge and General Harkins; that the Ambassador is resolute that the war cannot be won with the Diem regime while Harkins, although more emphatic regarding the undesirability of Nhu, differs in that he believes there should be another approach to Diem.

. . .

The President asked, based on the messages which had been received overnight, if anyone had any reservations concerning pursuing the project, or any recommendations for withdrawing from it. (There were no dissenting comments.)

. . .

General Taylor stated that we should ask ourselves exactly what position we wish to be in. In this regard, it is his view that we should first make sure that we have a good coup prepared. He said that he welcomed the CIA cable, which indicated we were going to get into the planning, which is a means of insuring that we will not be involved in something which we know too little about.

. . .

Mr. McNamara noted that Ambassador Lodge asks for authority to announce suspension of aid, but stated that we must be careful that this is not done too soon. General Taylor agreed, stating that this action should be reserved as a final shot in the arm.

. . .

Mr. McNamara recommended that General Harkins be authorized to endorse the U.S. position to the generals and that he be directed discreetly to acquaint himself with the plans. To this General Taylor added that he should also reserve his judgment as to proceeding further until he is satisfied with these plans.[14]

What had happened to the disunity earlier in the week? If Taylor and others still had strong reservations, they were certainly not apparent in the eyes-only cable for Harkins, Lodge, and Admiral Felt sent out by Taylor after the August 29 meeting:

The President is most desirous of receiving your personal views on this operation at this stage and as it may develop later. You should not be inhibited by concern over what the Washington view may be; we need your on-the-spot impressions of the best course of action. . . . In closing, let me say that while this operation got off to a rather uncoordinated start, it is now squarely on the track and all Washington agencies are participating fully in its support.[15]

On Friday, August 30, the advisers met for the fifth straight day, with Secretary Rusk presiding in the president's absence. The word from Vietnam was that the generals seemed to be unsure about a coup attempt and about American backing. Thus, by the time of Saturday's meeting (with Vice President Johnson replacing the president), the discussion changed somewhat—less on how to deal with an imminent coup and more on the long-range issues connected with a change in government and with winning the war.

Secretary Rusk stated that, in his judgment, we were back to where we were last week.

. . .

Mr. Kattenburg [director, under Hilsman, of the Vietnam task force] stated that as recently as last Thursday, it was the belief of Ambassador Lodge that, if we undertake to live with this repressive regime . . . we are going to be thrown out of the country in six months.

. . .

General Taylor asked what Kattenburg meant when he said that we would be forced out of Vietnam within six months. Kattenburg replied that in from six months to a year, as the people see we are losing the war, they will gradually go to the other side and we will be obliged to leave. Ambassador Nolting expressed general disagreement with Mr. Kattenburg.

. . .

Secretary Rusk commented that Kattenburg's recital was largely speculative; that it would be far better for us to start on the firm basis of two things—that we will not pull out of Vietnam until the war is won, and that we will not run a coup. Mr. McNamara expressed agreement with the view.

. . .

The Vice President stated that he agreed with Secretary Rusk's conclusions completely; that he had great reservations himself with respect to a coup, particularly so because he had never really seen a genuine alternative to Diem. He stated that from both a practical and a political viewpoint, it would be a disaster to pull out; that we should stop playing cops and robbers and get back to talking straight to the GVN, and that we should once again go about winning the war. He stated that after our communications with them are genuinely reestablished, it may be necessary for someone to talk rough to them—perhaps General Taylor. He said further that he had been greatly impressed with Ambassador Nolting's views and agreed with Mr. McNamara's conclusions.[16]

Accordingly, on August 31 Lodge was instructed to back off; the United States would not sponsor a coup at that point. The Washington decision makers had a temporary reprieve. Still, underneath, the malignancy was there, growing and spreading.

In September the debate about our role in Vietnam continued to rage back and forth. On September 2 and 9, President Kennedy was the television guest of CBS's Walter Cronkite and of NBC's Chet Huntley and David Brinkley. On Cronkite's program the president criticized the "repressions against the Buddhists." He suggested changes in policy and "perhaps in personnel" and concluded that, without some changes, the chances of winning the war would not be very good. With Huntley and Brinkley, the president confessed frankly to the "ambivalence" of "wanting to protect the area against Communists" and at the same time having "to deal with the government there." In these interviews, more than at any other time in his administration, Kennedy was specific on the nature of U.S. interest in Vietnam.

Early in September senior staff experts from Washington went to examine the situation. The task fell on Marine General Krulak, Taylor's assistant, and on Joseph Mendenhall of the State Department. They spent two days in Vietnam listening to many people's appraisals and perceptions. Krulak heard mostly from military men in the field; Mendenhall, from civilians in the cities. When the two returned to Washington, they reported opposite impressions: Krulak felt that the political crisis was temporary and that all was going well in the rural areas: Mendenhall concluded that the crisis went to the roots of the Diem regime—its doubtful capacity to govern and to knock out the Viet Cong. Their report to the president, at a September 10 NSC meeting, was in such disagreement that Kennedy asked, "Did you two gentlemen visit the same country?"

The following extracts from memorandum for the record of a meeting at the White House that same evening reveal how deep the divergencies were among Kennedy's advisers. The president himself was not present.

> The meeting was opened by Mr. Bundy, who stated that the obvious divergent views in both the Washington and the Saigon community needed to be resolved and that it was the purpose of this meeting to commence such a resolution.

> . . .

> Mr. McNamara proposed that we start with a clean slate and review the problem in terms of our objectives. To this Governor Harriman said that to start with a clean slate was not permissible; that we have to operate within the public state-

ments already made by the President; that we cannot begin afresh.

·   ·   ·

Mr. Bundy stated that he could not agree that we should fail to change our policies because of statements by the President, but we should have an open mind and recommend changes to the President if necessary. . . . Mr. Hilsman undertook to describe several variant courses of action. One involved the introduction of U.S. Armed Forces, to which General Taylor commented that he would not be associated with any program which included commitment of U.S. Armed Forces.

·   ·   ·

The Attorney General [Robert Kennedy] asked if it is the view of the State Department that we must get rid of the Nhus or lose the war. Governor Harriman responded in the affirmative. The Attorney General then asked Secretary Rusk if he agreed with Governor Harriman, and Mr. Rusk was less specific.

·   ·   ·

Mr. Bundy stated that the Group should meet the following day at 1800 with a series of papers.[17]

At the follow-through meeting the next evening, Kennedy was present.

The Secretary of State made introductory remarks. . . . Fundamentally, he stated we need to establish carefully the parameters. In this case, they appear, in his mind, to be that we should not abandon Vietnam, and that we should not apply force to achieve our objectives.

Mr. Rusk stated that he feels Nhu is in the center of our problem, that Diem is not; and that our objective should be to persuade Diem that Nhu is a prime impediment to the accomplishment of our joint purposes. He feels that Ambassador Lodge has not come fully to grips with Diem and that he must do so.

. . .

Mr. Gilpatric spoke concerning aid, stating that it is quite evident that suspension of military aid will collapse the whole battle.

. . .

To this General Taylor added that it is necessary for us to review the political aspect of the whole Buddhist matter and ask ourselves what we ourselves would do if, in the midst of a civil war, a group was organized for the specific purpose of destroying the government.

. . .

Mr. McNamara said he agreed with Secretary Rusk that there is great virtue in approaching the problem cautiously, and that there is no urgency for precipitate actions such as proposed by Ambassador Lodge where he wanted to make, as our national objective, the fall of the Diem government. In this regard, he advised the President that the Ambassador had never been out of Saigon and had never seen the real progress of the war in the countryside. Mr. McCone then expressed agreement with Mr. McNamara, stating that there is good reason to observe the development of affairs for some time.[18]

Thus, the president and his advisers faced difficult questions of judgment. Was the Diem regime, as it stood, on a losing course? Could Nhu be removed? Could Diem somehow be persuaded through quiet American pressures to make basic changes for the better? If not, should the United States make clear its support for a change of government?

To help resolve the situation, the president decided that McNamara should head a team, including General Taylor, to go to Saigon and to bring back both findings and a policy for JFK's approval. On September 23, 1963, the group left on its ten-day Vietnam trip.

The mission, which included representatives from agencies other than defense, had a busy itinerary. Reading it over, after all these years, one wonders how a group recovering from jet lag could have stayed awake through it all. In any event, they saved until late in the trip the major meeting with Diem, for which Ambassador Lodge and General Harkins joined McNamara and Taylor.

As usual, the meeting began with a long monologue by Diem. Eventually, McNamara was able to convey U.S. concerns over the political unrest in South Vietnam; then "Diem rebutted these points in some detail and displayed no interest in seeking solutions or mending his way." And so it went. In the end Taylor recapitulated McNamara's concerns and reminded Diem that "a serious crisis of confidence was developing in the United States"; it was vital that his government respond.[19]

On October 2, when the mission returned to the United States, the White House issued a press release on the findings. In the statement, as well as in the report itself, Pentagon optimism about the military situation was countered by the State Department's misgivings about the political side. Much to everyone's later regret, the White House announcement indicated that by the end of 1963 about a thousand American military personnel could be withdrawn and that most of the American forces would be home in about two years. The release went on: "The political situation in South Vietnam remains deeply serious. The United States has made clear its continuing opposition to any repressive actions in South Vietnam."

Not made public were other findings and recommendations, which included pressures on Diem. Foremost was a freeze in the commodity import program to drive home the point that American assistance was conditional on evidence that the insurgency was being defeated. It was also meant to show displeasure with Diem's political actions. Another pressure was the requirement that Diem send the Special Forces (his security) away from Saigon to the field. Because the presence of this force had deterred an August coup, its departure would be greeted with delight by the coup planners. McNamara and Taylor, however, actually believed that Diem still had time to shape up politically and to save his regime.

Kennedy was careful to instruct his advisers not to announce any official changes in policy. Changes would come about only as reactions to the continuing situation in Vietnam. But at this point Diem had less than a month to go.

TWO DEATHS IN NOVEMBER

Taylor and McNamara had the impression that the coup plotting in Vietnam was too fragmented to succeed in displacing Diem. In fact, the planners were getting organized, which became apparent as early as October 5, when the generals renewed the channel of contact, through the CIA, that had opened up in August. In the response to the generals' inquiry, Washington used the CIA channel to respond that the United States would support any South Vietnamese government that could govern effectively and that would continue the struggle against the Viet Cong.

From then until about October 22, the contacts were inconclusive. In Washington an interagency group deliberated as to whether cutting off the commodity impact program could be maintained beyond about two months. What steps could they take if by then Diem was unyielding? The United States had already cut funding support for the Saigon-based Special Forces.

The last ten days of October were confusing in both Saigon and Washington. Plots being hatched in Saigon were transmitted to Washington, where the main worry was about the outcome of a coup attempt. Debated back and forth with Lodge, the question was complicated by reservations that General Harkins had about encouraging a coup.

Looking back at this time a few months later, Robert Kennedy maintained:

> [Diem] was bad and it would be nice to have a better government, but we didn't want to have a coup when nobody knew what kind of government you were going to have and whether you'd just have a bloody riot out there. So we tried to throw some cold water on them by finding out who they had who was going to take over, what their forces were— asking all those questions.
>
> My impression was that Henry Cabot Lodge didn't pay much attention to it because he wanted a coup. But the President sent out requests for all that and got not very satisfactory answers, usually.
>
> And then, just suddenly, the coup took place.[20]

On October 29 the Saigon contact revealed that the generals expected to move within the next few days. Responding to inquiries from Washington, the generals expressed confidence in holding a decisive balance of force in the Saigon area.

Then, in the final days of October, Diem complicated the situation by inviting Lodge to visit with him in Dalat. The first communication between the two for many weeks, this overture meant that Diem probably wished to accommodate some of the points previously made by Lodge. However, the talks were vague. In any event, the generals' planning was now, as far as Lodge was concerned, at the point of no return.

The story of the coup has been told often and dramatically and need not be repeated in detail here. Through the last-minute switch of the Vietnamese general commanding the area that included Saigon, the coup generals did gain local superiority, as well as the assistance of the key person on whom Nhu had counted for a countercoup. The palace was quickly surrounded and by the early morning of November 2 the result was clear. Diem and Nhu had escaped during the night but were picked up at a hideout in the Cholon section of Saigon. While riding in an armored vehicle taking them to coup headquarters, they were killed.

Halfway around the world Taylor, awakened sometime after midnight, hurried to the Pentagon. Later he conferred with the other chiefs and, subsequently, McNamara. At 10 A.M. McNamara and Taylor went to the White House to meet with the commander in chief. Taylor saw how, when the president was passed a message that Diem and Nhu were dead, "Kennedy leaped to his feet and rushed from the room with a look of shock and dismay on his face which I had never seen before."[21]

Writing later, Taylor felt that the coup set in motion a series of events over the following two years "which eventually forced President Johnson in 1965 to choose between accepting defeat or introducing American combat forces." Further, he saw the episode as "one of the great tragedies of the Vietnamese conflict and an important cause of the costly prolongation of the war into the next decade."[22] As for the reactions of the chiefs of staff, one writer asserts that they "were shocked by the coup" and blamed their chairman "for not pushing their position with the president" against the coup strongly enough."[23]

Although no one at the time would say so, the reality was that what happened in the fall of 1963 deepened the American commitment to preserving South Vietnam. Americans in both public and policy circles were bound henceforth to feel more responsible for what had happened in South Vietnam. The policymakers had, too, the additional personal investment that comes from hoping to see one's past judgment proven right.

The South Vietnamese side, too, came to rely on American aid. After the fall of 1963 every American action was carefully interpreted in Saigon. The new leaders there were now convinced that the United States would have to act to help them. They reasoned that if American leaders had involved themselves at such risk for internal political change they would go to great lengths in other ways to preserve South Vietnam. The coup had made the United States more deeply involved than ever in the problems of Southeast Asia.

The report of the McNamara-Taylor mission had not mentioned this consequence, except that it rejected the notion of Uncle Sam's actually sponsoring a coup. Neither in that report nor at any other time in the August–October discussions did Washington decision makers face up to this natural result, which any political realist should have foreseen.

Three weeks after Diem's death, Chairman Taylor was conferring at the Pentagon with the outgoing and incoming West German chiefs of staff. About to take a nap after the lunch break, he was interrupted by an urgent phone call from the officer in charge of the National Military Command Center: President Kennedy had been shot in Dallas. The assembled Joint Chiefs, joined by Secretary McNamara, then received the next message: the commander in chief was dead. The new president of the United States was Lyndon Baines Johnson.

LBJ TAKES THE MANTLE

In his memoirs President Johnson says he was determined to see that John Kennedy's goals were achieved in his unfinished term. On November 27, 1963, speaking to a joint session of Congress, he named specific places in his pledge: "We will keep our commitments from South Vietnam to West Berlin."[24]

He became immersed in Vietnam problems immediately. Ambassador Lodge happened to be in Washington for scheduled conferences with Kennedy after a Honolulu meeting—also attended by McNamara and Taylor—that occurred just before JFK's death. Now conferring with the new president and top advisers, Lodge was optimistic. CIA Director John McCone was less so. Johnson, however, reaffirmed the American commitment: "I'm not going to be the President who saw Southeast Asia go the way China did."

The overall assessment of the Vietnam situation was basically the same, but the change of presidency necessitated an official document to show that the tiger had not changed its stripes. Accordingly, on November 26 Johnson approved National Security Action Memorandum (NSAM) 273. This, his first major decision on Vietnam as president, reads in part: "It remains a central objective of the United States in South Vietnam to assist the people and government of that country to win their contest against the externally directed and supported Communist conspiracy."

In the days following NSAM 273, the dark clouds of Vietnam closed in around the new president. He now realized that the situation was much more serious than he had first thought. As a result, Johnson asked McNamara to visit Vietnam again. His job was to look at all aspects of the conflict and then to give the president the most accurate report possible. Taylor was not along on this December 18–20, 1963, tour. On the twenty-first, McNamara gave LBJ a grim estimate: "The situation is very disturbing. Current trends, unless reversed in the next two or three months, will lead to neutralization at best and most likely to a Communist-controlled state.[25] One reason for the change from optimism to pessimism was the discovery that under the Diem regime the reporting system had resulted in great inaccuracies. After McNamara's trip the system was improved, but now the previously hidden disaster had to be dealt with as well.

We might ask ourselves at this point what effect Diem's overthrow had on North Vietnam's planning. Shortly after the coup, the Central Committee in North Vietnam met, making two important decisions: go on the offensive and give more assistance to the Viet Cong. The objective became a military victory. The Central Committee made this decision with a clear understanding of possible American intervention with combat troops later.

The Joint Chiefs were taking their own look at the Vietnam predicament in January 1964. Chairman Taylor, in a memorandum for the secretary of defense, set forth some actions that the Joint Chiefs felt were necessary. First, assign to the U.S. military commander responsibilities for the overall American program. That action would, in turn, require the South Vietnamese government to turn over the direction of the war to the U.S. military commander. This change never happened.

During all this, political tension abounded in South Vietnam. In late January 1964 a group of officers headed by Gen. Nguyen Khanh replaced, through a coup, the military junta headed by General Minh that had overthrown Diem. Although playing no part in this coup, the United States did manage to keep Big Minh in the government.

With increasing Viet Cong attacks and with anarchy in its own government, South Vietnam slid deeper and deeper toward the abyss of defeat. Because LBJ was a long way from all the distress, he asked McNamara and Taylor to go to Vietnam once more for a firsthand assessment. Just before this March 1964 trip, the president asked the chiefs' opinion on what should be done. Taylor recommended following a two-path military approach: "an intensified counterinsurgency campaign in the south and selected air and naval attacks against targets in North Vietnam."[26]

But 1964 was an election year; LBJ was not inclined to accept advice to attack North Vietnam just then. He was clear, however, in opposing any more coups; the United States had to do its best to support Khanh as the new national leader. Moreover, he wanted McNamara and Taylor to pose with Khanh as a symbol of unity between the United States and the new South Vietnam government. Indeed, the media did show several pictures of the two Americans holding Khanh's arm up campaign-style.

What Taylor found in Vietnam was much deadlier than it looked from the E Ring. The enemy was clearly gaining from the turbulence caused by the two coups in November and January. Obviously, with one-after-another changes in national government, the vibrations traveled down through the whole political structure.

The McNamara-Taylor report to the president contained many detailed recommendations. The essence of the report, though, was that U.S. policy should be continued as long as necessary to overcome the insurgency. The most important and enduring consequence of the trip was NSAM 288 of March 1964. If American commitment had been ambiguous until then, it certainly was not after this document, which is worth quoting here in part. For several years after, the Joint Chiefs of Staff and others used it as a basis for some U.S. actions.

> We seek an independent non-Communist South Vietnam. We do not require that it serve as a Western base or as a member of a Western Alliance. South Vietnam must be free, however, to accept outside assistance as required to maintain its security. This assistance should be able to take the form not only of economic and social measures but also police and military help to root out and control insurgent elements.[27]

During late March and April, South Vietnam became more and more a disaster area. The strength of its armed forces, instead of going up as planned, was dropping because of desertions. In the field the South Vietnamese forces were taking losses from Viet Cong activity and accomplishing very little. On the political front the Khanh government had problems of stability. Accordingly, in mid-May 1964 McNamara and Taylor were off again, at presidential request, on another trip to Saigon. They saw the grim reality there but did not come up with any new ideas.

Certainly unreal, however, was the response they received when conversing with the outgoing U.S. commander, General Harkins: "Paul," asked McNamara, "how long do you think it will take to wind up this war?" Harkins responded, "Oh I think we can change the tide in about six months." The incoming commander, Gen. William Westmoreland, who was also present, later wrote that he found this exchange incredible.[28] Incredible it was.

After reading the trip report, which was not encouraging, President Johnson asked Westmoreland and Ambassador Lodge to confer in Honolulu with his principal Washington advisers: Rusk, McNamara, Taylor, and McCone. At this meeting they did not change objectives but did discuss the problems incident to air attacks against North Vietnam. They included the need to prepare public and congressional opinion, which was becoming ever more divided, heated, and vocal about the Vietnam quagmire. With the Republican convention not far away, however, LBJ was not interested in setting up barn-sized targets for his opponents. November would be soon enough to complete planning for air operations.

Republicans needed Henry Cabot Lodge to participate in the presidential campaign, especially after he was the write-in choice of voters in the New Hampshire primary. He therefore, in the spring of 1964, submitted his resignation as ambassador to Vietnam. This change affected Maxwell Taylor's role in our Vietnam experience because then the president had to select a new ambassador. Offers to take the post came, interestingly enough, from members of the cabinet: Secretary of State Rusk, Secretary of Defense McNamara, and Attorney General Robert Kennedy. Taylor, somewhat reluctantly, also put his name in the hat, and the president decided to appoint him. The new ambassador was given a career foreign service officer, U. Alexis Johnson, as deputy ambassador. Taylor accepted on the basis that his Saigon assignment would be for only about a year. (The implications of this qualification we will consider at greater length later.)

Before leaving the JCS chairmanship in early July 1964, Taylor sent a memorandum to McNamara to give his thoughts on his tenure as chairman. Of particular interest is a section at the end called civilian-military relationships in the Pentagon.

> During my service as Chairman, I have worked to the best of my ability to attenuate or, if possible, to eliminate the differences—sometimes real, sometimes imaginary—between the civilians and military authorities in the Department of Defense. I hope that our own personal relationship, of which I have been very proud, has set an example for those around us and has contributed to proper team play. Inevitably, however, there are areas of potential friction where there is overlap or gray zone of common interests between subordinate elements of DOD. . . . While informal discussions have tended in the past to remove most of the abrasive corners, there are still potential difficulties arising from the fatal attraction which some of our civilians find in military planning.[29]

CHAPTER 5

Pearl of the Orient

$\mathbf{M}$axwell Taylor took the oath as ambassador to the Republic of Vietnam on the steps of the White House July 2, 1964. After Dean Rusk administered the oath and LBJ commented, the new ambassador made brief remarks. A wonderful photo on that bright, hot day shows the president looking on with the air of a master of ceremonies. Rusk holds the Bible, and in the background stand a corporate-looking Robert McNamara and a resigned Bobby Kennedy, playing out his role as one of the last survivors of the New Frontier.

Saigon in that summer was not yet overpowered by the American presence, as it would be, say, two years later. Truly the Pearl of the Orient, with its tree-lined boulevards, French architecture, and Western culture, Saigon still reminded visitors of Paris. The city of perhaps 1.5 million would soon expand dramatically as the war stepped up. Taylor's downtown headquarters (later, when replaced, known as the old embassy) was in a nondescript building, looking something like a furniture showroom in lower Manhattan. His residence, however, was an impressive white stucco villa in the old residential part of the capital.

MR. AMBASSADOR

Taylor's letter of instructions from President Johnson—drafted by Taylor himself—was the most powerful charter given an American ambassador to Vietnam. It read in part:

> As you take charge of the American effort in South Vietnam, I want you to have this formal expression not only of my confidence, but of my desire that you have and exercise full responsibility for the effort of the United States Government in South Vietnam.
>
> I wish it clearly understood that this overall responsibility includes the whole military effort in South Vietnam and authorizes the degree of command and control that you consider appropriate.[1]

Richard Holbrook, who served as Taylor's staff assistant, aide, and executive officer, thought that Taylor would have had more bureaucratic effectiveness by bringing along some of his own advisers, as he had at the White House and in the military.[2] However, two who arrived at their positions independently had Taylor's blessing: Deputy Ambassador U. Alexis Johnson and General Westmoreland.

Alex Johnson was deputy undersecretary of state when he accepted the assignment with Taylor. Max and Alex had studied Japanese together in Tokyo in the mid- to late thirties. Before their families arrived in Saigon, Taylor shared the ambassador's residence with Johnson, who helped his boss adjust to the foreign service mode.[3]

About Westmoreland and the military effort, Taylor had an ambivalent attitude. He respected the military chain of command—and, of course, Westmoreland was one of his protégés—but differences were to develop between the two by the fateful spring of 1965.

Westmoreland in that summer of 1964 was something to behold. At West Point he had been first captain of his class; as an officer he seemed to have stepped out of the Army career management manual. Maxwell Taylor, who first met "Westy" in Sicily in World War II, later wrote: "[His] sure-handed manner of command led to the entry of his name in a little black book I carried to record the names of exceptional young officers for future reference." After the war Westmoreland left the Field Artillery to become an infantryman parachutist; by the last year of the Korean War he was a young brigadier general commanding the 18th Regimental Combat Team in combat.

After a short stay at Harvard Business School, he became secretary of the Army General Staff; in 1957 he was the youngest major general in the Army. Thereafter came the superintendent's position of West Point and the command of the Army's Airborne Corps. After Harkins's departure, he was named commander, Military Assistance Command Vietnam (COMUSMACV).

Westmoreland's was a model career but not necessarily one of experience for grasping political subtleties, and at first President Johnson did not wholly accept him as Harkins's replacement. When Westy had gone to Saigon earlier as Harkins's deputy, he had not visited the White House; instead, some visitors, such as Bernard Fall, looked him over for the State Department (and probably higher) to estimate whether he had the political skill to carry off the task. Fall's report was favorable. It was not until the Honolulu Conference in 1966 that LBJ appraised Westmoreland and concluded that he was not the type to get involved in politics. "There's a lot riding on you," he told the general at that point. "I don't expect you to act like MacArthur."

Shortly after he arrived in Vietnam, Taylor held a staff meeting at which Westmoreland was present. Working from a paper that he had prepared in Washington, the new ambassador set forth his views on American objectives in Vietnam. One of those at the meeting interpreted these basic goals: achieving political stability in South Vietnam, preventing the enemy from taking over the country, and preparing the government of Vietnam (GVN) for a counteroffensive against the Viet Cong. Taylor went on to touch on some other considerations.

> The Sino-Soviet bloc is watching attentively the course of events in South Vietnam to see whether subversive insurgency is indeed the form which the "wave of the future" will take. In stating the U.S. objectives in South Vietnam, it is important to note . . . we are not seeking to reunify North and South Vietnam—our objective does not extend beyond enforcing the Geneva Convention of 1954.

> . . .

> Failure in Southeast Asia would destroy the U.S. influence throughout Asia and severely damage our standing elsewhere throughout the world. It would be the prelude to the loss or neutralization of all of Southeast Asia and the absorption of that area into the Chinese empire.[4]

One thorn in the side of American decision makers after Diem and for several years after was the so-called revolving door government of South Vietnam. The situation was particularly painful at the time of Taylor's arrival. The government at the moment was that of General Nguyen Khanh, the chairman of the Military Revolutionary Council, and four generals as his principal assistants. Technically, Gen. Big Minh was chief of state, but Khanh had deprived him of any real authority after seizing power the previous January. Constant changes kept the new ambassador on a merry-go-round, as noted in these extracts from his diary for the first two months in Saigon.[5]

JULY 14	Presented to General Minh, Chief of State.
JULY 17	Khanh Government at time of my arrival as Ambassador (Minh Chief of State). Khanh-Minh feuding. Khanh suspicion that I side with Minh.
JULY 20	Called on General Minh, at his suggestion.
JULY 27	I went to see General Khanh in Dalat.
AUGUST 12	Spent an hour with General Khanh regarding government organization and personnel.
AUGUST 14	Met with General Khanh in advance of NSC–Mission Council meeting regarding remodelling of his government.
AUGUST 16	Vung Tau Charter Constitution. Drafted in early August. Military Revolutionary Council to elect the new President.
AUGUST 16	The Military Revolutionary Council ousted Major General Duong Van Minh as Chief of State, elected Lieutenant General Nguyen Khanh President, and installed a new constitution.
AUGUST 25	Following a series of mass demonstrations and political pressure by civilian parties, Khanh promised liberalization of his government.
AUGUST 27	The new Vietnamese Constitution was withdrawn; the Revolutionary Council disbanded; and Khanh, Duong Van Minh, and Tran Thien Khiem were named provisional leaders.

AUGUST 29   Nguyen Xuan Oanh was named Acting Premier of Vietnam to head a caretaker government for two months. He stated that General Khanh had suffered a mental and physical breakdown.

SEPT. 5   General Khanh resumed the Premiership, dissolved the triumvirate provisional government established on August 27, and restored Minh to his former position of Chief of State.

SEPT. 6   My Estimate of Situation—Recognition of limits of perfectibility of government. No George Washington in sight. Best we can expect from government is a holding operation against VC. National Pacification Plan beyond its limits. Politicians feel political hassle is their field; battle with VC is for the Americans. A Popular Front adverse to U.S. interests may result. We can not accept this so we must assume greater responsibility.

On August 2, 1964, came an event that would have an explosive impact on the war: a North Vietnamese torpedo boat attacked the U.S. destroyer *Maddox* in international waters; what is controversial is whether the United States provoked the attack. The North Vietnamese may have confused De Soto, an electronic intelligence gathering operation, with Operation Plan 34A, in which the South Vietnamese, with American support, conducted minor raids against North Vietnamese coastal actions. Then, on August 4, North Vietnamese craft again attacked *Maddox* and *Turner Joy,* which had joined it.

In retaliation President Johnson decided to strike at the base of the attacking boats; and American carriers launched sixty-four sorties. But the more far-reaching result of the North Vietnamese attacks was the Tonkin Gulf Resolution, passed by Congress on August 10. The vote in the House was 416–0; in the Senate, 88–2. It empowered the president to use whatever force was necessary to assist South Vietnam and the other allies of the United States in Southeast Asia. The resolution, which the National Security Council had been preparing since June, was just awaiting the proper occasion. It reads in part:

The Congress approves and supports the determination of the President, as Commander in Chief, to take all necessary measures to repel any armed attack against the forces of the United States and to prevent further aggression.[6]

Nevertheless, the commander in chief was in the middle of an election campaign. For the moment he put the resolution in his pocket, but it was to appear dramatically the following year.

THE AUTUMN DEBATE

How to maintain political stability in Saigon was still the most crucial issue that autumn of 1964, but it was tied in with military matters. American decision makers felt that, in order to make the South Vietnamese government confident of American resolve, U.S. forces needed to hit the north. Leaders in both Washington and Saigon started debating just what kind of action to take.

The major "action officers" were William Bundy at State and John McNaughton at Defense in Washington—and Maxwell Taylor in Saigon. The president himself became involved when Taylor visited Washington on September 9; in early November, just after his reelection; and again in early December, when Taylor made his second visit.

Just before mid-August the Washington action officers had prepared a draft memorandum that considered a variety of military actions, including sustained air operations against the North. They would begin at the lower end of the spectrum and gradually work up—at first "tit-for-tat" air strikes in reprisal for major communist actions and then, by January, dramatic bombing of targets in North Vietnam, along with the mining of Haiphong Harbor. Taylor favored this strategy on the whole. He did not want any heavy action until January, when the Khanh regime would have had time to become stable. (And, one supposes, he had in mind that the American presidential election would be over.)

When Ambassador Taylor made his first return trip to Washington in early September, he stressed how unstable the Khanh government was.[7] Although fairly pessimistic about the war, he felt that the United States could not turn back. After hearing Taylor, the president approved NSAM 314 on September 10. The document gave priority to actions within South Vietnam but also approved resuming the clandestine activities along the North Vietnamese coast that had been suspended after the Tonkin Gulf incident. Moreover, it provided for reprisal air raids against North Vietnam in the event of major actions by the enemy.

During October the 1964 presidential election kept Vietnam policy decisions on the back burner. Then, on the eve of the election, the Viet Cong mortared the airfield of Bienhoa, destroying or damaging twenty-seven B-57s and killing four Americans. Cabling from Saigon, Taylor urged retaliatory strikes against North Vietnam. He considered this enemy action—deliberate targeting of a major American installation—a turning point in their tactics. Johnson, about to be reelected by a landslide against Sen. Barry Goldwater (who was alleged to be trigger-happy), rejected the ambassador's recommendation.

The president did, however, intervene a couple of days later by establishing an interagency working group chaired by William Bundy of State and John McNaughton of Defense. He asked them to review the situation and, by late November, to come up with an appropriate strategy to discuss with the NSC principals: Rusk, Ball, McGeorge Bundy, McNamara, McCone, and JCS Chairman Wheeler. They were to consider these three options: to continue along present lines, to embark quietly on systematic military pressures against the North designed to cause them to opt for negotiations, or to develop an in-between program of more limited and gradual military pressures.[8]

During the November review, Ambassador Taylor received information from Washington and cabled his own views. Just after midmonth Michael Forrestal went to Saigon to show Taylor the papers being developed, thus giving him a chance to feel out Washington thinking before his next trip there.

Taylor's own summation found a "mounting feeling of warweariness and hopelessness," particularly in the urban areas of South Vietnam. He noted that "there seems to be a national attribute which makes for factionalism and limits the development of a truly national spirit." Yet, for their part, the Viet Cong had shown "an amazing ability to maintain morale" and extraordinary staying power in the face of heavy losses. Without trying to explain reasons, such as ideology, for this Viet Cong toughness, Taylor focused on support from the North.

> If, as the evidence shows, we are playing a losing game in South Viet-Nam, it is high time we change and find a better way. To change the situation it is quite clear that we need to do three things: first, establish an adequate government in SVN; second, improve the conduct of the counter-insurgency campaign; and finally, persuade or force the DRV [Demo-

cratic Republic of Vietnam] to stop its aid to the Viet-Cong and to use its directive powers to make the Viet-Cong desist from their efforts to overthrow the government of South Viet-Nam.

If, ... as hoped, the government maintains and proves itself, then we should be prepared to embark on a methodical program of mounting air attacks in order to accomplish our objectives. We will leave negotiation initiatives to Hanoi.

Taylor suggested three principles to which the United States should adhere whatever the course of events:

a. Do not enter into negotiations until the DRV is hurting.
b. Never let the DRV gain a victory in South Viet-Nam without having paid a disproportionate price.
c. Keep the GVN in the forefront of the campaign and the negotiations.[9]

Reinforcing the work of the Washington group, the Taylor memorandum went at once to LBJ, who was in Texas. Perhaps more than any of the Washington papers, it influenced the president's decisions of early December.

Taylor arrived in Washington on Thanksgiving Day, November 26, 1964. The following afternoon he had a full meeting with these principals: Rusk, McNamara, McCone, Wheeler, McGeorge Bundy, McNaughton, Forrestal, and William Bundy. The ambassador told them that he must have a strong message to take back to Saigon. It should combine American resolve and readiness to act with specifics for the South Vietnamese government to carry out. The tone should be tough but reasonable. He felt that the correct approach would bring improvement, although slowly. In this, Taylor differed from McNamara, who was doubtful that the military situation would improve and who was pessimistic about the political side.

The group then turned to Taylor's two-tier approach. In the first phase, to last for a month or two, the government would expand American military actions and be prepared to conduct reprisals. Next, it would move to a systematic but gradual program of bombing and other military pressures.

What had to be determined at once, however, was the message for Taylor to take to the leaders in Saigon. It was what concerned the president the most as he met on December 1 with the full group of senior advisers. Focusing on what Taylor had to say, Johnson went

over in detail the political situation in Saigon. What could they do to
get South Vietnamese leaders to work together?

The president made clear above all else that he would never consider stronger action against the North unless he was sure that the
United States had done all it could to help in the South. In effect, the
president was saying to Taylor: If you want this bombing program,
you must get the Saigon political leaders in line. (Giving a personal
charge to his guidance was typical of LBJ.)

These discussions of December 1 were reflected in the instructions
to Taylor approved by the president on the third. "We should not
incur the risks which are inherent in such an expansion of hostilities
until there is a government in Saigon capable of handling the serious
problems involved in such an expansion and of exploiting the favorable effects which may be anticipated from an end of support and
direction by North Vietnam." In addition, the approved document
proposed that both South Vietnam and the United States should be
ready to execute prompt reprisals for any enemy action of an unusually hostile nature.[10]

Key to the president's message was the statement that the United
States was "prepared to consider" a second phase of direct military
pressure on Hanoi, to be carried out after the Saigon government was
firmly in control of itself. The conditional American intent to start
bombing the North was a major step—much further than LBJ had
ever gone in committing the United States to actions against the North.

After the December 1 meeting came a formal White House statement of a very general nature. Intended to convey a firm basic posture but no more, it said that the president had instructed
Ambassador Taylor "to consult urgently with the South Vietnamese
Government as to measures that should be taken to improve the
situation in all its aspects." Members of the press, who were there
mainly for taking pictures, overheard McNamara advising the president that Taylor should not give a press interview. "If these people
talk to Max, they will think the situation has gone to hell."[11]

The ambassador's subsequent conversations in Saigon carried out
to the full Johnson's instruction to "get the message across to everyone." Taylor met first with President Suu, Prime Minister Huong,
and General Khanh as commander of the armed forces, and then in
separate groups with the senior civilians and top military men. More
than ever, the United States seemed to be big brother, calling the
shots; undoubtedly, South Vietnamese pride, both personal and national, was wounded.[12]

A SHAKY DOMINO

The month after his return from Washington was a tough period for Ambassador Taylor. Through early December, the main threat to Prime Minister Huong's government had been from the Buddhists, although there was a suspicion that some generals were pulling the strings. For their part, the military was split; some supported Khanh, but others—"young Turks" who had saved him in September— thought him weak. Although Khanh had disposed of two potential problems in November (sending Big Minh packing on a ceremonial mission abroad and making Khiem ambassador to Washington), his authority was being challenged by the young generals. On the civilian side, the High National Council had set itself up, not very effectively, as the interim legislative body.

Then the generals stirred up all three groups by demanding that the High National Council adopt a law firing a group of senior generals; their object was to show their political power. When their demand was refused, the young Turks simply kidnapped many of their older colleagues and dissolved the council. In its place they set up a new Armed Forces Council, designed in part to deal with Khanh when the time came.

Taylor himself became involved in these dizzying events. He had dealt earlier with Generals Ky and Thieu, trying to impress on them the need for civilian control and political unity. Now, the kidnapping seemed a direct affront to the message Taylor had conveyed from President Johnson. The ambassador gave the young generals—and, later, Khanh—such a tongue-lashing that Khanh threatened to request Taylor's withdrawal as ambassador.[13] By the end of December, when the immediate crisis had eased, Khanh half-apologized; but the High National Council was defunct, and the Armed Forces Council retained the power to "act as an intermediary"—that is, to take over if necessary. On January 18, 1965, facing renewed Buddhist problems, Huong brought into his cabinet some of the young Turks, including Ky and Thieu.

The ambassador now had to concern himself with other matters. As the political crisis went on, the Viet Cong were still hell-raising while desertions abounded in the South Vietnamese forces. Through November and December, official and media reports from Saigon had been bleak about the future of South Vietnam. Then, on December 24, a violent action against Americans challenged the retaliation pledged by President Johnson earlier that month.

This Christmas Eve catastrophe occurred right in downtown Saigon at the Brink's Hotel, quarters for American bachelor officers. A Viet Cong squad detonated explosives that killed two Americans and wounded fifty-two Americans and Vietnamese.

Taylor promptly cabled his recommendations: use the new policy for an air strike just above the 17th parallel. The president, who was in Texas when the cable arrived, deferred a decision. By the end of December, when Secretary Rusk journeyed to Texas to see LBJ on this, the answer he sent to Taylor was no.

At this point the American public and Congress, for the first time since the election, stood up to be counted. An Associated Press survey published in early January showed that of eighty-three senators responding, roughly thirty-five urged doing everything possible to strengthen the South Vietnamese government. The majority rejected both extremes of either pulling out or taking stronger measures. As for the general public, a January Gallup poll revealed that by a margin of four to one, Americans felt that the war in South Vietnam was being lost; by four to three, they felt that the United States should be prepared to commit troops.

The beginning of 1965 meant the end of the thirty-day testing period for the South Vietnamese political climate. Taylor cabled his own strong view that, notwithstanding Saigon's political weakness, the United States should go ahead with the gradual bombing program against the North—the second phase of the plan decided on in early December. His point was that it might help stabilize the South Vietnamese government if its leaders saw America taking strong action when needed. Taylor's case for bombing, then, rested on morale and on political performance in the South. He did not feel that either the military results of the bombing or the effect on Hanoi's will would soon lead to a settlement or to putting down the Viet Cong threat.

On January 5, 1965, the day after his State of the Union message, the president met with his principal advisers for the first time since mid-December. The Joint Chiefs of Staff pointed out that, although the thirty days were up, they had no orders for stronger actions leading up to bombing the North. However, LBJ made clear at the meeting and repeatedly over the next two weeks (often using earthy terms to describe the behavior of the South Vietnamese) that he was not ready to make such decisions.

In mid-January the president spent most of his time on matters close to his heart and interests. He put finishing touches on his do-

Grandfather Milton T. Davenport in Confederate uniform.

Taylor's father, John Earle Maxwell Taylor—an easy-going, self-taught lawyer of modest means.

Taylor's mother, Pearle Davenport Taylor, who was instrumental in developing his early study habits and very possessive of her only child.

Taylor and friend in his Kansas City days, around 1910.

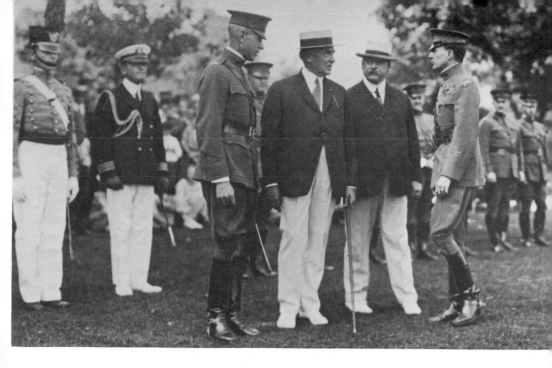

President Warren G. Harding and Superintendent Douglas MacArthur at June Week Review, West Point, 1922; Cadet Taylor is at far left.

The Taylors with family retainers in Tokyo around 1936. The Chilean minister's residence is in the background.

Winston Churchill, accompanied by Gen. Dwight Eisenhower and Division Commander Taylor, visits the 101st Airborne prior to D-Day.

General Omar Bradley and his corps and division commanders at Bristol, England, shortly before D-Day; Taylor is at far right.

Defense Secretary "Engine Charlie" Wilson is met in Seoul in May 1954 by Eighth Army Commander Maxwell Taylor; in the background (to Taylor's right) is Gen. John E. Hull, Far East commander.

Taylor as military adviser to Secretary of State John Foster Dulles at Baghdad Pact Conference, Ankara, in 1958.

Taylor with President John F. Kennedy at Hyannis Port in 1961.

En route to Vietnam on the Taylor-Rostow mission in the fall of 1961.

Taylor and Ngo Dinh Diem during the Taylor-Rostow mission in October 1961.

Taylor, Kennedy, and
Robert McNamara in the
Cabinet Room in the fall
of 1962.

Chairman Taylor and Defense Secretary McNamara at a news conference
following their fall 1963 trip to Vietnam.

Taylor in the Rose Garden after being sworn in by Dean Rusk as ambassador to South Vietnam, July 2, 1964; looking on are President Lyndon Johnson, McNamara, and Robert Kennedy.

Taylor reporting to President Johnson in August 1965 after returning from his post as ambassador to Saigon.

mestic program and on messages to go to Congress in late January and February. All other energies were reserved for the celebration of his inauguration on January 20—Lyndon Johnson's final moment of glory before the darkness of Vietnam enveloped him.

PLEIKU AND ITS AFTERMATH

In early 1965 a sense of crisis was building in South Vietnam. Clearly gaining in strength, the Viet Cong began operating as battalions and larger units as they employed Russian- and Chinese-made weapons. The embassy estimated that the Viet Cong had about 30,000 regular troops and 70,000 part-time guerrillas. There was no specific evidence that North Vietnamese units—as opposed to individual soldiers—were in South Vietnam, but communications intercepts suggested that they were.

South Vietnamese military and paramilitary forces were dispirited, and the government in Saigon had become a mélange of factions, all maneuvering for control but none exercising it. On January 27 General Khanh ousted Huong and named a new prime minister, Phan Huy Quat. Khanh, a source of turbulence, was to be removed the following month when a cabal of generals sent him packing out of the country. Still, the successor government seemed no more stable than those preceding it. To hold up American military action to await greater political stability in Saigon seemed less and less a good idea.[14]

Early in January, Westmoreland had sought and received the president's permission for American jets to support South Vietnamese troops on combat missions in border regions. By now the North Vietnamese had deployed up to six main force regiments there. The American involvement was beginning to accelerate.

Ambassador Maxwell Taylor became associated with the news from Vietnam—hardly ever good news. Toward the end of January, he received from Bobby Kennedy a handwritten letter that included this caution:

> I detect at least an effort on behalf of at least some important segments of the administration to place the blame on you. I notice it in the newspapers and I detect it in other ways. . . .
>
> And I don't think there is anyone back here who defends you or who speaks up on your behalf.[15]

(How Robert and Ethel Kennedy regarded their friend Max personally could be seen in a *New York Times* front-page photo on

January 18, captioned "Kennedy Baby is Named in Honor of Maxwell Taylor.")

In late January, McNamara and McGeorge Bundy requested a meeting with LBJ after they decided that more of a punch was needed to prevent a knockout in South Vietnam. Dated January 27, the memorandum initiating the meeting saw two alternatives: use American military power to force North Vietnam to change policy, or, in some other way, convince the other side to begin negotiations. They favored the first.[16]

Conferring with them that same day, the president agreed that the time had come to get tough militarily. First, though, he wanted to take stock of the Vietnam situation once more to demonstrate that he was considering every option. Earlier, Taylor had suggested that McGeorge Bundy come out to get a better grasp of Saigon's plight. An outcome of the January 27 meeting was the president's approval of this visit; thus, on February 2 McGeorge Bundy, McNaughton from Defense, and General Goodpaster from JCS left for Vietnam.

What Bundy saw in Vietnam led him to propose an ongoing reprisal program instead of the tit-for-tat actions that followed the Tonkin Gulf episode. In his memoirs, LBJ comments on Bundy's report.

> We were at a turning point. Though the Bundy report proposed a course of action we had considered and turned down only three months before, I was impressed by its logic and persuaded strongly by its arguments. I knew that the situation had changed and that our actions would have to change too.[17]

Actually, although LBJ needed very little convincing at this point, events themselves, rather than any particular report, were pushing him into directing a new strategy for Vietnam. One such event was the incident at Pleiku.

When Bundy was preparing to return to Washington early February 7, the Viet Cong made a mortar attack on an American base at Pleiku in the central highlands. They killed eight Americans, wounded more than a hundred, and destroyed ten aircraft. Bundy, Taylor, and Westmoreland—all together in Saigon—decided that the United States must retaliate, and Bundy telephoned that to Washington. About four hours after the attack, LBJ presided at an extraordinary meeting that included Speaker McCormack and Senate Majority Leader Mansfield. Only Sen. Mike Mansfield was opposed to retaliation. The president ordered an immediate attack on prese-lected targets, and more would be coming.

Taylor, delighted, wrote to his son that same week: "We finally seem to have turned a corner and adopted a more realistic policy to the conduct of the war. I have been working and waiting for a year and a half to get to this point."[18]

The NSC members huddled frequently during the days after the Pleiku incident. At a February 8 meeting, President Johnson summarized his position: In December he had approved a program to pressure North Vietnam but had delayed implementing it until the South Vietnamese could stabilize their government. "We are now ready to return to our program of pushing forward in an effort to defeat North Vietnamese aggression without escalating the war." After the meeting LBJ had a message for Taylor.

> I have today decided that we will carry out our December plan for continuing action against North Vietnam with mod-ifications up and down in tempo and scale in the light of your recommendations as Bundy reports them, and our own con-tinuing review of the situation.

Taylor's February 12 response offered thoughts about the strategy of graduated air reprisals.

> In review of the rationale for concept of graduated reprisals we are of the opinion that, in order of importance, it should have the following objectives:
>
> a. The will of Hanoi leaders;
> b. GVN morale; and
> c. Physical destruction to reduce the DRV ability to sup-port the VC.[19]

About the same time the Joint Chiefs of Staff, responding to an earlier McNamara request, came forward with an air strike schedule. They also proposed deploying a U.S. Marine brigade to Da Nang for securing an American air base for the attacks.

On February 13, 1965, President Johnson set in motion Rolling Thunder, a program of measured and limited air action against se-lected targets in North Vietnam. The first bombs fell on March 2 and would continue, with frequent pauses, for the next three and a half years. The administration called Rolling Thunder a response to "con-tinued acts of aggression by the Viet Cong and the North Vietnamese," but it was a new direction in American policy. The United States was, in fact, now at war with the Democratic Republic of Vietnam.

Would bombing provoke Chinese communists to march into Vietnam? With that fear in mind, the president and the secretary of defense kept a constant control over the air strikes. Shortly into the campaign, JCS Chairman General Wheeler judged that the bombing was not really breaking down North Vietnamese military capabilities or will. In keeping watch over the program, Lyndon Johnson leaned on his civilian advisers; for example, the staff of the Joint Chiefs, working with established guidelines (such as no bombing in the vicinity of Hanoi and Haiphong), would select targets but had to get them approved by both the secretary of defense and the president.

The dispute between LBJ's military and civilian advisers revolved around what the bombing was all about. In general, the civilians wanted gradualism—more than the Joint Chiefs did—both in pace and targeting; they believed that Hanoi would "get the signal": that the United States was serious about the war in Vietnam. As a result, the North would stop supporting the Viet Cong.[20]

Taylor, the four-star general in a diplomatic suit, was not for heavy bombing of North Vietnam. In that sense he was a gradualist, trying to pressure—but in a controlled way—Hanoi's leaders to negotiate. He did, though, become annoyed with the long delays between strikes and with the great behind-the-scenes diplomatic maneuvering, that by the British and French in particular ("our friends," as Taylor called them). An early March cable from Taylor to Washington gives the flavor.

> In my view current developments strongly suggest that we follow simultaneously two courses of action: (1) attempt to apply brakes to British and others in their headlong dash to conference table and leave no doubt in their minds that we do not intend to go to conference table until there is clear evidence Hanoi (and Peking) prepared to leave neighbors alone; and (2) step up tempo and intensity of our air strikes in southern part of DRV in order convince Hanoi they face prospect of progressively severe punishment. I fear that to date ROLLING THUNDER in their eyes has been merely a few isolated thunder claps.[21]

Taylor's other expectation for Rolling Thunder was, unfortunately, not met, that is, to slow down committing American ground forces to shore up the landslide in South Vietnam. The ambassador felt that the South Vietnamese should, if possible, fight their own war; further, to commit American troops was also to commit American prestige—and to a very tenuous situation indeed. This may seem at odds with his recommendation in the Taylor-Rostow report about three and a half years earlier, but there is a bureaucratic reality to consider. Maxwell Taylor was no longer a kibitzer from the White House staff on a field visit; he was the senior American in Vietnam, chartered by the president to be in charge of the U.S. effort.

Ironically, the earlier decision to use American close air support in the South was, when combined with the Rolling Thunder decision, what caused the American ground force deployment. After Pleiku it was clear that airfields with American aircraft could be secured only by ground troops—and that these would have to be American. Of three major U.S. air bases in Vietnam (two near Saigon and one at Da Nang), the one at Da Nang was the most vulnerable to enemy action.

Although Taylor continued to oppose introducing U.S. ground forces, he had to admit that some American troops were necessary to protect the Da Nang field. But when he agreed, the JCS cabled that they were sending an entire Marine brigade of more than 5,000 troops armed with artillery, tanks, and their own aircraft. Taylor objected. Washington compromised with two Marine battalion landing teams composed of about 3,500 troops. Almost immediately, on March 8, 1965, they came ashore in battle dress, flags flying, and with full media coverage. American prestige was now definitely committed.

Meanwhile, as Bobby Kennedy had warned, the Washington bureaucrats were taking potshots at soldier-statesman Taylor. McGeorge Bundy's memorandum to the president on March 6 said that, if it were up to him and McNamara, they "would bring Taylor back and put Alex Johnson in charge with a younger man."[22] (The younger man was presumably Assistant Secretary of Defense John McNaughton.) Although nothing came of the recommendation, it shows that some Washington insiders were getting frustrated with Ambassador Taylor. Probably they were not trying to replace him right away but wanted to make sure that the ambassador would stick to his announcement of a one-year tour only. In any event, the president was not part of the cabal.

Although Taylor's push for air strikes was now a reality, he was still trying to hold back American ground troops. That push came from the JCS and others in Washington, helped along by a recommendation from Army Chief Harold K. ("Johnnie") Johnson, a Vietnam visitor at LBJ's request. On March 16 General Johnson advised committing an Army division to Vietnam for security, plus up to four divisions of U.S. and allied SEATO forces along the demilitarized zone.

Moreover, Westmoreland was no longer in tandem with his old boss Taylor. The general was recommending that an Army division and a separate brigade, besides the Marines, be sent to Vietnam. Earlier, Westy and his former chief had bumped heads over the March 8 landing of the Marines. To tell it in Westmoreland's words:

> Circumstances of the landing led to the only sharp exchange I ever had with Ambassador Taylor. Word of the time of the landing got to me from the Joint Chiefs before it reached the Embassy, and even though I notified the Embassy, the word apparently failed to get to the ambassador in advance. He was visibly piqued, his upset accentuated because the marines had arrived with tanks, self-propelled artillery, and other heavy equipment he had not expected. "Do you know my terms of reference," Ambassador Taylor demanded sharply, "and that I have authority over you?" "I understand fully," I replied, "and I appreciate it completely, Mr. Ambassador." That ended the matter.[23]

For the moment Taylor parried the pressures for troops. He cabled the president his "devout hope that we were not about to rush in and take over the conduct of the war from the Vietnamese." But events were moving rapidly, and LBJ called his ambassador back for Washington consultations at the end of March.

THE APRIL DAYS

About the time Taylor descended on Washington, McGeorge Bundy wrote to LBJ about the scheduled March 31 meeting between the president and his ambassador.

> Max Taylor's visit this afternoon is the first of two. Today he comes privately. Tomorrow all the recommendations growing out of his visit will be available for formal presentation to you in the presence of the heads of the departments concerned. This will be quite a substantial meeting in numbers, but it is being kept off the record—and if it leaks it will be

billed simply as one more effort to make sure that we are doing everything we can to make our program more efficient and effective.

The three problems on Max's mind are these:

1. The timing and direction of attack on the North.
2. The timing, size, and mission of any U.S. combat deployments to Vietnam; and
3. The terms and conditions of a political resolution of the problem.
   He has done more thinking on (1) and (2) than on (3)—and so have we.[24]

Taylor had already left for Washington when Viet Cong terrorists detonated explosives outside his embassy. Two Americans and many Vietnamese died, and among those slightly wounded was Deputy Ambassador Alex Johnson. His boss, though, was receiving standing ovations, instead of slings and arrows, in Washington. In fact, when Taylor updated the Foreign Relations and Armed Services committees of Congress, he won, according to *Newsweek,* "warm praise . . . for his analysis of the situation in Vietnam."

President Johnson gathered his Vietnam advisers around him on the first and second of April. He wanted to talk over many matters, such as nonmilitary programs, the bombing campaign, and—what most concerned Taylor—whether he should send more troops to Vietnam. To that the ambassador was still opposed, despite urging from two important quarters: the report of Army Chief of Staff Harold Johnson, who had visited Vietnam on the president's orders, and the more direct pressure from MACV commander William Westmoreland, who was requesting two divisions.

Taylor succeeded—or felt that he had—in preventing that commitment, but he did go along with two more Marine battalions and more logistical troops. What really counted, though, was the president's decision to let the Marines patrol beyond the airfields they were guarding. Outwardly it was just a sensible precaution; in the real world it was a change of mission.

How that change of mission was to be handled with the public came up at an April 3 meeting in Secretary of State Rusk's office. Taylor, ready to return to Vietnam, heard Rusk say that he thought Ambassador Taylor now saw the problem U.S. political leaders had about Vietnam policy. The secretary said that the president felt that "he must not force the pace too fast." If so, Congress and the public, "held in line up to now through the President's strenuous efforts, would no longer support our actions in Vietnam."

> Ambassador Taylor agreed that he understood the situation in the United States. . . . There was agreement that the Marines should be used in (1) local counterinsurgency in a mobile posture and in (2) strike reaction, and that they should have an "active and aggressive posture." Secretary Rusk said later in the discussion that he did not yet want to give up the ability to describe their mission as defensive. . . . Mr. McGeorge Bundy emphasized the need for very tight public information control on these matters.[25]

A few days later the items agreed upon during Taylor's visit appeared in National Security Action Memorandum 328, which cautioned against premature publicity in the change of mission. For the moment, it worked.

Meanwhile, the president was warming to the subject. Taking McGeorge Bundy's place as speaker at Johns Hopkins University on April 7, LBJ made a major policy statement. He laid U.S. prestige on the line with this declaration:

> We are there because we have a promise to keep. Since 1954 every American president has offered support to the people of South Vietnam.
>
> Our objective is the independence of South Vietnam and its freedom from attack.

Now events began to move rapidly. On April 13 McGeorge Bundy informed Taylor, who was back in Saigon, that "additional troops are important, if not decisive." The next day Taylor picked up a JCS message that had been sent to him for information. It contained startling news: a U.S. Army airborne brigade was to be deployed to Vietnam as soon as possible. Alarmed, the ambassador cabled Washington immediately.

> I have just learned by the reference JCS message to CINCPAC that the immediate deployment of the 173rd airborne brigade has apparently been approved. This comes as a complete surprise in view of the understanding reached in Washington that we would experiment with the Marines . . . before bringing in other U.S. contingents.

. . .

Recent actions relating to the introduction of U.S. ground forces have tended to create an impression of eagerness in some quarters to deploy forces into SVN which I find difficult to understand. I should think that for both military and political reasons we should all be most reluctant to tie down Army/Marine units in this country and would do so only after the presentation of the most convincing evidence of the necessity.[26]

In an April 14 memorandum to the president, Bundy noted the ambassador's sensitivity. He cautioned about a cable that McNamara was planning to send to Taylor (and LBJ had approved the day before) that detailed the troop deployments.

Bob McNamara may bring over a cable to Taylor this evening which will rack up a number of instructions to the field to carry out some of the things that were discussed at lunch yesterday. . . . My own judgment is that direct orders of this sort to Taylor would be very explosive right now because he will not agree with many of them and he will feel that he has not been consulted. He heard about the airborne brigade by a premature JCS message of yesterday and has already come in questioning it. . . .

I am sure we can turn him around if we give him just a little time to come aboard.[27]

Then, on the next day, came the message from McGeorge to Max, telling him that in effect he had been overruled by his commander in chief.

The President has just approved an important cable to you on future military deployments. . . . President's belief is that current situation requires use of all practicable means of strengthening position in South Vietnam and that additional U.S. troops are important if not decisive reinforcement. He has not seen evidence of negative result of deployments to date, and does not wish to wait any longer than is essential.[28]

Taylor was not quite finished. On April 17 he had two more cables off to Washington. One noted Alex Johnson's observations against American troop commitment. The other, summarizing the instructions received over the past ten days, expressed astonishment at developments since the April 1 and 2 meetings with the president.[29]

To calm the ambassador, Bundy responded that after hearing Taylor's concerns the president was suspending action until after a high-level meeting in Honolulu on April 20. Taylor would be there, along with McNamara, Wheeler, Westmoreland, Bill Bundy, and others. In his diary Taylor tells about that conference and its decisions.

> We first considered the question of the introduction of additional U.S. and third country combat forces. There was no disagreement in estimating the situation. We all considered that since we could not hope to break the will of Hanoi by bombing alone, we must do better in the campaign against the Viet Cong in SVN.

He relates that no one expected an end within six months, no matter how the pressures were combined, and that "no one advocated attacking Hanoi." Air strikes on present targets plus other vital targets in the North would suffice for now. "I stressed that repetition of the same level of attack was in itself a form of escalation."

> With regard to the need for additional U.S. combat troops, in view of the inadequacy of ARVN units . . . we agreed on a Phase 1 which would call for the introduction into SVN of nine U.S. battalions and four third country battalions between now and the end of summer.
>
> With the present in-country strength of about 33,000 this reinforcement would bring the U.S. personnel to about 82,000, with something over 7,000 third country troops in addition. We recognized that it might be necessary to follow with a Phase II and III. . . . Final totals in that case would be 123,000 U.S. and about 22,000 third country combat forces.[30]

Powerful charter or not, Ambassador Taylor was now, after the Honolulu decisions, a background figure in Vietnam. Coming to the fore was the MACV commander, General Westmoreland. In that fateful spring of 1965, Mars was on the loose.

THE JULY DECISIONS

President Johnson was definitely open to the troop recommendations. First, though, he needed to have the escalation accepted by the

South Vietnamese government, in particular Prime Minister Quat. Realizing the significance of what was happening, the prime minister asked Ambassador Taylor for a little time to think about the matter. Quat took the weekend to meet with his civilian and military advisers, but the decision was his. Although he had serious misgivings, he was under pressure not only from the U.S. giant but also from his own military. That important part of his shaky political base agreed with the Americans. Thus, on April 28 Quat informed Taylor that South Vietnam went along with the American troop increase. (In the final government change of the series set up by the Diem assassination, Quat himself was to return power to the military on June 12. His successors Ky and Thieu, in one government or another, kept South Vietnam relatively stable until its final collapse almost ten years later.)

In early May LBJ sent a message to Congress requesting more money for the growing military requirements in Vietnam. He added that he could not guarantee that it would be the last request: "If our need expands, I will return again to the Congress for we will do whatever must be done to ensure the safety of South Vietnam from aggression. This is the firm and irrevocable commitment of our people and nation."

But would any Vietnam be left to support? By late May, that was the real question. The long-awaited Viet Cong summer offensive had jumped off on May 11. Everybody's nightmare of a speedy and total collapse of the South appeared possible. In June the communists pushed ahead in the central highlands and tried to cut the country in two.

By June 3 Taylor was cabling Washington his latest assessment of Hanoi's determination. If the United States were to bring the North Vietnamese around, bombing alone would not do the trick:

> Such a change in DRV attitudes can probably be brought about only when, along with a sense of mounting pain from the bombings, there is also a conviction on their part that the tide has turned or soon will turn against them in the South.[31]

Taylor was back on the team.

Westmoreland, wanting to take the offensive with large-scale reinforcements, asked for a speedy deployment of U.S. and third-country combat forces. He repeated his view that this was the only way South Vietnam could survive. These messages from the MACV commander put the issue directly to the president. Westmoreland was clearly in charge in Saigon, while Ambassador Taylor was by now playing for time; his agreed-upon one-year tour was almost up—much to his own relief and that of many others.

On June 7 Taylor was off to Washington again to take part in a debate about the proposed strength of U.S. forces by year's end. Westmoreland wanted the new air-mobile division and a total year-end strength of more than 100,000. He got approval from McNamara and the president for a lesser but sizeable increase, and the ambassador concurred.

Taylor also found himself sought out by the press (here was an expert in town) about the mission of American forces—was it defensive or offensive? Johnson's spokesman, Press Secretary George Reedy, equivocated, explaining that only Westmoreland could approve offensive missions without restrictions.[32]

Back in Saigon, although deprived of any real military authority, Taylor still saw himself as American proconsul. He had a long letter of advice off to his old adversary, the young Turk Nguyen Cao Ky, the new prime minister. As Taylor later stated in his memoirs, he was "hoping to direct [Ky's] energies into the most useful channels . . . pointing out the need to concentrate on . . . the improvement of security, [and] the restoration of combat effectiveness."[33]

With Taylor now supporting the program advanced by Westmoreland and the Joint Chiefs, there was a general call to arms. Only a few Washington leaders were still holdouts, most prominently Undersecretary of State George Ball. In late June, Ball wrote to the president that combat escalation was futile; he suggested instead that American forces stabilize at a low level and be restricted to base security; as a policy matter, the United States should seek as graceful an exit as could be arranged. Although LBJ listened, in the end Ball got nowhere. Others, such as Bill Bundy at State, were in between Ball and the military's position. Before Honolulu, Taylor may have supported the in-between approach effectively, but now he was silent. The old soldier saw the handwriting: the movement toward war was inexorable, and nothing was going to stop it. The question was how many troops and how soon.

By the beginning of July, the president's advisers were pressing him on all sides. He called for their opposing views at an NSC meeting not so much to decide at this point as to sharpen the issues. The day before this forum, McGeorge Bundy sent him the various positions and summarized the situation:

McNamara and Ball honestly believe in their own recommendations, though Bob would readily accept advice to tone down those of his recommendations which move rapidly against Hanoi by bombing and blockade.

Dean Rusk leans toward the McNamara program, adjusted downward in this same way.

The second-level men in both State and Defense are not optimistic about the future prospects in Vietnam and are therefore very reluctant to see us move to a 44 battalion force with a call-up of reserves. So they would tend to cluster around the middle course suggested by my brother. They would like to see what happens this summer before getting much deeper in.

The Joint Chiefs are strongly in favor of going in even further than McNamara.

My hunch is that you will want to listen hard to George Ball and then reject his proposal. Discussion could then move to the narrower choice between my brother's course and McNamara's. The decision between them should be made in about ten days, which is the point at which McNamara would like a final go-ahead on the air-mobile division.[34]

The problem now facing LBJ was more immediate and crucial than those faced by his predecessors. Obviously, South Vietnam would soon fall unless the United States made a substantial ground commitment. McNamara, his most influential adviser, developed three options for him:

1. Cut U.S. losses and withdraw with the best conditions that can be arranged;
2. Continue at about the present level, with U.S. forces limited to about 75,000, holding on and playing for the breaks while recognizing that the U.S. position will probably grow weaker;
3. Expand substantially the U.S. military pressure against the Viet Cong in the South and the North Vietnamese in the North. At the same time launch a vigorous effort on the political side to get negotiations started.[35]

McNamara supported the third option: a series of expanded military moves to set the stage for a negotiated settlement on U.S. terms. The defense secretary wanted to strengthen the U.S. military to the levels currently needed: forty-four battalions. To accomplish this, he would call up the reserves. After pondering this recommendation, the president decided to send McNamara to Saigon. There he should judge how a broadened U.S. role would affect the war and whether the president should delay his decision.

One member of McNamara's mission would be Henry Cabot Lodge, soon to be announced as Taylor's successor. The ever-efficient McGeorge Bundy notified LBJ about Taylor's acquiescence.

> Following two telegrams, to and from Max Taylor, show that we are over the hump on the Lodge transition except for details. Taylor accepts both Lodge appointment and McNamara/Lodge visit in good cheer and his preference for a short turn-around period is in accordance with ours.[36]

On July 16 McNamara, Lodge, Wheeler, and General Goodpaster arrived in Saigon. However, the purpose of the visit was suddenly eliminated when, on July 17, McNamara received a cable from his deputy, Cyrus Vance: the president had decided to go ahead with the forty-four-battalion proposal. Moreover, Johnson ordered McNamara to return home and complete his recommendations immediately. As Westmoreland later wrote, "Our July discussions turned out, in a way, to be moot." Lyndon Baines Johnson had already decided how to save South Vietnam.[37] Only about one matter was he unsure: should he accept McNamara's earlier recommendation to call up the reserve forces, or was there another way of getting young Americans to Vietnam?

He had also to consider how he would present his decisions to the public. Should he make a dramatic announcement, knowing that a congressional debate would ensue? Or could he prevent such a debate with a low-key announcement of escalation? The possibility of calling up the reserves was causing much of the anguish. Many presidential advisers felt that the reserve call-up would trigger a dispute that could go on for weeks.

And how, wondered Johnson, would his Vietnam decisions affect his domestic program—the Great Society? His memoirs tell how he felt about sacrificing that commitment to the war effort.

> The demanding decisions of those trying days relating to Vietnam were decisions involving our nation's integrity and its security. But they also involved what I considered to be the promise of the American future . . . we had begun the build-

ing of a better society for our people. The danger that we might have to slow that building, in order to take care of our obligations abroad, brought added anguish.[38]

Now, with McNamara back in Washington, the defense secretary was suggesting that "Congress be asked for the authority to call up 235,000 men in the Reserves and National Guard" and that the regular forces be increased by 375,000 (total 600,000). McNamara felt that the increase would offer a good chance for a favorable settlement in the longer view, while "staving off defeat in the short-view," and would imply a commitment to see a fighting war clear through. The Joint Chiefs of Staff agreed and opined that "mobilization unifies public opinion."

At an important meeting on July 21 after McNamara's return, NSC members considered four possibilities: all-out bombing of the North, withdrawal, standing pat, and full-scale reinforcement, including a reserve call-up. At the end of the meeting all present told the president that they favored the fourth option.

The president spent July 21–27 moving toward a policy decision and transforming that decision into a concrete program. On the weekend of July 25, he secluded himself at Camp David with McNamara. By that time the secretary of defense had done enough legwork to advise LBJ that the 600,000 additional troops could be raised without the reserve call-up. He gave the president several options—to speak loudly, softly, or in between, depending on what LBJ thought best for his foreign policy and his domestic responsibilities.

On Tuesday afternoon, July 27, came a final meeting on this subject at a full and formal gathering of the National Security Council. The commander in chief had them look at a fifth option: providing what field commanders needed without a call-up of reserves. In summarizing the options the president advocated the fifth, using all the persuasiveness for which he was noted. When all present accepted the fifth option, they were virtually rejecting what they had opted for at their previous meeting.

This conference was really for the benefit of those present who would have to implement the policy. The key moment was when LBJ came to the chairman of the Joint Chiefs of Staff and stood looking directly at him. "Do you, General Wheeler, agree?" Wheeler nodded his agreement. Everyone in the room knew that Wheeler objected—that the chiefs wanted a wartime footing and a call-up of the reserves.[39] This moment manifested Wheeler's frustration: he was unable to stand up and be counted when his job and responsibility required him to do so, even though he might have been overruled.

The president knew that Congress was holding itself aloof from decisions to wage limited war or to call up the reserves. On July 25 Congressman Don Edwards of California—also chairman of the Americans for Democratic Action (ADA)—had called a White House aide with a warning: if LBJ came to Congress for a reserve call-up, the president would have much more difficulty than in the past. Bill Moyers so advised McGeorge Bundy, who passed the word along to LBJ.

What was the role of Taylor—even though far away in Saigon—in shaping up LBJ for his decision on July 27? A memorandum to the president from McGeorge Bundy that day informs us. (The specific purpose of the paper was to prepare LBJ to meet with the congressional leadership on the evening of July 27 before the public announcement of his decisions the next day.)

> You will want to know, before you meet the Leadership, that Taylor and Johnson had a very good meeting with Ky, Thieu, and Co on strengthening our international political position at the same time that we move forward with the planned U.S. reinforcements in Saigon. Taylor and Johnson tried out on Ky and Thieu the political language which we drafted over the weekend. They did not call it a Presidential statement, but simply a draft U.S. position which might be stated at some point by a high U.S. official. Ky and Thieu accepted the entire position. This language takes us a long way forward and gives us a good political punch to go with our military decisions. . . . What is now in these paragraphs is the following:
>
> 1. An explicit affirmation that we are in favor of using the U.N. if we can get it into the act.
> 2. An explicit affirmation that we are in favor of free elections under international supervision.
> 3. Definite and clear-cut support for the purposes (but not the weak machinery) of the '54 agreements.
> 4. An offer of hope for the Viet Cong if they will turn from war to peace.
> 5. A concrete offer to discuss both their proposals and ours. . . .

All these are important from the point of view of men like Mansfield and Fulbright. A couple of them—like the offer to consider their proposals and the offer of hope for the Viet Cong after a peaceful settlement—may have real impact in Communist circles as well. Yet there is no weakness in them. And I repeat that Taylor has obtained Saigon's approval for them.[40]

On July 28, using a press conference to talk to the nation, the president spelled out his decisions with considerable frankness. The 28 million listening to their president that Wednesday noon understood that America was putting on more battle gear. He explained in full the reasons for his policy and made crystal clear that he intended to send American forces in the future as needed. The rhetoric supporting argument of his remarks was that of a war message.

There are great stakes in the balance.

· · ·

We did not choose to be the guardians at the gate, but there is no one else.

· · ·

Nor would surrender in Vietnam bring peace, because we learned from Hitler at Munich that success only feeds the appetite of aggression.[41]

Although the president used strong language, his specific proposals did not seem excessive. As the new program was less than expected, the country did not go into shell shock. Thus, what was a profoundly important and far-reaching decision seemed, in the way it was presented, to be moderate. Johnson's reason for posing the decisions as he did was to save his Great Society legislative program. The wily Texan hoped that, by leading gradually, he could persuade the public and Congress to support both the war and his domestic reform. It was a momentous step.

Now it was time for Taylor to depart from Saigon and to file the usual evaluation of the situation. He felt that the United States had during his tenure as ambassador developed a coherent strategy. If the United States persisted in the strategy, it could attain an independent South Vietnam free from attack. However, this had been the soldier-statesman's toughest year. Suffice it to say that when Taylor left

Saigon, we had begun an actual American war. By its end the number of Americans killed in action would be exceeded only by the two world wars and the Civil War. And by any fair standard, it was the only war the United States ever lost.

Just before he returned to Washington and a new assignment, Taylor was off to Cam Ranh Bay for the arrival of his World War II outfit, the 101st Airborne Division. The day was inspiring and clear, with the wind whipping in from the South China Sea. In an atmosphere of symbolism and irony, Taylor gave the welcome speech. Talking sternly of the traditions of the great division, he concluded with a World War II punch line relating to Bastogne: "The Germans have nine divisions surrounding us—the poor bastards." The scene was so much like a movie—all slightly unreal—that it could have been great fun, except for the reality of Vietnam.

CHAPTER 6

Mr. Johnson's War

Ambassador Taylor paid his
last diplomatic courtesy calls in Saigon, received a decoration from
President Thieu, packed his bags, and, after writing his final situation
report as ambassador, flew home on July 20, 1965.

He remained on the State Department payroll until September 14;
a contemporary White House memo noted that it was "customary"
for a returning ambassador to enjoy this perquisite.[1] He had expected to retire except for remaining on a few boards. However, the
president had other plans; late that summer Johnson asked him to
remain as a special consultant on a part-time basis. Taylor would
concern himself with auditing the Vietnam situation and reviewing
and advising upon all U.S. government policy and actions in "counterinsurgency," that is, resisting "wars of [national] liberation." He
would be paid by the White House after his State Department salary
ran out.

Taylor remembered later about his "half-time" job: "In the course
of the next few months I discovered that under this arrangement the
White House share of my time was the daylight half, and the dark
belonged to me."[2] He occupied the same suite in which he had
worked for JFK in the old wedding-cake Executive Office Building
(EOB), served by "one carefully selected Army officer ... rotated
about once a year"; and Ray Jones, his former Saigon secretary; and

163

a typist. Johnson also licensed him to hunt in any other government turf for information and temporary personnel as the situation dictated.

THE ADVOCATE

Although not specifying them on paper, LBJ had other uses for Taylor. As a new White House consultant, Taylor did meet ten times with the president in the latter months of 1965,[3] but Johnson's first design on the former ambassador was to send him out on speaking assignments: he was to be a public relations pointman for the administration's war policy.

Taylor's elder son John, then a middle-level foreign service officer, accompanied his father on one of the earliest speaking trips—and certainly the first tough one—a luncheon of the Commonwealth Club in San Francisco.

Meeting the Taylors at San Francisco International Airport, club officers informed them that local police predicted a demonstration. The son recounted that "our limousine had scarcely turned into the driveway at the Fairmont Hotel when we were surrounded by several hundred demonstrators, who spat, shouted obscenities, and climbed over the car, all the while waving placards that bore an unflattering likeness of America's erstwhile ambassador to Vietnam."[4] One such poster published by the Vietnam Day Committee across the bay in Berkeley showed a photo of Maxwell Taylor between the headlines "Wanted for War Crimes! Gen. Maxwell Taylor." Surrounded by the Fairmont's manager and some bodyguards, the White House consultant was hustled out of the car and rushed into the hotel lobby, also filled with protesters, to the manager's office. Taylor then went to the dining room to make his speech with an exterior chorus of protesters as background. It was the shape of things to come.

Taylor was a bit uncomfortable with his new role in the Johnson White House. Long before, under Kennedy, he had learned how officials regarded consultants. He would be shunned by those with more legitimate portfolios (cabinet officers, for example) simply because of his access. Taylor wrote in his autobiography about the consultant: "He is viewed by officials on the job as an irresponsible rival who can peddle his advice in high places and then disappear before its flaws appear," while the conventional official must survive both the results of his own actions and the consultant's, too.[5] Yet

Taylor seems often to have persevered by a certain hubris; having sipped the heady wine of White House insidership in Camelot, he still liked the taste of it.

One of Taylor's main roles remained the stump circuit. In October, giving the annual George Catlett Marshall Memorial Address, he quoted from Marshall's 1947 Harvard University speech about the media having too great an edge in shaping the public's view of government policy; the World War II chief of staff had believed that, despite all the press attention on any policy, ordinary citizens never got enough facts to make an informed opinion. But then Taylor nearly shot himself in the foot by remarking, "These words have an unusually pat application to the Southeast Asian scene." His speech almost said that these ordinary citizens were incapable of forming any sort of educated opinion on the war.[6] He went on to show why Hanoi's aggression in the South, aided by the Chinese, must be stopped. However, he still did not mention the historical endurance of Vietnamese nationalism and its search for autonomy; he still viewed international communism monolithically. He argued that the "civil revolt" in the South was merely a semantic nicety for guerrilla terrorism undermining a noncommunist government.

In Vietnam the stage was set for the first test of the new American strategy that had been in embryo form when Taylor left Vietnam. It came in November 1965, when units of the 1st Air Cavalry Division waged a particularly bloody battle at the Ia (River) Drang, where the North Vietnamese Army (NVA) chose to stand and fight. At this battle Americans found, for the first time, their mobility and firepower slung against the North Vietnamese manpower and terrain. In the end, the enemy scurried away.

The U.S. military success at the Ia Drang not only derailed Hanoi's hopes for an early victory but also made the Americans feel that they could lick the North Vietnamese. The goal had changed: whip the enemy rather than just keep South Vietnam from going down the drain. Obviously, winning is different from not losing, which, until the Ia Drang, was the principal concern. Now the objective became to devise a winning strategy.

General Giap, however, took another lesson from the Ia Drang: do not engage American forces head-on except at times and places of your own choosing. In short, retain the initiative, making maximum use of sanctuaries across the border.

Now American planners in Vietnam developed—and Washington

leaders worked over—not so much a strategic plan as a series of programs for force increases. They set certain minigoals and noted what troop increases they needed to accomplish these ends.

But Secretary of Defense McNamara was growing skeptical. Writing to Johnson on November 30, 1965, he suggested that, without any warning, Westmoreland would probably request another massive infusion of troops. This increase would raise the ante to, say, 400,000 by the end of the following year, 1966—and there was still no guarantee of success. Further, McNamara wrote, "U.S. killed-in-action can be expected to reach 1,000 per month."[7] The United States should present Ho Chi Minh with a respite and dangle an opportunity to negotiate, McNamara felt. He wanted the Rolling Thunder bombings of the North suspended; five days of suspension the previous May had not been enough of an incentive. He got his wish on Christmas Eve when the president halted the bombings. With Hanoi still uncooperative, though, Johnson ordered Rolling Thunder missions resumed thirty-seven days later, January 31, 1966. On Johnson's orders, McNamara tried to hold down Westmoreland's future importuning for more troops while paradoxically giving him most of what he wanted.

In December Maxwell Taylor sent the president four pages of suggestions for the coming year. However, they were largely theoretical, and Johnson reportedly never had the patience or the conceptual imagination for the abstract. In one of the letter's few pragmatic parts, Taylor did argue that Rolling Thunder raids had been effective. Curiously, he wrote nothing about the lessons of the Ia Drang and its wider consequences.

By mid-January Taylor sent another memorandum, this time fulfilling his second task as presidential consultant: to advise on all counterinsurgency actions. He argued that using Vietnam as a general model for future counterinsurgency efforts was difficult. The wider counterinsurgency problem covered a whole group of underdeveloped nations, each with its own specific conditions. The politico-economic evolution of these countries needed consistent monitoring by a specifically created bureaucratic mechanism capable of anticipating specific troubles in specific places.[8] But while Taylor was a consultant, Johnson was an operator. A very busy man these days, the president went to Congress on January 19, 1966, to request $12.8 billion more to fight the war.

With the long month of the bombing halt ending on January 31, the B-52s sortied once more against selected North Vietnamese targets. One week before, late in the afternoon of January 24, Mc-George Bundy had written a memorandum to the president stating the issues for Johnson's decision. The first reason for resuming bombing, Bundy maintained, was to outflank any future opponents of the action before they could make more headway with the public. News from Saigon of potential difficulties with the Thieu-Ky government precluded further delay. Also, the Republican party (GOP) could take partisan advantage, accuse the administration of hesitation, and assert that the bombing halt endangered U.S. troops in Vietnam. Finally, the successes of administration policy had exceeded expectations already; further delay would only signal "weakness in patience if we continue."

Bundy admitted that the counterarguments "are more subtle but they are not feeble"; many thought that continuing the bombing halt could yield open negotiations and greater foreign support for the United States. He also pointed out that North Vietnam actually might want the United States to resume the bombing. Lack of recent NVA action in the South could be construed as success for the December bombing halt. Bundy said that the American public believed in LBJ's strength and would hang with him a while longer. By his subsequent orders, Johnson accepted the memo's stronger earlier argument. So, with month's end, the bombs fell again on the North.[9]

Also in February 1966, Sen. J. William Fulbright, chairman of the Senate Foreign Relations Committee, gaveled down to begin televised hearings on the war. The president, no admirer of the senator from Arkansas, finessed him: Johnson left the continent for the first time in his presidency, towing behind him on Air Force One McNamara, Rusk, Wheeler, McGeorge Bundy, and a couple of other cabinet officers. Honolulu was the destination for LBJ's own war meetings with Prime Minister Ky, President Thieu, Westmoreland, Admiral Sharp, and a large delegation of South Vietnamese government officials. Not only did the Honolulu trip rob Fulbright of the testimony of several luminaries, but also it stole much of his media thunder. Headlines and broadcasts came from Honolulu instead of Washington; the powerful were all out in the sun, while Fulbright was left out in the cold.

In Honolulu, the president heard Westmoreland credit the July reinforcements for stopping a southern defeat. However, the general would not stop there to make do with what he already had. To establish the mythical "crossover" point from reactive defense of the South to initiating an offensive attack, he said that he needed more troops. The president probably winced at the nearly dead-on accuracy of McNamara's November prediction about Westmoreland; uncomfortably, he jumped the commitment from its current 184,000 to 429,000 by the end of 1966. In exchange, Johnson repeated his usual demand to Westmoreland: "Nail the coonskin to the wall." The goal was to reach the crossover point by December.[10]

Robbed of attention and stars for his show, Fulbright resorted to hearing testimony from lesser lights in the Washington cosmos, such as war critics Gen. James Gavin and diplomat George Kennan. Both had impeccable credentials, but neither held a current government post. There was, then, no way out for presidential consultant Taylor. Called for his testimony, he felt that the hearings provided a chance "to strike a blow for truth as I knew it." He went in with a chip on his shoulder, for, as he admitted later, "The committee was and remained loaded with doves, some bitterly hostile to the Administration's policy and all wanting to look good before the vast TV audience while making Administration witnesses look bad."[11]

Taylor prepared by himself, largely in his EOB office, and dry-ran his material publicly on February 3 in a speech before the Rotary Club of New York. He criticized the proponents of a new "holding strategy" to limit additional troop commitments and confining U.S. military presences to coastal areas; they were, he felt, unreasonably fearful of an outright Chinese entrance into the war. Creating American enclave bases solely on the coast would be tantamount to completely abandoning "many of the Vietnamese people whom we have promised to defend." A holding strategy would badly bruise "the morale of our proud United States forces," jeopardize any South Vietnamese government's survival, and cloud the future solidarity of United States–allied nations on the China rim. Likewise, it would threaten the acceptance of any future U.S. forces on the soil of those nations: Thailand, Malaysia, and the Philippines. "The 'war of liberation' would have been vindicated as the sure-fire formula for successful Communist expansion and we could expect to meet it again and again in Asia, Africa, and Latin America, just as the Communist leaders have been predicting."

Taylor's address continued that "to negotiate with Communists from a position of strength" was even very difficult. To retreat to the coast essentially would leave U.S. negotiators with nothing on which to bargain and would hamstring U.S. forces without recourse to "either their vaunted mobility or their modern firepower." It reminded him of the 1954 French experience at Dien Bien Phu (always a magic word in Washington in those days). For once, Taylor saw the greatest threat cited by the holding strategists in its true historical perspective: the ancient antagonism between Vietnam and China precluded Hanoi's acceptance of massive aid. The obligation would be too great for the North Vietnamese to bear, morally and otherwise. Further, if China entered the war, its action would erode the notion of a war of national liberation. Instead, two superpowers would be fighting against each other but using another nation as the battleground. And the Chinese would suffer a serious defeat in their ideological competition against Soviet communism's propaganda of "peaceful coexistence."[12]

Taylor established his framework in the New York speech, but his opening statement for the Fulbright committee two weeks later was far less aggressive. First, he reviewed the history of Vietnam since 1954 from both sides. He admitted that the United States, like the communists, had more than one reason for being involved. More than South Vietnam's democracy was at stake; the war was a contest. The communists wanted to prove the economy and effectiveness of wars of national liberation, whereas the United States had the responsibility to prove the opposite—that such conflicts are "costly, dangerous, and doomed to failure."

Taylor intelligently went on to criticize the buzzword "domino theory" as no "law of nature which requires the collapse of each neighboring state in an inevitable sequence." He stated that the United States could not tolerate North Vietnam being used as a "sanctuary" for operations against the South; he thus justified the returning Rolling Thunder. He claimed that even though recruitment of South Vietnamese forces outpaced similar Viet Cong recruitment by two to one, this ratio was insufficient for maintaining southern security; therefore, the United States could justify the more and more massive U.S. presence.

He cited Sen. Mike Mansfield's January estimate that 60 percent of the southern population lived under government control, 22 percent under the Viet Cong, and 18 percent in yet-contested areas, a 7 percent plus to the government side since Taylor's departure from Saigon the previous July. Then came an indirect reference to Ia Drang: "The prime target of our United States forces becomes the main-line enemy units which constitute the greatest threat to population." Nevertheless, Taylor thought these enemy units had serious logistics shortages caused by the expenditure of materiel and by U.S. air operations on their supply lines.

Whether he had heard the Honolulu news or not, Taylor told the Fulbright committee that these successes promised "to keep our troop requirement finite." Taylor again defended the bombing resumption, this time because it was a fair trade "on the source of the aggression." The bombing had boosted the morale of both the Vietnamese public and their armed forces. He repeated that the air strikes hampered the flow of combatants and supplies from the North. He claimed that both the bombings' effectiveness and the VC's failure to win the southern land war would convince Ho, Giap, Dong, and their subordinates of the error of their ways.

The president's special consultant painted another rosy picture—about the effectiveness of nonmilitary efforts to win South Vietnamese popular support—and he hoped that both military progress "and the slowly developing maturity of the civil leadership in Saigon" would permit "bringing the benefits of a comparatively normal life to these war-weary people." Taylor went on to warn that any expectation for a negotiated settlement still depended on convincing the enemy that the South and the United States meant business; otherwise, any peace talks would resemble the two-year-long Panmunjom stalemate in Korea.

He then summarized the "four-point strategy," a complicated effort to improve U.S. ground force success in the South, more demonstration of U.S. air superiority by more frequent and intense attacks on northern military targets, strengthening the nonmilitary factors in South Vietnamese life, and seeking a peaceful, negotiated settlement. He ended his statement by bashing the "holding strategy," just as he had done two weeks before in New York, but he tailored his congressional testimony with more circumspection. Almost all of his presentation accentuated the positive. Only at the end did he hit on the big negative of the holding strategy.[13]

Then, to nobody's surprise, the gloves came off. Senator Wayne Morse, the maverick Oregon Democrat who in 1964 had cast one of the two votes against the Tonkin Gulf Resolution, predicted that American citizens ultimately would disavow the war. Taylor hit back. "That, of course, is good news to Hanoi, Senator." The presidential consultant later asked Fulbright himself, equally rhetorically, "How do you compromise the freedom of 15,000,000 Vietnamese, Senator? I don't understand that." Here, perhaps, was a dramatic high-water mark for Taylor's consultant career. His experience, his belief, was clashing against the growing momentum of distrust for the war, for Lyndon Johnson, for the president's subordinates, and for all else that Maxwell Taylor represented.

THE THOUGHTFUL HAWK

The Fulbright hearings marked a transition in the role of Maxwell Taylor. Once the field expert just back from a year in Vietnam, he was now cast as a kind of publicist for a president trying to sell the public on the American effort in Vietnam. But he had as well his behind-the-scenes role, often a frustrating one, during the period of the major American buildup and the main force war—the grim months of 1966 and 1967. At the end of 1965 U.S. troop strength in Vietnam had been about 200,000; by the end of 1966 it was 400,000; and by the end of 1967, almost 500,000.

As 1966 began, American war strategy was firm and consisted of four elements. One was Rolling Thunder, the bombing campaign against North Vietnam. Inherent in it were two knotty problems that seriously strained civil-military relations. McNamara's staff favored gradualism in both the targeting and the pace of intensifying the bombing campaign. The professional fighters considered the gradual approach to be pointless. Another bone of contention was the value of the so-called bombing pause. Johnson's memoirs list fifteen of these before the final halt on November 1, 1968. These pauses were supposed to give the North Vietnamese an opportunity to slow down the war and to show that the United States was interested in peace negotiations—the carrot. The stick was that if Hanoi did not respond ARVN and U.S. forces were justified not only in resuming the bombing but also in accelerating it, with more targets and heavier bombing.

The other three elements of the 1966–67 war strategy employed were, as they developed, largely under the purview of Westmoreland (the air war was not). The first of these was the main force war: search and destroy and security missions by American, South Vietnamese, and allied (Australian, Korean, and Thai) forces. Next was the effort to develop the South Vietnamese armed forces. The third element, called the "other war," was pacifying and protecting the South Vietnamese population, usually the peasants.

How, then, did Maxwell Taylor, as presidential consultant, advise LBJ within these strategic guidelines? A good example is his reaction to a speech made by the president on August 20, 1966. About the bombing campaign, LBJ stated: "Both publicly and privately we have let the leaders of the North know that if they will stop sending troops into South Viet-Nam, we will immediately stop bombing military targets in their own country."

After reading the speech, Taylor quickly wrote to Johnson. This memorandum reveals how strongly the president's consultant felt about the bombing campaigns, and it came at a time when McNamara was beginning to doubt that the bombing was a good idea.

Referring to the president's statement, Taylor wrote: "I was not aware that any authorized U.S. official had either publicly or privately offered to trade the cessation of bombing for a cessation of infiltration into South Viet-Nam." He then made a cogent appeal:

> If the matter is still open, I would like to reiterate my opinion that the exchange of bombing for an agreement to stop infiltration is bad business from our point of view. . . .
>
> Our bombing of the north is, perhaps, our most useful bargaining asset since it represents the one means of hurting most directly the Communist leadership which will make the principal decisions in any settlement. . . . Ideally we should keep our adversary under constant pressure during negotiations and never let up our military actions. By this reasoning, the bombing of the north should be traded last and not first in any sequence of mutual concessions. . . .
>
> I realize that I may be "speaking from the jail" and that, unbeknownst to me, decisions may have already been taken on these matters. However, they are of such capital importance that I can not forbear expressing once more some of my views.[14]

Apparently, LBJ's consultant was indeed "speaking from the jail": a bombing *halt* began the next day and lasted until October 23—sixty days in all.

By the end of 1966, Taylor felt that no one paid attention to consultants. Frustrated, he proffered his resignation to LBJ in early January 1967.[15] After reviewing his contributions to the president during 1966, he felt "bound to admit that they have dwindled to the point that I doubt the propriety of continuing to bear the title of Consultant." With the letter was a three-page enclosure commenting on the role of U.S. ground forces in Vietnam and on "Preparations for a Viet-Nam Settlement."

On the troop question Taylor expressed his worries about expanding the involvement of U.S. forces.

> There is a clear trend toward an expanded role for United States Ground Forces during the coming year, a trend which results from the success of our offensive search-and-destroy operations and the sluggishness of the pacification program. . . . If this is not checked, it can result in the deep involvement of our forces in clear-and-hold operations, static security missions, and local civil administration.

. . .

> If no limit is set in principle, Washington will continue to receive from Westmoreland repeated requests for troops which it may be hard to decline. If he is not given policy guidance, Westmoreland will be justified in assuming that his concepts for the employment of our troops are consistent with Washington policy.
>
> I would think that, before accepting the inevitability of this expanded role for United States troops, we would leave no stone unturned to assure the Armed Forces of Viet-Nam have made a maximum contribution to pacification under the terms of their new assignment.

Taylor was also concerned about preparations for a settlement. The government needed to learn the painful lessons of the Korean settlement and to prepare the American public for the problems of negotiation.

> We must avoid the pitfalls of accepting a cease-fire, almost certain to work to our disadvantage, and seek instead to negotiate a complete package which will include a cessation of both military and terrorist actions. To avoid foot-dragging at a conference, we will be obliged to continue to keep military pressure on the enemy—on this point, we need to reread Admiral Joy's record of the stalemate at Panmunjom.

. . .

> My conclusion is that we need to . . . prepare our people in advance for the courses of action which we are likely to take—courses which many of our people will find unreasonably harsh.

The president's reaction to the proffered resignation was one of horror. By all means, he wanted to keep Taylor on the team and use him. That same month LBJ sent his consultant off on an eleven-day trip to Southeast Asia, where Taylor could get updated and then inform the commander in chief of his views. In all, Taylor spent five days in South Vietnam. His report to LBJ on January 30, 1967, was in the usual form of those times: an update on progress and problems in the four areas of the American effort. He also dwelt again (as in his letter to LBJ earlier in the month) on some fundamental questions about eventually settling the conflict. He ended on an upbeat note.

> There is an overall problem which is the critical one—how to make 1967 the year of victory in Viet-Nam. There is a fair chance to do so but it will require a maximum, simultaneous effort across the whole range of U.S./GVN activities. We must do better in our ground operations in the south, raise the level of the air operations in the north, inaugurate a constitutional president, hold the line against inflation and show significant progress in RD in the principal areas of population. If we can do these things in Viet-Nam while conducting ourselves at home in such a way as to show that, regardless of pressures, the U.S. will not change its course, I have the feeling that the Vietnamese situation may change drastically for the better by the end of 1967.[16]

That same winter, Taylor's talks on Vietnam at Lehigh the previous year were published in book form as *Responsibility and Response*. Because of Taylor's status (not because of the writing style, which was wooden), the book received perceptive reviews in such places as the *New York Times* and the *New Republic*. Sometimes confusing the messenger with the message, the reviews reflected how public opinion had turned against the war, but they were not wholly critical.

> It seems unlikely that General Taylor's book will change many opinions. Those who agree with current policies will perhaps find their agreement reinforced. Those who have doubts about current policies, as to their rightness or even what they are, will probably not find their doubts much eased. . . . Yet any book that enhances our understanding of public policy and stimulates interest in it is to be welcomed, and General Taylor's book, at the very least does this.[17]

By the spring of 1967 a wave of pessimism about the war swept over Washington. The president was aware of it, McNamara and his band were part of it, and Taylor was appalled by it. As the most salient target of the pessimists—both in and out of government—was Rolling Thunder, Taylor took that up in a letter to the president in mid-May. As usual, the consultant was both cogent (if one accepted his premises) and cautious.

> We tend to forget our own words used in the past when we express doubts about the justification of our bombing of the North. We have said repeatedly that we have never expected the bombing to *stop* infiltration, only to *limit* it—yet in our private councils I hear the results criticized on the score that infiltration continues in spite of all our efforts and, hence, that the game really is not worth the risks and international heat which it generates.

> . . .

> Having defended the need for continuing the bombing, I must say that I would be cautious in extending the target system much farther. Some of our bombing advocates still think in terms of World War II and forget another fact conceded in past discussions—that there is really no industrial target system in North Viet-Nam worthy of the name and no war-supporting industry which, if destroyed, will bear importantly on the outcome of the war. . . .

> Under these conditions, I do not think that it is worth the lives of our pilots, the loss of our planes or such political risk as may be entailed to enter heavily defended areas and strike or restrike targets which do not have a clear relationship to our bombing objectives. . . .

> We must pass this test of persistence—if we do not, we will be expected to give way at every other point on every other front in this conflict. It is concession which will make the enemy tougher—not the bombing, as some of the critics allege. If we yield on the bombing issue, we can be quite sure of no future "give" by Hanoi on any important point.[18]

Another wave of pessimism swept over the Potomac in April, when Westmoreland asked for an additional 200,000 American troops. On May 19, as the general pressed the request again, McNamara was opposed. In a memorandum to the president, his secretary of defense pointed out that the choice was one of "imperfect alternatives." Further, once the request was approved, there would be further pressures for extending the war into Cambodia and Laos and possibly for invading North Vietnam.[19] The only alternative seemed to be to dispatch McNamara off on another fact finder to Vietnam, but the June 1967 war in the Middle East delayed this trip.

Meanwhile, Westmoreland and his Saigon staff, without much real hope of success, developed a statistical briefing of the type dear to the defense secretary's heart. It was, of course, designed to show what previous troop commitments had accomplished and what could be expected from the requested increase. General Westmoreland; General Abrams, who was by then Westy's deputy; and Robert Komer, the pacification czar, served as the "murder board." Night and day they changed slides and rearranged rationales for the big day of their presentation, July 7, 1967, but McNamara was not impressed.

When McNamara returned to brief LBJ at the White House on July 12, Taylor was present and wrote his own memorandum for record:

MCNAMARA

With regard to U.S. troop increases, Westmoreland feels that he needs about 100,000 more in order to win faster. McNamara doubts that this total will be required, but some substantial increase will. . . .

THE PRESIDENT

In summing up the meeting, the President expressed his fear that U.S. patience would progressively decline and with it the will to continue the war in Viet-Nam. He feels that energetic, affirmative action is necessary to controvert the impression that we are not doing everything possible to gain a speedy success. He concedes that some troop reinforcement will be necessary but wants the Westmoreland requirement squeezed down to the absolute minimum acceptable.

He mentioned that he might call upon Clifford or Taylor to go abroad to visit Free World countries in the hope of getting additional troops for Viet-Nam.[20]

That trip did indeed take place. Both Clark Clifford and Maxwell Taylor traveled in August 1967 to South Vietnam, Thailand, Australia, New Zealand, and Korea. Two years later (in a memorandum to Henry Kissinger prompted by an article of Clifford's in *Foreign Affairs*), Taylor set down for the record his own more optimistic views, as contrasted with those of Clifford in hindsight. Taylor's traveling companion recalled having returned from the trip "puzzled, troubled, and concerned" with "nagging, not-to-be-suppressed doubts in my mind." Not so Taylor:

> While none of these governments were wildly enthusiastic over the thought of increasing their troop contributions, I certainly got no impression of indifference to the outcome of the war in Viet-Nam—quite the contrary. . . .
>
> While we got no promissory notes, we left these countries feeling that we had sown seeds which, in time, would produce results—as, indeed, they did. At the time of our mission, the total contribution of ground forces by the Troop Contributing Countries amounted to 54,000. Slowly, this figure rose until, in May 1969, it was over 70,000. While our mission may not claim all the credit, it was still a factor of considerable importance in setting this trend in motion. While this allied strength is still far lower than we would like, we should remind ourselves that in the Korean War the top figure for allied combat strength (less Korea) was about 39,000.[21]

Whether to bomb—and how much and where—became even more of a hot potato than the troop-ceiling issue. In the summer of 1967 the powers in the Pentagon were divided over the bombing issue. Whereas the military wanted to heat up the air campaign in North Vietnam, McNamara and many of his key civilian advisers favored a restricted campaign south of the 20th parallel. This important issue split not only the Pentagon but Congress and the public as well.

The matter was becoming so publicly controversial, in fact, that Sen. John Stennis of the Preparedness Subcommittee of the Armed Services Committee made a dramatic announcement. During August 1967 he would conduct a probe into the air war in North Vietnam.[22] McNamara was already working on a detailed analysis to show that stepping up the bombing would not accomplish U.S. objectives. Indeed, he felt that to de-escalate might help a negotiated settlement of the war.

McNamara began his testimony on August 25. This occasion was the only time he took a public position that, if not contrary to the president's position, probably hedged Johnson's future options. The official relationship between the president and his now dovish secretary of defense was never quite the same again. Nor was McNamara's influence with the president ever to be the same.

McNamara's testimony (which went on all day) had to convince both extremes: those who wanted more bombing should understand that it would be futile; those who wanted none should realize that bombing paid off in certain areas. The air war was not a substitute for the war in the South, as some believed it could be. Still, he pointed out, it had its objectives: to reduce infiltration to the South, to raise the morale of the South Vietnamese people, and to cause the North Vietnamese to pay enough of a price that they would finally conclude that negotiations were preferable.

Although his presentation was a real tour de force, McNamara did not win over the hawks in the Senate or anywhere else. The story on page 1 of the *New York Times* of September 1 gave the reactions of the Senate Preparedness Subcommittee: "Senate unit asks Johnson to widen bombing in North"; "Scores McNamara on policy of restricted air war in light of military views"; "Joint Chiefs supported."

What McNamara's August testimony did accomplish was to set the stage for a diplomatic initiative by the president. By challenging the military position on the bombing, McNamara had put the entire issue in a new perspective. Hence, when LBJ proposed to stop the bombing under certain conditions, perhaps leading to negotiation, the public reaction was muted. If the secretary of defense had not challenged the U.S. military position, reaction would have been much stronger.

The key part of this so-called San Antonio formula, delivered publicly by President Johnson on September 29, 1967 (and already unsuccessfully proposed to the North Vietnamese privately), read: "The United States is willing to stop all aerial and naval bombardment of North Vietnam when this will lead promptly to productive discussions. We, of course, assume that while discussions proceed, North Vietnam would not take advantage of the bombing cessation or limitation."[23] This formula somewhat relaxed a previous offer. Now North Vietnam was not required to stop all their military effort; the United States asked only that they not increase the effort. At the time the initiative led to nothing, but it did help to set the stage for the bombing halt the following fall.

Although their personal relationship was unaffected, Maxwell Taylor and Robert McNamara had long since parted company on the war. Still a hawk in most ways, the general took on the naysayers in a long article in the *New York Times Magazine* in mid-October 1967. He ended with the following charge:

> It would be hard for any serious student of American history to believe that the United States will fail to carry out its purpose with such preponderant strength and with such an impressive record of success since 1965 in overcoming formidable obstacles. The immediate stake in this conflict is the future of Southeast Asia and the worldwide credibility of the commitments of our Government. The outcome will determine the success or failure of the so-called "war of liberation" which Hanoi, Peking and Moscow have announced to be the favored technique for future Communist expansion. In such a contest for such stakes, as President Kennedy said in 1961: "We cannot stand aside." Having taken sides, this side can and must prevail.[24]

McNamara came up with still another initiative when he talked with the president on October 31, 1967 (and followed up with a memorandum the next day). Basically, at this point McNamara felt that to continue on the present course in Vietnam was fruitless. Without some initiatives, he foresaw more of the same—more troop requests, increased bombing requests—without decisive results. The secretary had three recommendations: stabilize the U.S. effort and announce that there would be no expansion of troop strength beyond that already planned and no expansion of the air effort; call a bombing halt by the end of 1967; and prepare a study of military operations in the South with the objective of giving the South Vietnamese greater responsibility.[25]

On November 2 Johnson consulted with several people whose opinions he respected: Dean Rusk, McGeorge Bundy, Walt Rostow, Maxwell Taylor, Abe Fortas, Clark Clifford, and two recalled from Vietnam—General Westmoreland and Ellsworth Bunker, who had replaced Lodge as ambassador in April 1967. In varying degrees, the advisers did not support McNamara's recommendations. Some disagreed on all points; some, just on the bombing halt.

In a follow-through memorandum to the president on November 6, Taylor strongly opposed McNamara's stabilization policy: "Of the alternatives (pull-out, pull-back, all-out, stick-it-out), this is one form of the pull-back alternative which would probably degenerate into pull-out." Although the proposal might allay the fears of those concerned over an expansion of the conflict, it would "provide fresh ammunition for the numerically larger number of critics who say that we are embarked on an endless and hopeless struggle or that we are really not trying to win."[26]

Finally, on December 18, 1967, President Johnson wrote a memorandum for the files with his own view of the McNamara proposals. In sum, Johnson rejected the bombing halt at that time; he rejected the notion of announcing a policy of stabilization, although he saw no need to increase the force level; and he agreed with studying ways to get the South Vietnamese to take over more responsibility.[27]

The preceding April Robert McNamara had been tentatively offered the presidency of the World Bank. In discussing the job with Johnson at that time, he got no direct response. In mid-October the president asked him if he was still interested. When McNamara said yes, Johnson indicated that he would help him. The president was true to his word, and the nomination went to the bank on November 22. The next week the announcement was made. Even Washington insiders, used to leaks of cabinet changes, were surprised.

At this point LBJ, desperate for public support, was fighting for his political life. With the first presidential primary only a few months off, Johnson needed Westmoreland on his bandwagon. In late April Westy had addressed a joint session of Congress and given an optimistic report on the Vietnam situation. Now it was time for a replay. Thus, when Westmoreland and Bunker were in Washington in November, their favorable accounts for LBJ were also delivered to the public. Optimism was the official mood when Westmoreland addressed the National Press Club on November 21.[28]

The MACV commander wound up his visit with a cable to his deputy, Gen. Creighton Abrams. It sums up Westmoreland's view of the situation at the end of autumn 1967.

> I was required to present my views on the situation in Vietnam to Highest Authority, Secretary of Defense, Joint Chiefs of Staff, Senate Armed Services Committee, and the House Armed Services Committee. In addition, I appeared on several nationwide television programs, addressed the National Press Club, and held an on-the-record press conference in the Pentagon. On each occasion, I presented in full or in part the following concept: we are grinding down the Communist enemy in South Vietnam, and there is evidence that manpower problems are emerging in North Vietnam. Our forces

are growing stronger and becoming more proficient in the environment. The Vietnamese armed forces are getting stronger and becoming more effective on the battlefield. The Vietnamese armed forces are being provided with more modern equipment. These trends should continue, with the enemy becoming weaker and the GVN becoming stronger to the point where conceivably in two years or less the Vietnamese can shoulder a larger share of the war and thereby permit the U.S. to begin phasing down the level of its commitment.[29]

TET 1968

Upon returning to Vietnam, General Westmoreland announced twenty-five goals for his command to accomplish in 1968. They included making all the enemy's main force units ineffective and inflicting casualties on enemy units faster than they could be replaced. His forces were indeed to knock out many enemy units, but not in the manner or with the outcome planned.

Not all observers of Vietnam in late 1967 were equally sanguine about the new year. David Halberstam, writing in the December *Harper's,* drew opposite conclusions from Westmoreland. "I do not," he wrote, "think we are winning in any true sense, nor do I see any true signs that we are about to win." He reflected the thoughts of a growing number of Americans in private and public life, even though they knew far less about the situation than Westmoreland did.

Soon after Westmoreland's return, the North Vietnamese were on the prowl around Khe Sanh. This important American outpost sat astride Highway 9 near the Laotian border in the northern part of South Vietnam. Originally established as a patrol base for blocking infiltration routes, Khe Sanh soon became a symbol of the American effort. It also had another purpose: to support strikes into Laos if Washington ever approved such operations. By late December 1967, with enemy forces massed nearby, Khe Sanh was in real danger of being overrun. Beginning around January 21, the NVA laid siege. The base could no longer block infiltration, but the real fear in Washington was that Giap intended to make it another Dien Bien Phu. At one point President Johnson extracted pledges from the Joint Chiefs that Khe Sanh was important and that the Marines could successfully defend it. The beleaguered outpost received great attention, including effective support by the Air Force, which brought supplies and struck at the besiegers from B-52s.[30]

But the high point of military action in the Second Indochina War was the Tet Offensive of early 1968. After all other Vietnam battles have been forgotten, it will be remembered as a watershed. Afterward, nothing in the war was ever quite the same. Although a military defeat for the VC and NVA in a technical sense, it was, ironically, a tremendous psychological victory for them with the American people. According to pronouncements of their civilian and military leaders before Tet, the war in Vietnam was about to wind down with a communist whimper.

Reality struck in the early morning hours of January 30, traditionally a holiday time known as Tet, or the lunar new year. Reports of enemy attacks began crackling into MACV; then, in the next two days, accounts of more attacks poured in. The enemy was evidently launching an enormous operation. Almost simultaneously (although with some coordination problems), assaults were taking place in over one hundred cities and towns, including Saigon! Even the American Embassy was briefly under siege. What, wondered the American people, was happening? Were we not supposed to be winning? How could an attack of such proportions be initiated by an enemy we were defeating?

The White House became a kind of military-political operations center, with the president as deeply involved in the entire operation as he was in the more limited Khe Sanh battle. His civilian consultant cum four-star general became a kind of senior military adviser for the commander in chief. On February 9 a Taylor memorandum to the president speculated on a possible enemy scenario for the immediate future.

> I would guess that, several months ago, the enemy high command abandoned any thought of continued reliance upon prolonged conflict and the progressive attrition of our forces and our will. Instead, they decided "to go for broke" prior to our national election, taking advantage of the turmoil of an election campaign and the anticipated difficulties for the Administration in taking critical decisions in the election atmosphere.
>
> .   .   .
>
> Assuming the validity of the foregoing hypothesis, one can show . . . the possible course of events. . . . five phases which information leads us to believe to be in their plans.

The attack of the cities.

The winter-spring offensive in the North and Northwest.

Negotiations while fighting (they would hope to take place under conditions of no bombing in North Viet-Nam).

A coalition government emerging from negotiations, under Communist domination.

The eventual withdrawal of the U.S. military presence from South Viet-Nam following our elections.[31]

Not a bad guess, considering what actually happened later.

Shortly after the Tet Offensive began, JCS Chairman Wheeler sent a message to COMUSMACV to encourage Westmoreland to ask for the forces he felt he needed to cope with the new situation. Westmoreland's thinking along these lines was initially conservative. He cabled Washington that, although he could use additional troops, he was not making a firm demand for them. He did, though, want to accelerate the arrival of those forces (about 25,000) already programmed for Vietnam.

On February 9 McNamara and Wheeler discussed this request with the president, who asked Taylor's opinion. The response came by memo the next day.

> With regard to the broad overall question of whether we should send additional forces to Southeast Asia at this time, my answer would be affirmative.
>
> .   .   .
>
> If we decide to send these reinforcements, then the next question is their replacement in the strategic reserve at home. I would support the argument which I understand the Chiefs have made that three reserve divisions be called to active duty and I would hope that they would be a balanced force in the sense of having the necessary supporting units to permit their prompt deployment overseas if required.
>
> .   .   .
>
> Whether or not you decide to send further reinforcements, I would recommend consideration of conveying new strategic guidance to Westy and Admiral Sharp. . . . Such a document, I believe, should include the following point. . . . The most pressing matter at this moment is the suppression of the at-

tacks on the cities and the restoration of order. . . . We should
not undertake to hold exposed outposts unless their value is
equal to the anticipated cost and unless reinforcements are
available if needed for the defense.

Throughout the coming months, we should maintain the
bombing of the north at maximum levels of effectiveness. We
should devise a political track parallel to the military which
would include a joint US/GVN assertion of the principles
which must govern any terminal settlement to which we
would agree.[32]

At this point the troop issue began to take a curious turn. In a
message and follow-up telephone call to Westmoreland, Wheeler
elicited from the American commander the statement that "he desperately needs the troop elements requested." Wheeler's hidden
agenda was a reserve forces mobilization and a reconstitution of the
American strategic reserve. By getting Westmoreland to increase the
urgency of his troop requirement, he was putting pressure on a commander in chief still very reluctant to call up the reserves. Immediately picking up the change in Westy's tone, Taylor commented to
the president about this development.

It is hard to believe that this cable is written by the same man
as the preceding one, which we discussed at our meeting
yesterday. This new one is clear, crisp and sounds an unam-
biguous call for additional help in minimum time. I agree
completely with Westy that this is a new ball game which he
faces in which the enemy is playing for high stakes in a short
span of time and that we should meet this challenge by a
commitment of all necessary resources. This is a great opportunity if we use our resources correctly and not a cause for
regret.

.   .   .

In conclusion, I recommend approving the dispatch without
delay of the additional forces which General Westmoreland
requests. I would accompany this approval with new strategic guidance conforming to the new situation and would send
General Wheeler at once to see him to make sure that there
are no misunderstandings.[33]

On Taylor's last point LBJ did indeed want Wheeler to visit Vietnam. The chairman of the Joint Chiefs of Staff could not only confer with Westmoreland but also get a feel for the situation at first hand. Mulling over that trip, Taylor gave the commander in chief some points to pass on to Wheeler.

> Reflecting on the possible objectives of General Wheeler's visit, I would hope that he would obtain answers to some of the fundamental questions which are troubling us, derived from detailed private discussions with General Westmoreland and his staff. The questions which need exploring appear to me to include the following:
>
> > What are Westy's operational plans, force requirements, and force availabilities for:
> > A spring-summer offensive by friendly forces to regain the initiative and to exploit the weakened condition of the enemy when his offensive has run out of steam?
> > What reinforcements will General Westmoreland need during this calendar year?
> > What grounds are there for the allegation of an "intelligence failure" at the time of the first wave of attacks on the cities?
> > How does General Westmoreland feel about the functioning of his own and the Vietnamese intelligence services in connection with this situation?
>
> These are all hard questions for which there are probably no final answers at this time but whatever Bus can bring back will be most helpful.[34]

The JCS chairman had his marching orders and on February 23 arrived in Saigon. The trip was to set in motion a chain of events that would dramatically affect both the American war effort and the Johnson presidency.

POST-TET ASSESSMENTS

Briefings began for Wheeler immediately after his arrival in Saigon, and he met at length the following day with Westmoreland.[35] The chairman of the Joint Chiefs of Staff—responsible for U.S. troops worldwide, not just in Vietnam—had a hidden agenda: how to use the Vietnamese situation to build up a U.S. Army depleted by this

war. If he could encourage COMUSMACV to request a maximum
force, Wheeler would be justified in asking for a call-up of reserve
forces. Westmoreland's estimate, originally an optimistic one,
changed after the two generals conferred. Examining force requirements to meet any contingency, even the most extreme, they came
up with a requirement of about 206,000 troops. The first increment
of somewhat more than 100,000 was to be in Vietnam by that
spring; the rest were to come in two increments later in the year if
required.

Now Wheeler's task was to sell the Washington decision makers
on the 206,000 potential increase for Vietnam, which would indeed
require a substantial call-up of reserve forces—perhaps 400,000.
Stopping at Honolulu on February 26 en route home, Wheeler cabled
the president his troop request, along with his own evaluation (but
not Westmoreland's less pessimistic version) of the situation in Vietnam. Omitted but implied in the message was a statement that Westmoreland shared the chairman's assessment. Significantly, no copy
went to Westmoreland. The chairman of the Joint Chiefs of Staff was
playing fast and loose for big stakes.

On February 27 Rusk hosted a farewell luncheon for outgoing
Defense Secretary McNamara. Attending was McNamara's replacement, Clark Clifford, who was to take over on March 1. When the
discussion turned to the Wheeler cable, the now dovish McNamara
made a strong plea for a "hard-headed" look at requests for more
American troops in Vietnam. He maintained that additional forces
were simply not the answer to the problem.

Wheeler arrived back in Washington early on the morning of February 28 and went immediately to a White House breakfast. Besides
the president and vice president, one of those in attendance was
Maxwell Taylor. Others included Rusk, McNamara, Clifford, and
Rostow. They heard Wheeler express the same gloom as was in the
cable.

A worried LBJ then directed Clark Clifford to set up a task force
to analyze the situation and to advise him by Monday, March 4,
what should be done. The group had its first huddle on that same
day. The principals, as Taylor recalls them, in addition to himself and
Rostow from the White House, were Rusk, Nicholas Katzenbach,
and Bill Bundy from State; Clifford, Paul Nitze, Paul Warnke, and
Phil Goulding from Defense; Wheeler from JCS; and Richard Helms
from CIA. Several papers on relevant subjects were to be completed
and discussed by the task force on Saturday, March 2. Taylor's as-

signment was to come to grips with the question, What alternative courses of action are available to the United States?

At age sixty-one, Clark Clifford was no stranger to government service or to defense matters. He had served in Truman's White House from 1945 until 1950, had been part of Kennedy's transition team, and had served on the Foreign Intelligence Advisory Board. The president valued his advice on many matters; hence, no one was surprised when he was offered the position of secretary of defense. When the task force began its work, Clifford's views on Vietnam were probably not fully matured. Although he had always supported Johnson on Vietnam, apparently he was becoming apprehensive about the American commitment there. The seeds of doubt had been sown on his trip to Asia with Maxwell Taylor in the summer of 1967.

More doubts arose as the new secretary listened to some civilian advisers in Defense. Among those concerned about the U.S. commitment in Vietnam were Paul Warnke, his assistant for international security affairs, and, for different reasons, Phil Goulding, his public affairs officer. Clifford's daily contact with them probably helped shape his views more than the task force meetings did. Another task force member, Secretary of Treasury Harry Fowler, saw serious economic problems in meeting Wheeler's requirements. Not only would taxes go up but also Congress would insist on reducing domestic programs, including the Great Society programs dear to Lyndon Johnson.

Taylor was surprised that "some of the civilians in the Department of Defense were taking a new tack." They appeared to feel that "success in Vietnam could never be attained by military means. Hence, we should cease sending reinforcements, minimize our losses, try to stalemate the situation with the resources presently committed, and hope for a break."[36]

With his own position, Maxwell Taylor had no problem. His required memorandum to Clifford on March 2 set forth his views on alternative courses of action. He favored giving Westmoreland his 25,000 troops now, and he supported General Wheeler's desire to call up the reserves in order to reconstitute the strategic reserve. Taylor went on to propose that Westmoreland be given new strategic guidance, which "should make it clear that Westmoreland's mission was primarily the suppression of attacks on the cities, the restoration of order . . . and the creation of a mobile reserve ready to pass to a vigorous offensive with the resumption of favorable weather in the spring."[37]

Taylor was not involved in drafting the formal report of the task force. Warnke and Bill Bundy did that and gave it to the president on March 4. The report was a compromise between the views of the Joint Chiefs and the defense civilians led by Warnke. In effect, it went along with some additional troops for Westmoreland, about 22,000, and recommended a call-up of about 245,000 reserves. It deferred for further reassessment the issue of new strategic guidance to Westmoreland.

As Warnke later put it, "The actual recommendations were a small part of the report"; the main goal was to get the president to focus on the wider issues of the war. Clifford's subordinates used the report to plant doubts about American strategy in Vietnam in the mind of the new secretary of defense.[38]

The task force had not solved the president's problems; it merely postponed solving them. On March 9 Taylor was summarizing the diversity of views that LBJ faced and combining them into A and B groupings. The A group view was that the enemy had been beaten at Tet and that the United States should exploit the situation, whereas the B view held that in reality the enemy had won and that the United States should hedge its bets. While pointing out that he leaned more toward being an A than a B, Taylor admitted, nevertheless, that "the returns are not all in and we cannot be entirely sure of the outcome." Further, he had doubts about "the feasibility of any strategy which depends for its success upon the willingness of the American people to wage a prolonged, limited war of stalemate."[39]

Taylor was not the only skeptic. On March 12 the New Hampshire presidential primary showed that Democrat Eugene McCarthy had a surprising 42 percent of the vote as compared to 48 percent for the incumbent president. On March 16 Taylor's old friend Bobby Kennedy—with whom Taylor had agreed to disagree on American Vietnam policy—declared for the presidency. Johnson was beginning to have his doubts also and decided to reconvene the "Wise Men" who had supported his Vietnam policies the previous November. In addition to Taylor, this group included Acheson, Robert Murphy, Ball, McGeorge Bundy, Lodge, Clifford, and Fortas. This time Johnson was in for some surprises from the group.

The Wise Men assembled on March 25 at the State Department for dinner with Rusk. They received briefings from Philip Habib, a Bundy deputy; Maj. Gen. William De Puy, Wheeler's special assistant; and George Carver, a CIA analyst. According to Taylor, their presentations were "temperate and thoughtful." The next day the group met at the White House for lunch and then conferred with the president.

Each member gave his views to LBJ. McGeorge Bundy, the group's informal spokesman, told how they had shifted views since the previous November; as a group, he said they were no longer hopeful about the results in Vietnam. General Matthew Ridgway, for example, opposed more U.S. troop increases; rather, the United States should support the South Vietnamese for two years, during which it would expect them to develop their own defense capability; then, American troops could begin to phase down. In short, the group in general felt that the United States ought to find a way out. Disagreeing strongly with these views, however, were three of the advisers: Murphy, Fortas, and Taylor. The discussion, nonetheless, brought home to the president what was happening in the country: mainstream America would not accept further escalation.

What, asked Taylor later, accounted for the change in these advisers since the previous November? He felt certain of two answers: the news media, especially the *New York Times* and the *Washington Post,* and (as he called them) the Pentagon doves such as Paul Warnke.[40]

Now LBJ had the ball. For some time, in the wake of Tet, he had been considering an address to rally the American people. But that talk, now scheduled for March 31, was to take a different turn. It would become one of the most dramatic presidential addresses of the 1960s.

Work on it went apace between LBJ's meeting with the Wise Men and March 31. Only Johnson and a few of his very close advisers knew about its surprise ending. First, a somber president announced three decisions:

- Only a token increase would be made in the American forces in Vietnam along with a small reserve force call-up.
- Expansion and improvement of the South Vietnamese forces would be the first priority from this point on.
- He would stop the bombing of a major portion of South Vietnam in order to move toward peace. He went on to say that Hanoi would match this restraint and that both sides would soon begin to bargain for peace.

Then came the bombshell. Taylor and all the rest of the country watching that night were amazed at LBJ's coda: "I shall not seek, and I will not accept, the nomination of my party for another term as your President."

All this was the end result of the Tet Offensive. That significant military action had caused the U.S. leaders to reconsider and alter their strategy in Vietnam. In changing American public opinion, Tet had led to negotiations, to the downfall of a president, and, eventually, to a plan for U.S. withdrawal.[41]

LAME DUCK CONSULTANT

Taylor's immediate reaction to Johnson's abdication speech was a rational one, perhaps too rational. In a memorandum to the president the day after, he even had a political proposition: "Might it not be possible to assemble several leading members of both parties at the White House and get them to issue a joint statement endorsing the peace overture contained in your speech last night. . . ? I have in mind such men as . . . Nixon, . . . R. Kennedy, and McCarthy. . . ."[42] (But, obviously, no other politician was going to let himself get tarred with Lyndon Johnson's war.)

The beleaguered president had for a time to direct his thoughts and energies elsewhere. On April 4, the assassination of Martin Luther King, Jr., triggered rioting and looting in many cities, including Washington, D.C., where flames erupted within seven blocks of the White House.

As the immediate reaction to the King assassination subsided, Johnson and others turned their attention to the negotiations with Hanoi, which began in Paris on May 12. The American delegates were W. Averell Harriman as chief and as deputy Cyrus Vance (who, Taylor felt, was more reliable than Harriman). Taylor believed that Harriman—one of those he held responsible for Diem's overthrow—was more interested in removing Vietnam as an issue in the U.S.-Soviet dialogue than in the terms of agreement on a Vietnam settlement.[43]

Regarding the negotiations, Taylor had some advice for the lame duck president.

> We are reacting far too little, it seems to me, to actions of Hanoi in raising the level of military action in South Viet-Nam while heckling us to stop the bombing. By our quiescence, we seem to accept as a matter of course the continued high rate of enemy infiltration and repeated acts of accentuated violence . . . and no strong protest to indicate that we take these things seriously. In their fight-talk campaign, the

other side is increasing the fighting in the South while trying to talk us out of our freedom to retaliate in the North.[44]

The military actions of the enemy that Taylor was referring to was another countrywide attack, which became known as "mini-Tet." The attack on Saigon was, however, stronger than the one in February. Never one to let up, Taylor prodded LBJ to get started again on the bombing.

> My proposal would be first to launch the public campaign which we need so badly setting forth with specific examples the tremendous efforts of the enemy to escalate the war in South Vietnam. Then, on the occasion of the next spectacular act of violence or escalation by the enemy . . . we should announce the lifting of all territorial restraints on our bombing and our intention to adjust it henceforth to the scale of war in the South and the behavior of the enemy . . . we should eliminate territorial restrictions and go for the most remunerative targets wherever found outside immediate urban areas.[45]

To a country already traumatized over bloodshed and confusion at home and abroad, in June 1968 came another blow: the assassination of Robert Kennedy. To Maxwell Taylor came the shock of losing his close young friend. Later he wrote: "I shall always be indebted to him for changing the course of events in a way which allowed me to play a small part in the historical drama of John F. Kennedy, to know Ethel, Jackie, and the others of his extraordinary family and to have my life enriched by the friendship of Bobby Kennedy."[46]

All that summer of 1968, fighting continued in South Vietnam, but the media shifted the spotlight toward the talks in Paris. Going against the widespread feeling that these negotiations would end the war, Taylor was not sanguine in his advice to LBJ. He could give no certain answers, but he had explicit warnings.

> In spite of occasional "straws in the wind," there is very little of substance to show for more than two months of negotiations in Paris.
>
>   .   .   .
>
> It would be timely, I think, to ask ourselves how long we should accept this kind of stalemate.

. . .

At home, we have to contend both with the national impatience of our people and with the repercussions on the Presidential campaign which will rise from a stalemate.

There are probably more reasons for Hanoi to be content with a stalemate than to oppose one. It gives them time to rebuild and refit their forces in South Viet-Nam and to chip away at the GVN. Likewise, it gives them time to study the reactions of the U.S. domestic front and to reflect on the probable consequences of Presidential alternatives.

. . .

As a military move, we always have the option of extending the bombing beyond the currently restricted limits. Indeed, this is our most powerful tool and should never be given up without reservation.

. . .

In the present circumstance, I suggest that you ask the Secretaries of State and Defense for their views on this subject. . . . As for the U.S. domestic and political fronts, I am afraid, Mr. President, that only you can evaluate the probable effects of a prolonged stalemate in Paris.[47]

In the fall of 1968 the presidential election took over. If any doubts remained about the impact of the war on American politics, events at the Democratic convention in August at Chicago erased them. Vice President Hubert Horatio Humphrey won his party's nomination, but bitter disputes inside the convention hall and clashes outside between antiwar protesters and the police left a bad impression. Humphrey, of course, was plagued by the war; despite the president's October 31 announcement of a complete bombing halt, LBJ's vice president was unable to defeat Richard Milhous Nixon. The Republican candidate, whose campaign promises included "a plan to end the war," became president-elect by a narrow margin on November 5.

The consultant remained an unregenerate hawk to the end. On December 3, he had a few remaining words of advice to the now truly terminal president.

In reading the cables and listening to discussions, I frequently get indications that some of our serious officials hold views on the conduct of the Paris negotiations which to me seem highly fallacious. Three of them are of especial concern.

The first is the proposition, supported I believe by Averell Harriman, that we should withdraw at an early date some of our forces in Viet-Nam as a unilateral gesture. I would consider such an action to be a very unfortunate step for a variety of reasons.

. . .

A second fallacy is the belief that it is to our interests to deescalate the fighting in South Viet-Nam. I would take the opposite view and say that it is to our interests to increase continuous pressure on the formed bodies of the enemy forces and, in particular, on the Viet Cong infrastructure.

. . .

A third fallacious view which is often implied rather than expressed is that we should avoid suggesting the possibility of a return to bombing North Viet-Nam. Here again I take the opposite view, feeling that we must awake and keep alive in Hanoi a constant fear of our resumption of attacks against military targets anywhere in North Viet-Nam.[48]

Taylor's final word on Lyndon Johnson—whom he advised on Vietnam, in one capacity or other, during LBJ's entire tenure as president—comes toward the end of his own memoirs.

So President Johnson retired to private life, unhappy at having left the nation at war in spite of his unceasing efforts for peace. I suspected that he regretted the unilateral concessions he had made to Hanoi in deference to the urging of most of his advisers, but that he had felt obliged to run the risks of trying them for the sake of national unity. In any case, he had left the seeds of victory implanted in the soil of Vietnam for cultivation and harvesting by his successor—if Mr. Nixon could hold the country together for the time required for the reaping.[49]

For all practical purposes, Nixon's inauguration ended Taylor's public career, although he did remain for about a year as a member of the presidential Foreign Intelligence Advisory Board.

CHAPTER 7

Afterward: The High Song Is Over

axwell Taylor left his consultancy at the end of the Johnson administration with neither army nor bureaucracy to command, but he still commanded attention. Because of his close relationship with the Kennedy clan, Taylor departed unsure if Lyndon Johnson had really trusted him; the uncertainty haunted him long afterward. (Walt Rostow claimed that LBJ had told him privately that, despite the Kennedy-Taylor relationship, the president never had doubted Taylor's loyalty to the administration[1]). Despite giving up his chairmanship of the Foreign Intelligence Advisory Board, he retained his membership at the behest of the new president, Richard M. Nixon; he did not, however, remain on that job after the first year of the Nixon administration. In 1969, too, he resigned the presidency of the Institute for Defense Analysis to concentrate on his writing.

He may have left these responsibilities somewhat reluctantly; maybe the urge to remain at the center of power still burned brightly. Perhaps seeking to elongate his White House affiliation, he dangled bait in a long letter to Henry Kissinger, then national security adviser in the new administration. The letter detailed his ideas on defense and foreign policy priorities and named alternative agencies for researching and implementing them. Dragging the fly across the pond slightly, Taylor also mentioned his willingness to meet with Kissinger. If this letter was bait, Kissinger did not bite.[2]

Taylor just would not fade away; his habits of a lifetime were too ingrained. He would continue to grasp and build on whatever life had to offer, living up to Gerald Higgins's memory of him as "always doing the best he could, and looking for ways to improve performances." He went on the lecture circuit, with mixed results. His son wrote of a sign of the times: protesters preventing Maxwell Taylor from speaking at the University of Rochester in May 1969. He fell back to confer with a small group of students and faculty at President Wallis's home, taped by the student radio station.[3]

With the frustrations of contemporary public appearances, Taylor increasingly concentrated his efforts on his writings. Throughout 1971 he toiled on his magnum opus, the autobiographical *Swords and Plowshares;* in his neat handwriting (he had never learned to type), he penned reams of legal paper. But he put down his autobiographical pen and picked up a polemical one in June 1971 to excoriate the *New York Times* for its decision to publish the Pentagon Papers as edited by Taylor's old media antagonist, reporter Neil Sheehan. Although unsullied by these revelations, Taylor nevertheless chastised the *Times* for consorting with national enemies by taking this action.

Taylor's book was conceived as a tract on his Vietnam experience, but Evan Thomas, his editor at W.W. Norton, joined Taylor's family and close friends in calling for a full-fledged autobiography. The author compromised, writing about many of his earlier experiences; but of the book's thirty-five chapters, fourteen were primarily about Vietnam. To his credit, he avoided discussing personalities pro or con, save for "testifying to the author's admiration and affection for the Kennedy family."

As the manuscript mounted up and was forwarded to his publisher, the Norton editors found that Taylor, in their opinion, was insufficiently contrite in his Vietnam recollections. One anonymous top Norton staffer wrote a scathing memorandum that the embarrassed Evan Thomas sent on to the book's author. It warned that Taylor had not defended his reputation nearly enough and further opined that "forty-five thousand American lives" were too great a price to pay "to guarantee a life free from oppression to illiterate peasants on the other side of the world."[4]

Published in 1972, *Swords and Plowshares* never climbed to best-sellerdom, nor was it ever filmed by Hollywood. It did inspire considerable differences of opinion by reviewers. Marvin Kalb of CBS News praised it, along with Herbert Cheshire in *Business Week*. A surprising supporter emerged: John Kenneth Galbraith, a prominent war critic, wrote very positively. The naysayers, as expected, largely knocked Taylor for a lack of contrition. These included David Halberstam, the early leader of journalistic criticism against the war, and Neil Sheehan, another veteran of the Vietnam correspondents' war with the U.S. government. Son-biographer John M. Taylor's later account views Sheehan's review as more negative than it actually was. John Taylor quotes only two words—"bad history"—from Sheehan's review of *Swords and Plowshares*, but Sheehan actually wrote: "This book is bad history, but in its own way, a good memoir, for it tells a great deal about General Maxwell Taylor and those other statesmen of the 1960s who led us into the Indochina war."[5]

The book does exhibit some tunnel vision with its media comments:

> Biased reporters found no good to say about our Vietnamese allies, whom they held up to scorn in a way which led the American people to believe that our allies were not worth the sacrifices we were making in their behalf. Such selective and slanted reporting spread defeatism among the tender-minded at home and provided enormous encouragement for Hanoi to hold fast and concede nothing.[6]

Was Taylor unaware of all the endemic corruption in both the government of Vietnam and its military (RVNAF), or had he remembered his Korean experience more than two decades before and chalked it all off to the natural Asian order of things? Even a Vietnam insider like Robert Komer wrote: "Perhaps the greatest flaw was the failure to come to grips directly with the gross inadequacies of GVN and RVNAF leadership at all levels. U.S. advisers early recognized that this was the critical problem."[7]

Taylor also commented: "Every war critic capable of producing a headline contributed, in proportion to his eminence, some comfort if not aid to the enemy."[8] This attitude tends to dismiss legitimate policy questions and equally legitimate dissent. As a former high official, albeit experienced and sophisticated, Taylor probably should not have drawn this line between the free expression of dissent and outright collusion with a foe. A professional soldier may at times possess clear insights into a politico-military situation but is still wise to be evenhanded in his judgment of the media and public opinion. Media bashing in *Swords and Plowshares* solved no problems.

Late in 1972, after the book's publication, Henry Kissinger telephoned Taylor at home. As national security adviser, Kissinger wanted Taylor to send him a letter analyzing and criticizing the current North Vietnamese peace proposals. Taylor went to work. When he wrote, he complimented Kissinger on the progress of the Paris peace talks. Drawing on his own experience relating to Panmunjom two decades earlier, Taylor reiterated a warning about future impediments to a settlement. He saw "ambiguities which, if not clarified, will invite chicanery on the part of our communist opposites after the Americans depart":

- North Vietnamese troops, probably 150,000, remained in the South, "ready to make exorbitant claims to territorial control," and were unmentioned in the Hanoi document.
- Vietnamization would be interrupted by the removal of U.S. advisers "and limiting the introduction of equipment to replacement issues."
- According to Taylor's earlier Korean experience, a cease-fire announced before the arrival of international observers would only hasten violations because of the observers' ignorance of original troop dispositions.
- The agreement specified two equal governments: the Provisional Revolutionary Government of South Vietnam and the regular GVN. Taylor predicted that its adoption would only strengthen Prime Minister Thieu's intractability.

Taylor also advised Kissinger to deal with the problems of repatriating communist prisoners of war (POWs), who might not, by then, necessarily want to return to the North. He closed the letter by continuing to encourage Kissinger's efforts.[9]

Kissinger replied on November 9. The lopsided, controversial election of 1972 was then over, and he had time for considering the pressing matters of foreign policy. Thanking Taylor, Kissinger promised not to agree to anything in Paris "until we are satisfied that the provisions are right."[10]

Whether satisfactory or not, the final settlement was signed by Kissinger and Le Duc Tho in 1973, and the remaining American troops were out two months later.

The Second Indochina War ended in April 1975. American television viewers mutely watched choppers lumbering off the U.S. Embassy roof in Saigon to airlift the last U.S. personnel and a few privileged Vietnamese. Then the North Vietnamese tanks crashed through the gate of the National Palace. Out at sea, sailors shoved multimillion-dollar helicopters off the decks of aircraft carriers to make room for incoming helicopters with more escapees. It was the lowest point for the United States since the domestic turmoil of 1968. Taylor remembered the words of World War I veterans when he told an interviewer, "We all have a share in it, and none of it is good. There are no heroes, just bums. I include myself in that."[11]

The next year Taylor published the last of his three books, a short collection of defense and foreign policy essays called *Precarious Security*. With a global viewpoint he predicted (correctly) that domestic problems would increasingly preoccupy Soviet leadership and lessen its threat to the United States. Seeing the growth of world population as the enemy of world peace in the future, he continued his plea to Congress and the general public for more population control.

This championing was sometimes buried in other themes, articles, and speeches, such as that given at Columbia University in October 1977. In that one he also warned: "In all quarters, the United States suffers from its image as the archetype of selfish, affluent capitalism, one that makes it a natural target for the resentment of the underprivileged world." Merely by having when others have not, he maintained, the United States becomes perceived as responsible and therefore vulnerable to threats initiated by the USSR but executed by surrogates, merely to economize on Soviet commitments.[12] Taylor's comments, though, failed to examine the other side of the coin—the desire of millions around the world to emulate the American way of life.

General Omar Bradley, Taylor's old boss, had told a London *Daily Express* interviewer in 1959, "The best service a retired general can perform is to turn in his tongue along with his unit, and mothball his opinions." If Maxwell Taylor ever heard this, he never accepted it. With extraordinary frequency he came out with written and spoken opinions. Self-criticism and national criticism on the Vietnam issue echoed the Chinese martial philosopher Sun-Tzu. Taylor said:

> First, we didn't know ourselves. We thought we were going into another Korean war, but this was a different country. Secondly, we didn't know our South Vietnamese allies. We never understood them, and that was another surprise. And

we knew even less about North Vietnam. Who was Ho Chi Minh? Nobody really knew. So, until we know the enemy and know our allies and know ourselves, we'd better keep out of this dirty kind of business. It's very dangerous.

(A half-century before Christ, Sun-Tzu said, "Know the enemy and know yourself. . . . When you are ignorant of the enemy but know yourself, your chances of winning or losing are equal. If ignorant both of your enemy and of yourself, you are certain in every battle to be in peril."[13])

Then there were the immediate foreign policy and defense issues. Taylor supported President Carter's stand for a treaty giving the canal to Panama "in a partnership based on reciprocal self-interest." In the midst of the 1980 presidential primaries, Carter ordered a military rescue for American hostages in Tehran. When it failed at Desert I—the intermediate refueling point where eight servicemen died in the helicopter crashes—many observers likened the operation to the Bay of Pigs disaster. Taylor, in one of his many contributions to the *Washington Post,* analyzed the plan and its aborted execution for similarities and differences. He concluded: "In both cases, the decision to act was not accompanied by a determination to succeed, followed by an allocation of resources more than enough to assure success."[14]

Long an advocate of universal national service, Taylor writing in the *Washington Post* added to the defense debates heating up in the year before the 1980 election with this advice: "We can swallow hard and restore some form of conscription. . . . No other action we could take would so clearly demonstrate our seriousness of purpose." Clearly to him, a poignant lesson from our Vietnam experience had been the disproportionate number of the poor and minorities in uniform. The unfairness of it continued later when the all-volunteer Army in its early days overwhelmingly attracted the same type of enlistees. This increase in illiterate recruits created havoc with training programs for more sophisticated machinery and weaponry. Not only was Taylor arguing for shared danger across the board for all socioeconomic strata but also he was demanding increased educational levels needed for competence on computer keyboards, steering wheels, and firing buttons.

Another Taylor target was the National Security Council. He suggested replacing it with a new entity, the National Policy Council, with broader responsibilities and powers for integrating civil and political priorities with military ones. Taylor called, too, for a new standard in military appropriations and manning; he called it "task adequacy."[15] He argued against the MX missile and for the Joint Chiefs. In the latter case, he fought a congressional bill that would have created a Senior Strategic Advisory Board, interposing another screen between the president, the secretary of defense, and the chiefs.[16]

Maxwell Taylor had, ironically, long lambasted American journalists for what he saw as their interference with the Vietnam War and often equated them with the enemy. Now, after failing to lick them, he joined them. As an "irregular columnist," he saw the press as a convenient vehicle for his opinions simply by publishing them with the frequency that he did in the *Washington Post*.

He continued to garner attention, sometimes in unlikely places. An August 1979 Soviet magazine article headlined Taylor as "The Unlucky Trumpeter." TASS correspondent Nikolay Portugalov wrote:

> He has aged considerably and looks quite peaceful. Retired American Gen. Maxwell Taylor is still considered to be "one of the best strategic heads in the United States." He is even now busy at his favorite occupation—working out net strategic formulas "adapted to the changing situation," at the behest of the military-industrial complex, of which Taylor himself is an integral part.[17]

At home, too, he was remembered. Commentator Edward P. Morgan told National Public Radio listeners in September 1980 that defense was the singular issue in the presidential campaign that "desperately needs a referee . . . and . . . I nominate for the role, General Maxwell Taylor, one of the more sophisticated and civilized military men extant." The listeners heard Morgan continue: "No hawk with talons bared, he is as much of a dove as an attack-trained Doberman pinscher. That is why I consider him eminently fit to referee presidential exchanges." Morgan concluded that Taylor "may not have all the answers, but he certainly produces sounder logic to apply to our national security problem than Carter or Reagan and I think he is eligible to blow the whistle on both of them."[18]

Morgan's somewhat facetious paean arrived a little late in the game. Increasingly troubled by arthritis, Taylor finally had to resort to a walker. A visitor, historian Forrest Pogue, asked if the infirmity came from "jumping out of too many airplanes." "No," replied Taylor. "It came from playing tennis on too many hard courts." His tennis-playing days were over, and he had to resign from several boards that met in New York City; he restricted his travels outside Washington. As if this infirmity was not enough, his doctors then discovered that the arthritis camouflaged something more frightening: amyotrophic lateral sclerosis (ALS, also known as Lou Gehrig's disease). A degenerative attack on the nervous system, ALS does not affect mental function but does result in restricted movement, interfered speech, and—in older patients like Taylor—a decreased sensation of vibration in the feet that inhibits the ability to walk.

On January 23, 1982, Mike Wallace narrated a CBS News documentary greatly criticizing Gen. William Westmoreland. It accused him of manipulating statistics and other intelligence reports between 1966 and 1968 to deceive President Johnson, Congress, and the general public about the progress of the Vietnam War. Even conservative writer William F. Buckley, Jr., was impressed with the program and wrote so in his syndicated column.[19]

Taylor was incensed, both at CBS and at Buckley. He soon jumped into the controversy to take both to task. He called the telecast "a hatchet job," dismissed both its allegations and Buckley's support of it, and defended Westmoreland as "a long-time respected friend of the utmost integrity."[20] Taylor even donated to Westmoreland's legal fund when the controversial commander sued CBS for libel and sought $120 million in damages. Taylor believed that Westmoreland had little chance of being a successful David against the CBS Goliath, but he did see some good in what he interpreted as revelations of CBS's "shoddy standards." Taylor wrote Westmoreland, when the latter dropped the case, "after taking on too big an opponent, CBS, on the wrong battlefield, the courthouse, you have achieved important effects that will make for a worthy victory over the enemy."[21]

Heeding Dylan Thomas's call to "rage against the dying of the light," Taylor continued to write as long as he could; activity, doctors feel, is the only therapy for ALS patients. He continued to churn out his thoughts and recollections for the *Washington Post* and any professional magazine that would have him. Celebrating the fortieth anniversary of D-Day in the *Post,* he remembered his experience jumping into France in command of the 101st Airborne. *Post* readers also read his memories of the Battle of the Bulge in commemoration of its fortieth anniversary.

By 1985, the year of his eighty-fourth birthday, his ability to speak had all but disappeared. Still, for the fortieth anniversary of the end of World War II, he managed another commemorative article for the

Post. In it he reminded readers of much that happened in the days after May 8, 1945. Especially notable was his account of a visit on June 27, 1945, from Gen. George Marshall. Taylor and Gen. George Patton heard the chief of staff's sudden announcement at lunch about the results of a recent test in New Mexico. The plan was to use two of the tested weapons to bomb Japanese cities beginning "on the first moonlight night in August." According to Taylor, Marshall said that it "would end the war."[22]

Taylor's condition finally deteriorated so much that he could no longer write for the *Post,* and he had to give up an idea for a book of personal anecdotes perhaps modeled after Dwight Eisenhower's *At Ease,* as I suggested.[23] Despite these frustrations he continued to write and study, often translating English works into French or Spanish. In a 1985 Christmas card to me, Taylor wrote regretfully, "I'm afraid I must confess to old age," followed by a doggerel "not for publication" modeled after the rhyme schemes of his favorite poets, the English Romantics:

> I walk not badly with a cane,
> With specs I'm just half blind.
> My dentures hold and cause no pain
> But I sure do miss my mind.

One night in January 1987, he tried to mount his walker but fell, striking his head and breaking his collarbone. The District of Columbia ambulance took him to Georgetown Hospital instead of to Walter Reed. The emergency doctors who treated the unconscious patient were ignorant of his controlling condition. Transferred to Walter Reed the next day, he was found to have contracted pneumonia, the most dangerous illness for ALS patients. Remaining at Walter Reed, he regained consciousness but in mid-March became comatose. On Easter Sunday, April 19, 1987, Maxwell Taylor died.

One of the more fitting tributes sent to Diddy Taylor was written by Jacqueline Kennedy Onassis:

> His intelligence, the optimism and gaiety of his charm—this soldier, scholar, statesman, linguist, author—one found all these qualities in one man in the early days of this country, not in the twentieth century.[24]

Thursday, April 23, 1987, was an overcast, drizzly day in the Washington area. In the New Chapel at Fort Myer, son Thomas

Taylor, a West Pointer and 101st veteran himself, eulogized his father:

> One of his grandchildren, Alice, lives in London and could not be with us today. She has left for us a description of Grandy [Taylor] which I would like to share: "He was as tall, straight and full-sapped as a young oak tree. He had eyes resonant with laughter, eyes that crinkled like my father's eyes, eyes that could warm a room. He was agelessly handsome, well-knit to the bone, and he radiated that kind of inner certainty that many people seek and some are born with."[25]

The mourners then traveled to Arlington National Cemetery, where Maxwell Taylor was buried near the tombs of the Unknowns. Nineteen guns boomed, and the bugler played taps. A group of 101st veterans stood at attention and gave a final salute with "the cocky air of elite troops," reported the *New York Times*.

> The high song is over.
>   There was a thing to say, and it is said now.
>
> Winners and losers—they are only a theme now.
>
> There is no need for blame,
>   Nothing to hide, to change.
>
> The high song is over.[26]

CHAPTER 8

Maxwell Taylor—An Interpretation

The main subject of this book is the American experience in Vietnam. The public life of Maxwell Taylor is used as a prism to tell the story of high-level American decision making and its consequences in Vietnam.

To understand Taylor, we needed first to look briefly at the forces shaping the man and his career—especially the interwar Army of the 1920s and 1930s; the heady days of World War II, when he served as an airborne general; his tour as commander of the Eighth Army in the Korean War; and his four frustrating years as Army chief of staff in the Eisenhower administration.

But central to this book was Taylor's post-Army career: eight years from the time he was called back to high government service by a shaken John F. Kennedy—smarting from the Bay of Pigs failure—until he retired, along with LBJ as, in his own words, "a lame-duck adviser."

Maxwell Taylor was a transition figure. The last of the World War II heroic generals, he was at the same time the first of a new breed—the managerial generals. He was willing to adopt new technologies, management modes, and strategic concepts. Further, he was unique in having achieved substantial power without ever seeking, much less holding, public office.

There was no precedent for a retired chief of service to be recalled as a personal military representative, with his own White House staff, to advise the president. Nor was there a precedent to recall a retired general to America's highest military position, but, after his White House years under Kennedy, Maxwell Taylor did indeed become chairman of the Joint Chiefs of Staff.

Equally unique were his two subsequent appointments: ambassador to Vietnam with an unlimited charter of power during the critical time of decisions to commit troops and then a four-year stint as consultant to LBJ on the Vietnam War. In these capacities, but mainly as ambassador, he was involved not only in strategic decisions but also in domestic and international matters associated with the war.

This chapter brings the story together, to sum up and interpret and, in so doing, to confront the following questions:

- In what ways did Taylor's early years and his career in the interwar Army shape his development and outlook as a professional soldier?
- How did Taylor's experiences as an airborne general in World War II and as the American Army commander in the Korean War focus his ambition and shape his strategic outlook?
- Why did he fail to achieve his goals for the Army when he held its highest position as chief of staff from 1955 to 1959? How did he then capitalize on this experience to develop into an adroit political-military figure and thus set the stage for a prominent position in the next administration?
- If it is true, as Gen. Earle Wheeler said, that "Taylor had an influence with President Kennedy that went far beyond military matters; [Kennedy] regarded him as a man of broad knowledge, quick intelligence, and sound judgment," then a fundamental question of civil-military relations arises. Does the American system have a place for an unelected, not congressionally confirmed military careerist of four-star rank to hold a position as influential as military representative of the president?
- What, in fact, was Taylor's influence on presidential decision making in the 1960s concerning Vietnam while he served as military representative of the president (1961–62), chairman JCS (1962–64), ambassador to Vietnam (1964–65), and presidential consultant on Vietnam (1965–68)?

• Finally, there is the central question, one that up to now has been the most elusive concerning Taylor, whose eight-year involvement with Vietnam was longer than that of any other senior American official: How much of the burden of the war must he bear as compared with those whose careers were permanently marked by the tragedy—Lyndon Johnson, Robert McNamara, and William Westmoreland?

In Maxwell Taylor's early development, as set forth in the Prologue, a few matters stand out: The loner personality is not unusual for an only child, in his case conditioned by a possessive mother. His innate intelligence and competence also were evident, especially during his cadet years.

How, we wonder, did the student and then the young officer adapt so easily to foreign languages—Asian as well as European—that he was able to communicate effectively in them? Facility in learning languages is difficult to predict. Some can acquire a vernacular ability quickly but cannot, for example, use specialized verb tenses. Apparently Taylor learned languages rapidly and precisely. His proficiency seems especially remarkable when we recall his partial deafness suffered after a Hawaiian tunnel explosion in 1924 (a matter he does not take up in his autobiography).

Taylor began his studies in the classical languages (on his mother's insistence), as well as Spanish and French, while still in high school. He continued Spanish in junior college and then took more Spanish and French at West Point. The internal music of language, as well as its internal symmetries, thus became a facility relatively early in his life.

Besides creating his own style for the presentations that command and leadership demand, Taylor clearly developed his oral expression consummately, despite the hearing problem that caused him to appear detached and aloof from those around him. In meeting this communication problem, he combined a congenial, interested, nearly professorial pose with psychological and physical distance. Perhaps this was to allow him to lip-read, to gauge facial reactions instinctively, and, ever so quickly, to adjust his response. This ability to handle his hearing problem without mechanical assistance was remarkable, but it did change his relationship with people.

The other aspect about Max's early development that bears repeating is the amount of time the young officer spent as either teacher or student. In the 1927–40 period, he was a teacher for five years and a student for eight. All this academic effort was bound to have certain effects. We can speculate about three of them.

First (although the hardest to prove) is that he approached problems and programs in a way that carried logic, unconditioned by pragmatism, to an extreme. This inclination may partially explain his infatuation with organizational solutions to problems.

The second facet, also intangible, is the effect on an impressionable lieutenant of the tough two-year Leavenworth course he undertook in 1933–35. Recall that he was one of the youngest officers in the course and had the lightest background in troop experience. Leavenworth developed and stressed such Clausewitzian maneuvers as grand turning movements, which, although they helped win World War II, perhaps embedded students too deeply in a certain concept of warfare. Would he have not been better equipped for the 1950s, and especially the 1960s, with a little less Clausewitz and a greater dose of Sun-Tzu?

The final consideration (also from the Leavenworth experience and the easiest to prove) is that Taylor made important contacts that would help send him on his way in World War II. In particular, Walter Bedell ("Beetle") Smith brought him to George Marshall's office in 1941, and Matthew Ridgway brought him to the 82d Airborne in the summer of 1942.

Taylor's service in World War II in the 82d Airborne in the Mediterranean and subsequently as commander of the 101st Airborne in northern Europe have been covered extensively in the Prologue and elsewhere. However, two matters merit further comment: his behind-the-lines mission to Rome in September 1943 and his command style in the 101st.

The one World War II decision for which Taylor was later criticized was his recommendation to Ike to cancel a planned airborne drop near Rome. There was no question of Taylor's personal courage in undertaking this mission; he was throughout World War II a soldier of valor, who dropped into Normandy with his division on D-Day. The question is, Was he too cautious in calling for cancellation when boldness might have shortened the war in Italy? My own feeling is that the operation was not feasible to begin with and that, indeed, all concerned owe a debt of gratitude to Taylor for his prudence. He prevented what would probably have been a bloodbath and might not have changed the outcome of subsequent events one iota.

As for his command style in the 101st—he was an iceman. As

Frank Moorman put it, partly in jest, in his comments to writer Clay Blair, "Taylor would cut your throat and think nothing about it." This comment was in comparison to Ridgway, who "would cry," and to Gavin, who "would laugh" under similar circumstances— exaggerated of course, to make a point. All the senior officers of the wartime 101st note in their interviews that Taylor, whatever his competence, lacked warmth in his leadership personality, a marked contrast with his predecessor, Bill Lee. As Harry Kinnard described him to me, Taylor was a cold potato as compared to Lee.

Gerald Higgins, who knew him as well as anyone in the 101st, wrote to me that Taylor was respected and liked in the sense that one appreciated his competence but not in a personal sense. He added that Taylor "did not make 'close' friends." Was he the loner from Kansas City again, with the added restriction of his impaired auricular abilities? We will never know for sure. What is significant is that both personality and impairment affected his outlook, relationships, and method of doing business.

For the Army careerist during World War II, Europe had been the place to be; as a young general of forty-three when the war ended that summer of 1945, Taylor was clearly a front-runner in a profession at the height of its prestige. His image had been further heightened in and out of the Army by his heroic mission behind the lines for Ike and, however one measures his talents in that role, by his division command. Fortunate enough to head the 101st Airborne Division on D-Day, Taylor was the first American general to land on the continent in that most memorable military action of World War II.

After the war the victorious generals went on to new assignments, but none was better suited to the man, his career, or the times than Taylor's appointment as the superintendent at West Point. Comparisons with MacArthur's arrival at the academy just after World War I were inevitable and did not hurt Taylor's reputation.

Aside from his well-known tilting with the academic board, his superintendency was fairly conservative, and he made no dramatic innovations of the type one might expect during that watershed period.

He did, though, have a bully pulpit and made the most of it. The young and handsome superintendent's public relations flowered. Taylor was an effective and frequent public speaker who was convincing, active, and energetic, "the very model of a modern major general." Making the most of the generous entertainment facilities, he had an unsurpassed guest list—Truman, Eisenhower, and Herbert

Hoover, to cite three. In all respects he was becoming quite prominent, and conventional wisdom already had him installed as a future Army chief of staff.

After he left West Point in early 1949, Taylor had three principal assignments: U.S. commander in Berlin, Army deputy chief of staff in the Pentagon, and commander of the Eighth Army in Korea. The last one deserves additional comment.

During the Korean War, the Eighth Army had four commanders. The first, Walton Walker, led the Army out of the Pusan perimeter but was killed in an accident in December 1950. Next came Matthew Ridgway, who molded the Eighth Army into a fighting army before he replaced MacArthur in Tokyo. The next was James Van Fleet, an excellent commander whose semipublic and critical assessments of Washington's war management helped Ike's 1952 campaign. (Van Fleet was especially bitter that, in his twenty-two-month command of the Eighth Army, he was not allowed to conduct a general offensive against communist Chinese forces.) Then, in February 1953, Maxwell Taylor took command.

Of the four, Taylor was the least tested in Korea, both in the duration of command—action ceased that summer—and, more important, in the lessened intensity of action during that period. For those in field units, Taylor was almost invisible, even during the last big battle of the Kumsong Salient. Perhaps this absence would have been true of any commander at that stage, but what comes through is that Taylor did not project as effectively as an Army commander in combat should.

When he arrived in Washington to be Army chief of staff in the summer of 1955, Taylor had an adequate, but not extensive, Washington background, and his outlook on budgetary and strategic issues was rational and highly professional. But his goal—to modify the Eisenhower military strategy—would have threatened the president's own budgetary goals, which were absolutely central to Ike's overall objectives.

Taylor approached his goal rationally as he developed a national military program setting forth his strategic views and introduced a supporting paper into the JCS arena. His colleagues on the Joint Chiefs of Staff, however, were not impressed. Whatever the logic of his argument, they saw it as essentially partisan for the Army.

Soon thereafter, Taylor tried to solve the problem in another way— what might be called an organizational-psychological approach. To create a forward-looking image, he wanted to embrace at least the appearance of a new technology by organizing Army divisions to fight on an atomic battlefield. He reasoned that the president would support this concept and consequently loosen the purse strings for the Army. Eisenhower thought the idea a good one, especially because he perceived a savings in personnel—a consideration quite opposite to what Taylor had in mind.

For his proposed program Taylor did secure some bureaucratic allies: the Navy, for its own reasons, and the lower levels of the State Department. However, none of this really influenced Eisenhower or his programs. Outside the administration—most notably Congress in 1959—Taylor was more successful but in an indirect way. Without getting more money for the Army at that time, he did help set the stage for the 1960 presidential campaign, in which defense issues played a prominent part.

Taylor's final effort, his publication of *The Uncertain Trumpet* after he left the Pentagon, played a part in Kennedy's 1960 campaign rhetoric. Moreover, it essentially brought about his return to office in a very influential military-political role in the Kennedy administration.

For Taylor the entire episode as Army chief of staff was not the end of a lesson; it marked both an end and a beginning. Although the exit for his military career, or at least for the standard one, it was the entryway into a new career of government service. The sound of *Trumpet* heralded Taylor as a kind of political-military figure.

His failure as chief of staff to meet the Army's goals was, in retrospect, understandable. He was pitted against one of the most formidable political-military figures of his time, Dwight Eisenhower. This president was superbly equipped, in fact and in his public image, to deal with military matters; as chief executive, he thoroughly dominated the civilian relationship with the military. In fact, Ike's presidency strengthened the civilian hand and lessened the influence of the senior military on major policy decisions. This impact would affect Taylor and others during the next decade—the decade of Vietnam.

For his part, Taylor came back to government service more politicized and more sophisticated in the ways of the Washington jungle. Whether these new qualities were desirable for a military man in the decade of Vietnam is an open question.

As Chapter 2 shows, Taylor's arrival in Kennedy's White House occurred because JFK felt that the CIA director and the Joint Chiefs had given him poor advice on the Bay of Pigs invasion. During the work of the subsequent Cuba Study Group, Taylor, as its head, had fit in well with the new White House leadership. When the group's work ended, he went on to become the first and only military representative of the president. Thus began his association with the trauma of Vietnam.

Recall that in June 1961 Diem, following through on LBJ's visit, had written Kennedy to ask for his support in expanding the South Vietnamese Army and for more American advisers. The president's query on this letter to his new military representative began, to use Taylor's own words, "an involvement in the Vietnam problem to which I was to commit a large part of my life during the next eight years."

Although JFK may not have recalled it, he already had the benefit of some of Taylor's thinking on Vietnam. In *The Uncertain Trumpet* (which had first brought Taylor to Kennedy's attention and was responsible for his new role), the outgoing chief of staff had some words on Vietnam and on Eisenhower's failure to intervene. In view of what happened later, we should look at Taylor's words in 1959.

> The ink was hardly dry on the New Look before the episode of the fall of Dien Bien Phu. . . . The deteriorating situation of the French defense there in early 1954 led to discussions in the Pentagon and White House of possible United States intervention.
>
> During these deliberations, the need was apparent for ready military forces with conventional weapons to cope with this kind of limited-war situation. Unfortunately, such forces did not then exist in sufficient strength to offer any hope of success. In May, Dien Bien Phu fell and in the following July in Geneva, Indochina was partitioned between Communism and Freedom at the 17th Parallel.[1]

Taylor seems to be saying that American forces in sufficient numbers could have prevented the fall of Dien Bien Phu, which is possibly true. He also implies that this intervention would have been worth its cost to the United States; on that point Eisenhower would not have agreed. Even if he had had sufficient American forces available, Ike would never have committed American combat forces to this kind of enterprise. The difference between their two views is dramatic, both politically and strategically.

What came out of Taylor's early assignment on Vietnam from JFK was the Taylor-Rostow mission in the fall of 1961, his high point of influence as a member of the Kennedy White House staff. The presidential decisions based on the mission report were among the great milestones of American involvement in the war.

The lightning rod for Vietnam analysts looking back at the report has always been Taylor's proposal for an American combat force of 8,000 (which Kennedy turned down), but the document is much more significant than that. Kennedy vetoed the troop proposal in such a way as to leave open its possible implementation later. Moreover, the debate on the combat force distracted the decision makers from what was really happening—a significant increase of American advisers, support personnel, and resources to Diem. By ignoring the Geneva Accords, Kennedy set in motion a chain of events whose outcome had to be further escalation. The only questions were when and how much.

All in all, the report was an extraordinary one, emanating as it did from perhaps the most prestigious member of the White House staff. Taylor was a natural for Camelot, but whatever the external trappings of urbanity and sophistication, he was a military man. Surely such a document, which focused on military problems (as contrasted to the more important political ones), would have received greater scrutiny by the political leadership had it emanated from the Joint Chiefs.

It was, further, a great contrast to Ridgway's report to Ike during the Dien Bien Phu crisis, which had emphasized the risks of an American commitment. Taylor's report to the inexperienced president was more optimistic; specifically, it substantially underestimated the enemy.

When Taylor's White House tenure ended with his becoming chairman of the JCS, he was returning to a world he knew well. The chairmanship was a job that he had wanted earlier but that Eisenhower had denied him, basically because of his opposition to Ike's strategy. Taylor is the only person to have served as chairman who was recalled from retired status. The advantages of just having worked near the Oval Office are obvious: he knew the president and understood his policies.

Less obvious is the major disadvantage: he was more politicized than any chairman to date, and the other members of JCS considered him a White House man. Still, they had to depend upon him; he was their only conduit to influence administration thinking. The Vietnam War presented a general problem for the chiefs during Taylor's tenure and even more so later in regard to their disagreement with both Kennedy's and Johnson's notions of gradualism. The problem came to the fore later when the bombing campaigns began. To the other members of the Joint Chiefs, Taylor always appeared ambivalent when dealing with the White House on this and other policy questions relating to Vietnam.

The major event in Vietnam during Taylor's two years as chairman was the Diem coup. Recall the key initiating event: the infamous August 24, 1963, cable. Unquestionably, Taylor was opposed to the cable, once he became aware of it. Where he has been faulted on this matter by his JCS colleagues is immediately afterward, specifically for not taking a stronger position against U.S. support of a coup. Such a policy change would have required new instructions to Lodge. Whether a reversal was feasible and, in particular, whether subsequent events could have been changed are problematical. With regard to Taylor, however, the incident does illustrate a bureaucratic proclivity—a failure to stand up and be counted when in the minority—that apparently began, or at least became operational, with his White House service.

Between the cable and Diem's assassination on November 1 came the first of three trips Taylor and McNamara made together to Vietnam during Taylor's tenure in the E Ring. The two would eventually part company over their Vietnam views, but during this trip (which turned out to be the final precoup assessment of Diem), they papered over their differences. Taylor was the more optimistic of the two about the Vietnam situation and slanted his report to the president that way.

After this trip the White House announced that most American military forces could be removed in about two years—an assessment that some called Harkins's rosy view. Taylor's response to senior JCS officer Gen. Bruce Palmer's assessment that Taylor was playing presidential politics with this optimism was that, although he supported this view publicly, he did not privately. He went along, he said, to put pressure on Diem and added, "if it was Presidential politics it was also a useful effort in national policy." The trumpet was playing a more political tune by this time.

His tour as ambassador to Saigon in 1964–65 was Maxwell Taylor's high noon in relation to Vietnam. It was also the most important year for presidential decisions leading to the U.S. combat role. In the summer of 1964 most options were still open for Lyndon Johnson; by the following summer there were none—except to escalate the war.

When Taylor arrived in Saigon in July 1964, his charter was the most powerful ever given an American ambassador. In effect, he was in control of American military forces in that country. Had this charter been granted to a "true" civilian, the American military undoubtedly would have objected. Actually, Taylor never made full use of the charter. Instead, he created a Mission Council composed of the senior U.S. officials of the various government agencies represented in Saigon, including MACV. In theory this council was the forum for working out decisions. In fact everyone looked to his own fiefdom in Washington for guidance and instructions.

By creating the council, Taylor accepted bureaucratic realities, whatever his charter, but two mistakes he made at the outset cut deeply into his effectiveness: not bringing his own team with him and announcing in advance that his tour would be for only one year. The weakness of the second error is too obvious to labor; the first requires some comment.

Taylor, the organizational man, had in 1962 adjusted rapidly to his JCS role—a situation he knew well—but the Saigon ambassadorship provided no such certain base. On the one hand, he was not a State Department careerist, and on the other, the JCS were not particularly prone to support this civilian "general." For one thing, the military felt that to give an ambassador such a strong military charter established a bad precedent. Moreover, his White House base began eroding by the spring of 1965. Recall McGeorge Bundy's memorandum to LBJ, probably to ensure that Taylor did not stay beyond his year and, no doubt, to push his own man as ambassador (Bundy described Taylor as "rigid, remote, and sometimes abrupt"). However, LBJ needed Taylor's public image as a senior soldier-statesman, so nothing much came of Bundy's initiative except that Taylor received no inducements to stay on past the one year.

As for the strategic views of Ambassador Taylor, two should again be stressed: the role of bombing and the employment of American combat troops. Taylor's views on both matters are not exactly what one would suppose, given his background, and he did not fully prevail in either area. Still, he had become a kind of icon for the president to display when LBJ needed credibility on Vietnam, at least with a certain constituency.

Taylor as JCS chairman, as ambassador, and later as consultant strongly advocated the efficacy of bombing the North. He saw it both as a deterrent to Hanoi's aggression in the South and as a way to prod the North to the negotiating table. This view explains the ambassador's early attempts, albeit unsuccessful, to get LBJ to bomb the

North as retaliation for the VC mortaring of Bienhoa and the explosion in the Brink's Hotel. Particularly noteworthy was his delight when the president finally did approve bombing after the Pleiku incident in early February; for this, Taylor had been "working and waiting for a year and a half to get to this point." Although a gradualist, to a point, in the application of bombing, he did not support the notion of the bombing pauses. In this sense he was his own man, somewhere between the JCS, who wanted all-out bombing, and the Defense Department civilians, who viewed it as a kind of faucet to turn on and off; their assumption was that Hanoi leaders understood what their Washington counterparts were doing and would respond in a reasonable way—which they did not.

Taylor's real bête noire, however, was the ground force commitment. The spring of 1965 made clear that American bombing had not broken the will of the North Vietnamese; thus the U.S. Marines, introduced to protect the airfields of the Rolling Thunder aircraft, were permitted to maneuver in the countryside.

On an April trip to Washington when the Marines' decision was made, Taylor resisted the commitment of additional American ground forces that Westmoreland was urging. Up to the end of his trip, Taylor felt that he had carried the day. But such a commitment also turned out to be desired by a more formidable opponent: "Highest Authority," meaning, in the lexicon of cable traffic, Lyndon Baines Johnson. At this evidence that LBJ was assuming the initiative, the ambassador was astonished. He had a brief sparring match on the issue with McNamara and Westmoreland during the Honolulu meeting later in April. Taylor lost. This momentous defeat finished the fiction of the all-powerful ambassador. Always flexible in the long run, however, Taylor later modified his position, saying that perhaps the United States had waited too long to commit American ground forces.

Despite defeat on the troop commitment matter, Taylor finished his year as ambassador and, on returning to the United States, was still willing to serve the president. His letter of resignation indicated that he was ready to assume new responsibilities for his commander in chief. Surely that was a flexible response.

In the three and one-half years of Taylor's consultancy to President Johnson, he played the role of senior statesman. His advice for LBJ focused on the Vietnam issue, which more and more became the president's preoccupation. Determining Taylor's direct influence on events in that period is not easy. He was not involved directly in the decision-making process, and his input was episodic—the wont of consultants in any case.

Taylor himself found the work "frustrating in the sense of no base of authority"; while people listened, "follow-through was another matter." Bruce Palmer, who was involved both in Vietnam and Washington planning on the war, later wondered why Taylor, during that period, was "not more successful in bringing about a sounder strategic approach to the war." To this, Taylor responded in a letter to me, "I tried to influence the strategy of the war with much less than total success." He went on to lament the weakness of the consultant's role "with no battalions, neither in the military nor diplomatic, to support him." Still, he hung on. A little power is better than no power at all.

In the early part of the consultant period, his public advocacy of the president's strategy was effective with at least a portion of the public. He did, however, develop very strong antimedia feelings, once opining to a small group of senior officers that he thought the greatest mistake of the Vietnam War was "the failure to impose censorship on the news media." This view was probably not unusual in some ways, given Taylor's military background. Still, it does indicate a fundamental lack of understanding, both of the nature of the American polity and of the sociopsychological dimension of strategy—in this case, domestic support for a limited war.

Taylor's blind spot is illustrated by other statements as well. Appearing before the Fulbright committee in early 1966, he admonished the committee that France had lost the First Indochina War in Paris, not in Vietnam. (Where else would a major power lose a limited war except on the home front?)

Later, in his memoirs, Taylor stated that he could not understand why the North Vietnamese launched the Tet Offensive and sacrificed so many of their troops. Again, he seems to have failed to grasp Hanoi's real target: the American home front, not the Vietnam battlefield. In fact, Tet 1968 collapsed that home front. The North Vietnamese understood only too well the sociopsychological dimension of strategy, as Taylor seems not to have.

With characteristic tenacity, Taylor remained an unregenerate hawk to the very end of the consultant period. For example, during the post-Tet assessment, he was one of the few of the "Wise Men" who supported the president's strategy; here he was willing to stand up and be counted. Perhaps, ambition now behind him, this was the real Maxwell Taylor, the most experienced, even if not the most philosophical, of his peers.

An overall Vietnam War problem that we have previously touched on should be highlighted at this point. My own research and the writings of many others show that military leaders in the war were dissatisfied with its management at the Washington level. It is a major theme in William Westmoreland's memoirs.

The military's main thesis is that the incremental application of power in Vietnam and the constraints placed on the use of power were the product of poor decision making by civilians. Furthermore, they believe that this approach led to a no-win situation. It permitted North Vietnam to marshal its resources in what that vastly smaller country perceived to be a total war and to prolong the conflict until the patience of the American people was exhausted.

We will never know what the result of a different strategy would have been. We do know that a graduated response did not work. Whatever else might be said about the approach taken, however, it did prevent the war from escalating beyond Indochina.

Another side of the civilian-military relationship is also pertinent. Traditionally, an adversarial relationship has long existed between American civilian and military leadership, and it continued during the Vietnam War. We are not dealing here with whether the civilians were ultimately in charge. They were. The question is one of communication.

There are, it seems to me, two reasons for this relationship of caution and bargaining. In the first place, the power bases of the two groups are different. The civilians—at least, the appointed and elected ones—have to keep in mind issues of an immediate nature bearing on domestic policy. The military leadership represents an entrenched bureaucracy who must live with decisions once they are made; meanwhile, they watch the civilians, who do not always have to live with their own decisions, come and go.

Whatever the reasons for the adversarial relationship, we should consider how it affected the Vietnam War. The war understandably minimized the adversarial relationship as compared, say, with a peacetime budget struggle. The manner in which it was minimized, however, was to paper over the real issues of the war rather than to face up to them.

In this area of military-civilian rapport where the role of soldier-statesman Taylor became critical, he was unfortunately never really able to serve as an honest broker between the two. In his military representative days, the senior military perceived him to be a de facto civilian. Later, when he returned to the Pentagon, they did not fully trust him because of his residual White House connection. Still later, as ambassador, he was somewhat resented by the senior military, who feared that his strong charter would make him operate as the "general" in charge. For better or worse, he never did attempt to play that role.

The broker role that he did try was, in any case, not effective with the military. In part this was a matter of Taylor's personality. Although nothing is inherently wrong with a senior military person's being appointed to major civilian roles (such as, in Taylor's case, the Kennedy White House or the ambassadorship to Saigon), returning to the military, especially at the level of chairman JCS, is perhaps a mistake. Taylor never was able to bridge the civilian-military gap that developed during the Vietnam War, and he may, in fact, have made doing so more difficult.

Insofar as Taylor participated in key decisions on Vietnam in 1961, 1965, and 1968, his record varies over time. His 1961 mission with Rostow was a benchmark in U.S. involvement. Despite his urbanity and impressiveness to the Kennedy White House, Taylor thought in standard military terms, and the president knew that when he assigned him the mission. Taylor's recommendation for combat troops was not really unusual, given his background, nor was the president's turning down the proposal. The real decision was the enormous increase in advisers and support personnel that Taylor proposed and that Kennedy approved. It is what JFK was anticipating when he dispatched his military representative, and it is what he got.

In the Diem coup, a watershed in U.S. involvement, Taylor was not directly involved, but when he became aware of the August 24 cable, his objections were muted. What Taylor did here is not what mattered; the problem was what he failed to do at this time—to be counted and to force the issue with the president. Perhaps he felt that doing so was not really his responsibility as JCS chairman, and in any case the certain trumpet had long since played its last note. Perhaps, given his role, Taylor was correct in this instance. In any case, Kennedy, whatever his ambivalence toward Diem, again got what he asked for.

Taylor's major setback in Vietnam decision making was the spring 1965 buildup of American forces. He was correct in his judgment to hold off the American commitment. (Think of what might have been prevented had he prevailed!) By spring, however, he was standing on an eroding power base, and his many opponents on this issue included Westmoreland. But his chief opponent was LBJ himself, who took the initiative and forced the troop commitment. In time, further escalation was inevitable. Again (as in the two previous cases with Kennedy), the president got what he wanted.

Regarding the final major decision—involving Johnson's post-Tet actions leading ultimately to U.S. withdrawal—Taylor opposed the consensus for withdrawal; he remained a hawk. With his views so far out of the mainstream and his power base so tenuous, however, he knew he had no chance to prevail.

Maxwell Taylor was one of the major American military figures of the twentieth century. He was more soldier than statesman. His major involvement in the American political scene was the Vietnam tragedy, in which his role was central but not decisive. His views were generally better than the views that did prevail. Had Diem not been eliminated and had American combat troops not been committed in 1965, who knows what might have been the result? The failure of Taylor in Vietnam decision making was not in what he did, but what he failed to do.

Taylor possessed a vision and, more than most, the ability to communicate it. Perhaps his vision was sometimes flawed or perhaps he failed to communicate it when it really mattered—during Vietnam. Others may judge that for themselves. Of one thing I am certain: few twentieth-century Americans have lived fuller or more dedicated lives.

Notes

PROLOGUE: THE SOLDIER

1. Maxwell D. Taylor, *Swords and Plowshares* (New York: W.W. Norton, 1972), p. 22.
2. John M. Taylor, *General Maxwell Taylor: The Sword and the Pen* (New York: Doubleday, 1989), p. 11.
3. Taylor, *Swords*, p. 24.
4. *Howitzer* (1922 USMA yearbook), p. 217.
5. Ibid., p. 191.
6. Taylor, *Swords*, p. 22.
7. Major J.M. Moore, Efficiency Report on Maxwell D. Taylor (MDT), Taylor 201 file.
8. Captain J. R. Bibb, Efficiency Report on MDT, Taylor 201 file.
9. Taylor, *Swords*, p. 30.
10. Samuel B. Griffin, trans., *Sun-Tzu—The Art of War* (London: Oxford University Press, 1963), p. 101.
11. Taylor, *Swords*, p. 32.
12. Ibid., pp. 33–34.
13. Barbara W. Tuchman, *Stilwell and the American Experience in China, 1911–45* (New York: Macmillan, 1971), p. 170.
14. Colonel Joseph W. Stilwell, Efficiency Report on MDT, Taylor 201 file.
15. Maxwell D. Taylor, "Japan (Combat)—Tactical Doctrine of Japanese Army," Report #9755. Tokyo: Military Attaché, April 1, 1939.
16. Taylor, *Swords*, p. 37; also Clay Blair, *Ridgway's Paratroopers: The American Airborne in World War II* (Garden City, N.Y.: Dial Press, 1985), p. 11.
17. Taylor, *Swords*, p. 38.
18. Ibid., pp. 39–40.

221

19. Ibid., p. 41.
20. Ibid., p. 43.
21. Blair, *Ridgway's Paratroopers,* p. 30.
22. Ibid., pp. 33–34.
23. Ibid., pp. 39–40.
24. Ibid., pp. 40.
25. Maxwell D. Taylor, letter to George Marshall, December 12, 1942, Marshall Foundation Archives, Lexington, Va.
26. Taylor, *Swords,* p. 46.
27. Blair, *Ridgway's Paratroopers,* p. 69.
28. Taylor, *Swords,* p. 50.
29. Commanding General, Hq., Seventh U.S. Army, September 3, 1943.
30. Dwight D. Eisenhower, *Crusade in Europe* (Garden City, N.Y.: Doubleday, 1948), pp. 183–84.
31. William Tudor Gardiner served as governor of Maine from 1929 to 1933. He learned to fly in the mid-1930s and in 1942 received a wartime commission in the Air Force. He died in 1953.
32. M.D. Taylor and W.T. Gardiner, "Memorandum for AC of S G-3, Allied Forces Hq., September 9, 1943," pp. 56–67.
33. Taylor, *Swords,* pp. 56–63.
34. Kenneth Strong, *Intelligence at the Top* (Garden City, N.Y.: Doubleday, 1969), pp. 159–61.
35. Taylor, *Swords,* p. 70.
36. Blair, *Ridgway's Paratroopers,* p. 197.
37. Taylor, *Swords,* p. 79.
38. Maxwell D. Taylor, letter from Gerald J. Higgins to author, July 20, 1981.
39. Ibid.
40. Ibid.
41. Taylor, *Swords,* p. 97.
42. Higgins letter.
43. Taylor, *Swords,* p. 110.
44. Quoted in K. Bruce Galloway and Robert Bowie Johnson, Jr., *West Point: America's Power Fraternity* (New York: Simon and Schuster, 1973), p. 45.
45. Taylor, *Swords,* p. 113.
46. Ibid., p. 112. Eisenhower's influence on both the concept and its ultimate actualization is further verified by a letter to the author from Col. Red Reeder, October 30, 1983.
47. Higgins letter.
48. Maxwell D. Taylor, letter from General Harbord to Gen. John J. Pershing, June 10, 1946, General Correspondence, John J. Pershing Papers, Library of Congress, p. 2.
49. J. Taylor, *General Maxwell Taylor,* p. 155.

50. Log sheet, "Addresses of Major General Maxwell Taylor," Taylor Papers, National Defense University Library (NDUL).
51. Taylor, *Swords*, p. 179.
52. J. Taylor, *General Maxwell Taylor*, p. 150.
53. "Soldierly Conduct," letter from David K. Carlisle to the *New York Times Book Review*, June 30, 1989.
54. Taylor, *Swords*, pp. 119–22.
55. Walter Millis, ed., *The Forrestal Diaries* (New York: The New York Herald Tribune and the Viking Press, 1951), p. 194.
56. Taylor, *Swords*, p. 122.
57. Ibid., p. 123.
58. Ibid.
59. Ibid., pp. 123–30.
60. J. Taylor, *General Maxwell Taylor*, p. 160.
61. Taylor, *Swords*, pp. 130–32.
62. Ibid., p. 132.
63. Accounts by Jim Lucas and Bob Considine of interviews with MacArthur in 1954, the *New York Times*, April 9, 1964, p. 16.
64. Ibid.
65. Taylor, *Swords*, pp. 135–37.
66. Ibid., p. 137.
67. J. Taylor, *General Maxwell Taylor*, p. 183.

CHAPTER 1 · THE GENERAL AND THE PRESIDENT

1. Maxwell D. Taylor, *Swords and Plowshares* (New York: W.W. Norton, 1972), p. 168.
2. Key appointments were John Foster Dulles as secretary of state, George Humphrey as secretary of the treasury, Charles Wilson as secretary of defense, and Arthur Radford as JCS chairman. Ike also appointed new military chiefs of service shortly after taking office: Gen. Matthew B. Ridgway, Army; Gen. Nathan B. Twining, Air Force; and Adm. Robert B. Carney, Navy.
3. John S.D. Eisenhower (JSDE), interview with author, April 1972, and unpublished manuscript by JSDE in his private papers.
4. Douglas Kinnard, *The Secretary of Defense* (Lexington, Ky.: The University Press of Kentucky, 1980), p. 51.
5. Memorandum of record of Taylor's meeting with the president (hereafter cited as MR or MCP, memorandum of conference with the president), February 24, 1955. Taylor tells the story in more general terms in *The Uncertain Trumpet* (New York: Harper, 1959), p. 28. In view of later events, I find the two versions significantly different on the question of what Taylor's interpretation of what agreement, if any, he was making with the president on support of his views.

6. Memorandum to Adm. Arthur Radford, chairman Joint Chiefs of Staff from Col. Andrew Goodpaster, defense liaison officer (White House), February 14, 1956.
7. Douglas Kinnard, *President Eisenhower and Strategy Management* (McLean, Va.: Pergamon-Brassey's, 1989), p. 51.
8. MCP, March 30, 1956.
9. MCP, May 24, 1956. Taylor describes the background for this conference in *Uncertain Trumpet,* pp. 36–46.
10. MCP, October 11, 1956.
11. MCP, December 19, 1956.
12. MR (December 29 meeting in Pentagon), dated January 12, 1957.
13. Statement contained in Taylor papers, National Defense University Archives, Fort McNair, Washington, D.C.
14. MCP, October 30, 1957. The Eisenhower papers have dozens of guest lists for stag dinners of various types. Typically, after dinner the group would gather for discussion in the White House living area. Eisenhower consistently directed the conversation toward matters of interest to himself, either to obtain information or to convince others of the validity of his own views.
15. MR of stag dinner, November 4, 1957.
16. MR of meeting in Pentagon, April 7, 1958.
17. Taylor, *Uncertain Trumpet,* pp. 59–65. Gerard Smith, who was present, confirms that the secretary of state failed to support Taylor on this occasion. Gerard Smith transcript, Dulles Oral History Project, Firestone Library, Princeton University.
18. Taylor, *Uncertain Trumpet,* pp. 70–71.
19. MR, December 3, 1958.
20. After six years in office, and with Congress heavily controlled by the Democrats, Eisenhower was well aware of the need for carefully thought-out legislative tactics. Apropos of this, an informal body of rules had been developed to guide executive leaders appearing before congressional committees. They were designed to convey the impression of a united administration and to prevent executive personnel from providing gratuitous information to Congress. No testimony was allowed on matters under consideration by the administration but not yet resolved or released or on how particular determinations had been made by the president. MR, March 7, 1958.
21. Taylor, *Uncertain Trumpet,* p. 78.
22. MCP, March 9, 1959.
23. MCP, March 6, 1959.
24. Interview with Bruce Palmer, Jr., February 1989. Writing a book for commercial publication using government resources during working hours and while drawing a government salary for another job would be ethically unacceptable by today's standards. Substantively,

the book covered the arguments against reliance on massive retaliation and the need for a strategy of flexible response; it stressed limited war in which the Army would play the prime role. Taylor also called for a major overhaul of the organization of the Joint Chiefs. Stylistically, *The Uncertain Trumpet* left much to be desired, being jargonistic and repetitive and resembling a series of Army briefing papers.

CHAPTER 2 · A SOLDIER IN CAMELOT

1. The Bay of Pigs episode has been extensively documented and commented upon. The most recent comprehensive treatment, containing an excellent bibliography, is Trumbull Higgins's *The Perfect Failure* (New York: W.W. Norton, 1987). The only important, although brief, commentary on the Bay of Pigs since Higgins's book is in Thomas Schoenbaum's biography of Dean Rusk, *Waging Peace and War* (New York: Simon and Schuster, 1988).
2. Arthur M. Schlesinger, Jr., *A Thousand Days* (Boston: Houghton Mifflin, 1965), p. 238.
3. General Taylor's letter to President Kennedy, with accompanying memorandum and testimony obtained during the investigation by the Study Group, is contained in *Operation Zapata*, ed. Luis Aguilar (Frederick, Md.: University Publications of America, 1981).
4. Author's interview with Gen. Lyman Lemnitzer, April 1981.
5. Working paper, Taylor Papers, NDUL, Washington, D.C., with the following notation in Taylor's hand: "This was read by President Kennedy to JCS about May 27, 1961."
6. What Taylor himself hoped for in the way of a charter he never made clear in his later writings or interviews. However, a letter from Maj. Gen. Chester Clifton, military aide to JFK, to his one-time associate (in possession of the author) James M. Connell, is revealing.

When it was agreed that Taylor would be called back to active duty and put on the White House staff, the next question was what would be his duties, where would he fit in, and what would be his title. Max was asked to draw up a memo recommending the duties he would be assigned, and the title he thought he should have. JFK was very leery of getting a "super chief" between him and the Chiefs.

The outlined duties were O.K. and then Max suggested the title that Leahy had had with FDR in World War II. But Kennedy said that this was before a JCS organization was in place, and a Chairman had been established by law. Furthermore, he didn't want Max to get the idea that he "ranked" the Chairman, or any of the chiefs.

When it came down to the last moment of announcing this appointment, JFK called me in and said to take General Taylor into Pierre Salinger and check over the press release and the title. He told me to see that General Taylor didn't come out with the Leahy title, and to let it be something "less than that." Hanging in there until the last minute, Max Taylor finally agreed, just minutes before the morning briefing, to the title he finally was given.

7. Letter from President John F. Kennedy to Gen. Maxwell Taylor, dated June 26, 1961, Taylor Papers, NDUL.
8. The president's letter to the JCS is National Security Action Memorandum (NSAM) 55, June 28, 1961, "Relations of Joint Chiefs to the President in Cold War Operations."
9. Quoted in *Time,* July 28, 1961, p. 10.
10. Much of the material on the White House bureaucratic politics of the MILREP period is contained in formal notes and memorandums deposited in Taylor Papers (NDUL). The author supplemented this with interviews.
11. Oral history interview with Roswell Gilpatric, May 27, 1970, by Dennis J. O'Brien for the JFK Library, p. 70.
12. Interview with Robert McNamara by author at World Bank, December 11, 1980.
13. Remarks by Maxwell Taylor at a symposium held at the Marshall Foundation, Lexington, Va., March 25, 1977, at which the author was present.
14. The most complete bibliographical essay on the event is Lester H. Brune, *The Missile Crisis of October 1961* (Claremont, Calif.: Regina Books, 1985). For more recent commentary see Raymond L. Garthoff, *Reflections on the Cuban Missile Crisis* (Washington, D.C.: The Brookings Institution, 1987); and "Cuban Missile Crisis: The Soviet Story," *Foreign Policy* 72 (Fall 1988): 61–80.

CHAPTER 3 · THE INHERITANCE AND THE MISSION

1. One irony of these developments, which resulted from the outbreak of the Korean War, is that they came at a time when French public opinion was wavering on support of the war in Indochina and served to strengthen those interests in France committed to achieving "victory" there. These interests merged with U.S. perceptions that the preservation of a noncommunist Indochina was vital. The combination of a wavering French home front and American perceptions gave French officials leverage on U.S. policymakers (by threatening directly or indirectly to pull out of Indochina) that permitted retention for a time of a colonial Indochina, contrary to American policy.

2. The origin of the talks was a meeting in Berlin in January and February between the foreign ministers of the United States, Britain, France, and the Soviet Union. Agreement was reached to hold an international conference in Geneva beginning in April to deal first with Korea and then with Indochina. The United States was strongly opposed to including Indochina; but the French were adamant and were supported by the British.

3. A vast amount of writing, including accounts by the principals themselves, concerns this mission. In the State Department, *Foreign Relations of the United States, 1961–1963, Volume 1, Vietnam, 1961* (Washington: Government Printing Office, 1988), 358 of the 768 pages of text are concerned with the mission and its immediate aftermath.

4. Lansdale was not one of Taylor's favorites. He considered many of Lansdale's ideas to be not feasible. In the early 1950s Lansdale had been an adviser to Philippine Defense Minister Ramon Magsaysay in the successful campaign against the communist guerrilla movement.

5. The formal decision paper approved at the NSC meeting was NSAM 111, published on November 22, 1961. It was essentially the same recommendations contained in the Rusk-McNamara memorandum, with the categorical commitment to save South Vietnam deleted. It is printed in *Foreign Relations,* pp. 656–657.

CHAPTER 4 · VIEW FROM THE E RING

1. Of the vast body of books that touch on the American experience in Vietnam during the 1962–64 period, I found the following most useful in the context of this chapter: William Colby, *Lost Victory* (Chicago: Contemporary Books, 1989); William Gibbons, *The U.S. Government and the Vietnam War, Part II, 1961–1964* (Princeton: Princeton University Press, 1986); Lyndon Johnson, *The Vantage Point* (New York: Holt, Rinehart and Winston, 1971); Frederick Nolting, *From Trust to Tragedy* (New York: Praeger, 1988); William J. Rust, *Kennedy in Vietnam* (New York: Charles Scribner's Sons, 1985); and Thomas J. Schoenbaum, *Waging Peace and War* (New York: Simon and Schuster, 1988).

2. Maxwell Taylor, *Swords and Plowshares* (New York: W.W. Norton, 1972), pp. 257–60.

3. Neil Sheehan, *A Bright Shining Lie* (New York: Random House, 1988), p. 99.

4. William Hammond, *The Military and the Media* (Washington: Government Printing Office, 1988), pp. 28–38.

5. Gibbons, *U.S. Government and Vietnam War,* II, p. 134.

6. Ibid., pp. 134–35.

7. Ibid., pp. 137–39.

8. The best account of the events of 1963 in South Vietnam leading up to Diem's assassination is contained in Ellen Hammer, *A Death in November* (New York: Oxford University Press, 1987). An excellent journalistic account is "Untold Story of the Road to War in Vietnam," *U.S. News and World Report,* October 10, 1983.

9. Maxwell D. Taylor, "Memories of Peace and War," *American Heritage* (April/May 1981). See also Taylor, *Swords,* pp. 291–95.

10. MR by Maj. Gen. V.H. Krulak (VHK) of White House meeting of August 26, 1963. This and subsequent MRs are contained in the Taylor Papers, NDUL.

11. MR by VHK of White House meeting, August 27, 1963.

12. *U.S. News and World Report* (October 10, 1983): 8 VN.

13. MR by VHK of White House meeting, August 28, 1963.

14. MR by VHK of White House meeting, August 29, 1963.

15. Back-channel message, August 29, 1963, Taylor Papers, NDUL.

16. MR by VHK of White House meeting, August 31, 1963.

17. MR by VHK of White House meeting, September 10, 1963.

18. MR by VHK of White House meeting, September 11, 1963.

19. Extract from memorandum of conversation with Diem, Taylor Papers, NDUL.

20. Interview with John Barlow Martin, in *Robert Kennedy in His Own Words,* ed. Edwin O. Guthman and Jeffrey Shulman (New York: Bantam Books, 1988), p. 399.

21. Taylor, *Swords,* p. 301.

22. Ibid., p. 302.

23. Mark Perry, *Four Stars* (Boston: Houghton Mifflin, 1989), p. 130. Perry is a Washington reporter who specializes in military and intelligence issues.

24. Johnson, *Vantage Point,* p. 43.

25. Ibid., p. 63.

26. Taylor, *Swords,* p. 309.

27. *Pentagon Papers,* Gravel ed. (Boston: Beacon Press, 1971), vol. 2, p. 412.

28. William Westmoreland, *A Soldier Reports* (Garden City, N.Y.: Doubleday, 1976), p. 67.

29. Maxwell Taylor, letter to Robert McNamara, July 1, 1964, Taylor Papers, NDUL.

CHAPTER 5 · PEARL OF THE ORIENT

1. Letter quoted in *Pentagon Papers,* Gravel ed. (Boston: Beacon Press, 1971), vol. 3, p. 79.

2. Richard Holbrook, interview with author, April 13, 1981.

3. Johnson gives his view of his experience as deputy ambassador in *The*

Right Hand of Power (Englewood Cliffs, N.J.: Prentice-Hall, 1984), Chapter 11.

4. Paper, "U.S. Objectives in Southeast Asia," contained in Taylor Papers, NDUL.

5. *Chronology of Events while Ambassador to the Republic of Viet-Nam July 1964–July 1965*, Taylor Papers, NDUL.

6. Public Law 88-409, passed August 10, 1964.

7. Taylor tells his version of the trip in *Swords and Plowshares* (New York: W.W. Norton, 1972), pp. 320–21. In chapters 25–28 he discusses at some length the personalities of the South Vietnamese government leaders with whom he had to deal.

8. From the unpublished manuscript of William Bundy, which he made available to me at the Council of Foreign Relations Building. It is now deposited in the John Kennedy and Lyndon Johnson presidential libraries and was of considerable assistance in clarifying President Johnson's actions on Vietnam during the 1964–65 period.

9. *Pentagon Papers*, Gravel ed., vol. 3, pp. 666–73.

10. William Bundy papers, pp. 9–13, 14, 15.

11. Ibid., pp. 9–18, 19.

12. Taylor's message to the South Vietnamese leadership is contained in "Report on Washington Attitudes," Taylor Papers, NDUL.

13. Taylor's version is in *Swords*, Chapter 26. That of his deputy, U. Alexis Johnson, is in *Right Hand of Power*, pp. 417–19; Ky's is in *Twenty Years and Twenty Days* (New York: Stein and Day, 1976), pp. 53–57 and passim.

14. An interesting perspective of the Quat period from a Vietnamese point of view is in Bui Diem, *In the Jaws of History* (Boston: Houghton Mifflin, 1987), Chapters 17 and 18.

15. John M. Taylor, *General Maxwell Taylor: The Sword and the Pen* (New York: Doubleday, 1989), p. 311.

16. William Conrad Gibbons, *The U.S. Government and the Vietnam War, Part III, January–July 1965* (Princeton: Princeton University Press, 1989), pp. 47–51.

17. Lyndon Baines Johnson, *The Vantage Point* (New York: Holt, Rinehart and Winston, 1971), p. 128.

18. J. Taylor, *General Maxwell Taylor*, p. 308.

19. Gibbons, *U.S. Government and Vietnam War, III*, p. 67.

20. Phillip B. Davidson, *Vietnam at War* (Novato, Calif.: Presidio Press, 1988), pp. 336–42.

21. *Pentagon Papers*, vol. 3, p. 335.

22. Memorandum to President Johnson, March 6, 1965. See Gibbons, *U.S. Government and Vietnam War, III*, p. 153, especially n. 67.

23. William C. Westmoreland, *A Soldier Reports* (New York: Doubleday, 1976), p. 125.

24. Memorandum to the president, March 31, 1965. NSC History, Deployment of Major Forces to Vietnam, vol. II, LBJ Library.
25. MR, meeting in Secretary Rusk's office, 10:30 A.M., April 3, 1965, Taylor Papers, NDUL.
26. Cables, American Embassy, Saigon, to secretary of state, 5 P.M. and 8 P.M., April 14, 1965. Cited in Gibbons, *U.S. Government and Vietnam War, III*, pp. 226, 227.
27. Memorandum for the president, April 14, 1965. Cited in Gibbons, *U.S. Government and Vietnam War, III*, p. 228.
28. Ibid., p. 228.
29. Ibid., pp. 228–30.
30. Diary entry, April 18–22, 1965, Taylor Papers, NDUL.
31. Larry Berman, *Planning a Tragedy* (New York: W.W. Norton, 1982), pp. 64, 65.
32. Taylor, *Swords*, p. 344.
33. Ibid., p. 345.
34. Memorandum for the president, July 1, 1965, LBJ Library.
35. Gibbons, *U.S. Government and Vietnam War, III*, p. 383.
36. Cable to president, July 4, 1965, 1:10 P.M., NSC Histories, Deployment of Major U.S. Forces to Vietnam, vol. VI, Tabs 357–83.
37. Cyrus Vance, cable to McNamara 172042Z, July 17, 1965. Westmoreland's comment is in *A Soldier Reports*, p. 143. Some doubt exists, however, as to whether LBJ had really made up his mind yet. This question is discussed with additional documentation in John Burke and Fred Greenstein, *How Presidents Test Reality* (New York: Russell Sage Foundation, 1989), p. 215.
38. Johnson, *Vantage Point*, p. 324.
39. David Halberstam, *The Best and the Brightest* (New York: Random House, 1969), pp. 599, 600. Mark Perry in *Four Stars* (Boston: Houghton Mifflin, 1989), p. 156, tells how Gen. Harold K. Johnson, Army chief of staff at the time, almost resigned his position over the president's failure to mobilize the reserves. Johnson told me somewhat the same story in an interview in my home in Burlington, Vermont, on September 12, 1981.
40. Memorandum to the president, Subject: Progress on Vietnamese Diplomatic Front, Tuesday, July 27, 1965, 4:30 P.M.
41. Gibbons, *U.S. Government and Vietnam War, III*, pp. 437–38.

CHAPTER 6 · MR. JOHNSON'S WAR

1. Lou Schwartz, White House memo to John Macy, September 2, 1965, Taylor Papers, NDUL.
2. Maxwell D. Taylor, *Swords and Plowshares* (New York: W.W. Norton, 1972), p. 359.

3. Presidential Office Log, 1965, LBJ Library, Austin.
4. John M. Taylor, *General Maxwell Taylor: The Sword and the Pen* (New York: Doubleday, 1989), p. 325.
5. Taylor, *Swords,* p. 359.
6. Maxwell D. Taylor, "George Catlett Marshall Memorial Address," October 27, 1965, p. 4.
7. Neil Sheehan, *A Bright Shining Lie* (New York: Random House, 1988), p. 579.
8. Taylor, *Swords,* p. 360.
9. McGeorge Bundy, memorandum to the president, "Pros and Cons of Immediate Resumption of the Bombing," January 24, 1966, LBJ Library, Austin.
10. William P. Bundy and John McNaughton, memorandum to Gen. William Westmoreland, February 8, 1966. Given to author by General Westmoreland.
11. Taylor, *Swords,* p. 365.
12. "General Taylor Hits 'Holding Strategy,' Defends Vietnam Policy," *U.S. News and World Report* (February 14, 1966): 20.
13. Maxwell D. Taylor, statement to Fulbright Committee, February 17, 1966, in *Department of State Bulletin,* March 7, 1966.
14. Maxwell D. Taylor, memorandum for the president, "Cessation of Bombing Attacks on North Vietnam," August 23, 1966, Taylor Papers, NDUL.
15. Maxwell D. Taylor, letter to President Johnson, January 3, 1967, Taylor Papers, NDUL.
16. Maxwell D. Taylor, letter to President Johnson with attached memorandum for record of Vietnam visit, January 30, 1967, Taylor Papers, NDUL.
17. *New York Times,* January 30, 1967, p. 27.
18. Maxwell D. Taylor, letter to President Johnson, May 11, 1967, Taylor Papers, NDUL.
19. Cited in Larry Berman, *Lyndon Johnson's War* (New York: W.W. Norton, 1969), p. 44.
20. Maxwell D. Taylor, MR, "Meeting with the President, July 12, 1967," Taylor Papers, NDUL.
21. Clifford's comments are in "A Viet Nam Reappraisal," *Foreign Affairs* 47 (July 1969): 66. Taylor's memorandum for Kissinger, dated June 26, 1969, is in Taylor Papers, NDUL.
22. A good inside account of these hearings is in Philip G. Goulding, *Confirm or Deny* (New York: Harper and Row, 1970), Chapter 6.
23. Lyndon Baines Johnson, *The Vantage Point* (New York: Holt, Rinehart and Winston, 1971), p. 267.
24. Maxwell D. Taylor, "The Cause in Vietnam Is Being Won," *New York Times Magazine* (October 15, 1967): 36.

25. Johnson, *Vantage Point,* pp. 372–77.
26. Maxwell D. Taylor, letter to President Johnson with enclosure, "An Estimate of the Vietnam Situation, November 1967," November 6, 1967, Taylor Papers, NDUL.
27. Reproduced in Johnson, *Vantage Point,* pp. 600–601.
28. The night before, Westmoreland had a private session with the president. In view of later events, the general's diary entry for November 20, 1967, is worth quoting (Westmoreland Papers, History File, LBJ Library).

> That evening we had a family visit with President and Mrs. Johnson which was also attended by Senator Russell. After dinner Senator Russell departed early and the ladies retired. [He and the president put in an appearance at a dinner for Senator Dirksen and then returned to White House.]
>
> The President and I resumed our discussion and talked until after 11 p.m. The President let his hair down. He told me that Secretary McNamara was leaving to take advantage of a "big job." . . . The President expected to appoint Clark Clifford to replace him. The President did not plan to be a candidate in the 1968 presidential election. He asked me what would be the reaction of the troops. I responded to the effect that if the troops were told why the President had made his decision they would understand and it would not adversely affect their morale. President explained that his health was not good and that he and "Lady Bird" were tired and recalled the fact that the Constitution did not provide for an invalid President—and referred to the illness of President Wilson and President Eisenhower. The President emphasized the sensitivity of our discussion. I stated that I would not mention it before his announcement to anyone.

29. Cable, Westmoreland to Abrams, 252203Z November 1967, Westmoreland Papers, Message File, LBJ Library.
30. Early in the Khe Sanh siege, Westmoreland had his staff look into the possibility of using tactical atomic munitions there (code name Fractured Jaw). This contingency plan, based on a discussion between LBJ and Wheeler, was leaked to the press on the same day, February 9, that Westmoreland approved it. The furor over the press leak forced LBJ, through Wheeler, to tell Westmoreland to stop the planning. About the same time Giap, for whatever reason, seemed to lose his determination to overrun the base at Khe Sanh, although the battle continued in one form or other until early April. In time the base was evacuated. Throughout, the siege itself was overplayed by the media. Giap mismanaged the battle but so—to a lesser extent—did Westmoreland, though by chance Khe Sanh turned out to be perhaps Westy's best battlefield success in Vietnam.

31. Maxwell D. Taylor, paper for president, "Enemy Scenario of the Future," February 9, 1968, Taylor Papers, NDUL.
32. Maxwell D. Taylor, memorandum for the president, "Further Reinforcements for Viet-Nam," February 10, 1968, National Security Council Histories (NSCH), LBJ Library.
33. Wheeler message to Westmoreland (JCS 01695, 1201082); Wheeler memorandum for the president on the telephone call (CM-3003-68 of February 12, 1968); and Maxwell D. Taylor, memorandum for the president, "Comments on General Westmoreland's Cable of February 12, 1968," February 12, 1968, are all in NSCH, LBJ Library.
34. Maxwell D. Taylor, memorandum for the president, "General Wheeler's Visit to Viet-Nam," NSCH, LBJ Library.
35. Of the numerous good interpretations of events connected with these reassessments, the most authoritative coverage remains Herbert Y. Schandler, *The Unmaking of a President* (Princeton: Princeton University Press, 1977). An excellent later analysis, particularly as to the motives and actions of JCS Chairman Wheeler, is in Phillip B. Davidson, *Vietnam at War* (Novato, Calif.: Presidio Press, 1988), Chapter 18.
36. Taylor, *Swords,* pp. 387, 388.
37. Maxwell D. Taylor, memorandum, "Vietnam Alternatives," March 2, 1968, NSCH, LBJ Library.
38. Schandler, *Unmaking,* pp. 175, 176.
39. Maxwell D. Taylor, letter to president, March 9, 1968, NSCH, LBJ Library.
40. Taylor, *Swords,* p. 391.
41. Earlier that month, General Westmoreland received word from the president that shortly he would be departing Vietnam to become the chief of staff of the U.S. Army. Apparently McNamara had recommended the change in January, before Tet, and Clifford in March made a similar recommendation. General Creighton W. Abrams, Westmoreland's deputy and West Point classmate, was his successor in Vietnam.
42. Maxwell D. Taylor, memorandum for the president, April 1, 1968, Taylor Papers, NDUL.
43. J. Taylor, *General Maxwell Taylor,* p. 356.
44. Maxwell D. Taylor, memorandum for the president, "Negotiations," May 23, 1968, Taylor Papers, NDUL.
45. Maxwell D. Taylor, letter to the president, May 31, 1968, Taylor Papers, NDUL.
46. Maxwell D. Taylor, "Bobby Kennedy," September 3, 1968, Taylor Papers, NDUL.
47. Maxwell D. Taylor, memorandum for the president, "The Stalemate in Paris," July 17, 1968, Taylor Papers, NDUL.
48. Maxwell D. Taylor, memorandum for the president, "Negotiation Fallacies," December 3, 1968, Taylor Papers, NDUL.

49. Taylor, *Swords,* p. 398.

CHAPTER 7 · AFTERWARD: THE HIGH SONG IS OVER

1. John M. Taylor, *General Maxwell Taylor: The Sword and the Pen* (New York: Doubleday, 1989), p. 360.
2. Maxwell D. Taylor, letter to Henry Kissinger, December 26, 1986, Taylor Papers, NDUL.
3. J. Taylor, *General Maxwell Taylor,* p. 359.
4. Ibid., pp. 362–63.
5. Neil Sheehan, quoted in Josephine Samudio, ed., *Book Review Digest—1972* (New York: H.W. Wilson Co., 1972), p. 1278.
6. Maxwell D. Taylor, *Swords and Plowshares* (New York: Doubleday, 1972), p. 408.
7. R.W. Komer, *Bureaucracy Does Its Thing* (Santa Monica, Calif.: Rand Corp., 1972), p. 124.
8. Taylor, *Swords,* p. 408.
9. Maxwell D. Taylor, letter to Henry Kissinger, October 30, 1972, Taylor Papers, NDUL.
10. Henry Kissinger, letter to Taylor, November 9, 1972, Taylor Papers, NDUL.
11. Daniel F. Gilmore, "No Heroes, Just Bums: I Include Myself," United Press International, May 4, 1975.
12. Maxwell D. Taylor, "The Reality of the Soviet Threat," address at Columbia University, October 17, 1977.
13. Samuel B. Griffith, trans. *Sun-Tzu—The Art of War* (New York: Oxford University Press, 1980), p. 84.
14. Maxwell D. Taylor, "Analogies (II): Was Desert I Another Bay of Pigs?" *Washington Post,* May 12, 1980.
15. Maxwell D. Taylor, "How Reagan Can Pull Policies Together," *Washington Post,* December 19, 1980.
16. Maxwell D. Taylor, "This Is No Way to Reform the Joint Chiefs," *Washington Post,* September 10, 1982.
17. Nikolay Portugalov, "West Europe Should Cure Itself of Strategic Schizophrenia," *USSR International Affairs, Western Europe* (Wire dispatch, Moscow TASS International Service, LDO 91114, August 9, 1979).
18. Edward P. Morgan, "In the Public Interest" (National Public Radio Commentary #516), recorded September 15, 1980, p. 1.
19. William F. Buckley, Jr., "The Uncounted Enemy," *Washington Post,* February 2, 1982, p. A15.
20. Maxwell D. Taylor, "The Hatchet Job on Westmoreland," *Washington Post,* February 5, 1982.
21. J. Taylor, *General Maxwell Taylor,* p. 383.

22. Maxwell D. Taylor, "It Wasn't Over on May 8," *Washington Post,* May 8, 1985, p. A24.
23. Maxwell D. Taylor, letter to author, July 9, 1985.
24. Quoted in J. Taylor, *General Maxwell Taylor,* p. 386.
25. Thomas Taylor, Eulogy for Maxwell D. Taylor, April 23, 1987.
26. From Humbert Wolfe, *Requiem* (London: Ernest Benn, 1927), p. 123.

CHAPTER 8 · MAXWELL TAYLOR—AN INTERPRETATION

1. Maxwell Taylor, *The Uncertain Trumpet* (New York: Harper, 1959), pp. 24–25.

Sources

Because of the vast, ever-growing amount of material available to researchers on the American experience in Vietnam, a comprehensive bibliography could become a major work in its own right. My purpose here is merely to indicate the sources I utilized in my research on this book.

A. INTERVIEWS

1. I conducted twelve interviews with Maxwell D. Taylor in the winter and spring of 1981 at his apartment at 2500 Massachusetts Avenue in Washington, D.C. Each was about two hours.

2. I conducted the following interviews with other principals generally in the same time period and of about the same duration: George Ball, Martin Blumenson, Hugh Bullock, McGeorge Bundy, William P. Bundy, Arleigh Burke, Bruce Clarke, J. Lawton Collins, Charles Daniel, Julian Ewell, Michael Forrestal, James Gavin, Edward Gillette, Robert Ginsburg, Andrew Goodpaster, Richard Holbrook, Harold K. Johnson, U. Alexis Johnson, Phelps Jones, Ethel Kennedy, Harry Kinnard, Robert Komer, William Lawton, Lawrence Legere, Lyman Lemnitzer, William McCaffrey, Mark McClure, Robert McNamara, Carter Magruder, Frederick Nolting, George Olmsted, Bruce Palmer, Thomas Parrott, Walter Poole, Red Reeder, Walt Rostow, John Taylor, Arthur Trudeau, Paul Warnke, and C. Tyler Wood.

3. Interviews of Taylor contained in the Taylor Papers (described below under "Documents") that were most useful to me were by Richard Polak, Charles R. Smith, Steve Feinberg, Elspeth Rostow, Richard A. Marion, and BDM Tapes.

I also conducted correspondence with a number of individuals who knew Taylor. One of great value was with retired Maj. Gen. Gerald Higgins, who knew Taylor in World War II and when he was superintendent at West Point. His comments were detailed and perceptive.

I also conducted a correspondence (although not in depth) with Taylor from about 1979 until a few months before his death in 1987. It was not of great direct use in my research.

4. Oral histories in the presidential libraries that were especially useful are:

John F. Kennedy Presidential Library: Roswell Gilpatric, Roger Hilsman, Earle Wheeler, and Maxwell Taylor.

Lyndon Johnson Presidential Library: Michael Forrestal, Roger Hilsman, U. Alexis Johnson, Maxwell Taylor, John Roche, Earle Wheeler.

B. DOCUMENTS

1. I enjoyed access to General Taylor's personal papers, which are deposited in the National Defense University Library (NDUL) at Fort McNair, Washington, D.C. These comprise some 33 linear feet. They are well catalogued, and a small percentage are very useful for researchers.

2. Other collections containing Vietnam documents that I found useful in a less systematic way than the NDUL documents are at the Army Center of Military History in Washington; the Library of Congress; the National Archives; the Washington National Records Center at Suitland, Maryland; and the Military History Institute at Carlisle Barracks, Pennsylvania; the last deserves special note for the Vietnam researcher. They can be conveniently divided into two parts.

Private Collections. There are about seventy-five individual private collections of retired senior Army officials—almost without exception general officers—who were connected with or served in Vietnam. These number some 846 boxes of material. Included are completed oral history transcripts, although some of these are still closed because of donor restrictions or incomplete processing. The Senior Officer Oral History Project has interviewed more than 150 officers, the majority of whom saw service in Vietnam.

Documents Collections. There are two basic document collections of Vietnam: the Basement Collection contains approximately 70 linear feet; the E Level Collection has approximately 58 linear feet. The Basement Collection consists primarily of five file cabinets of MACV and USARV (U.S. Army, Vietnam) records. The E Level Collection is much wider in scope, consisting of Vietnam documents and reports that were sent to the Army War College as part of normal or special distribution. They are filed by actual reporting unit. A very valuable card catalog is located in the Main Reading Room.

3. Holdings at the John F. Kennedy and Lyndon Baines Johnson libraries are essential; they have generally been available through such works as

William Conrad Gibbons and to a lesser extent Larry Berman (both listed in "Books").

4. I used earlier research I conducted on the Eisenhower period, most importantly the private papers of John S.D. Eisenhower, which are now deposited in the Eisenhower Library in Abilene.

C. BOOKS (only those most relevant to this work are listed).

Acheson, Dean. *Present at the Creation: My Years in the State Department.* New York: W.W. Norton, 1969.

Aliano, Richard A. *American Defense Policy from Eisenhower to Kennedy.* Athens: Ohio University Press, 1975.

Asprey, Robert B. *War in the Shadows: The Guerrilla in History.* Vols. 1 and 2. New York: Doubleday, 1975.

Ball, George. *The Past Has Another Pattern.* New York: W.W. Norton, 1982.

Bodard, Lucien. *The Quicksand War: Prelude to Vietnam.* Boston: Little, Brown, 1967.

Braestrup, Peter. *Big Story: How the American Press and Television Reported and Interpreted the Crisis of Tet 1968 in Vietnam and Washington.* Vol. 1. Boulder, Colo.: Westview Press, 1977.

Brandon, Henry. *Anatomy of Error: The Secret History of the Vietnam War.* London: Andre Deutsch, 1970.

Brodie, Bernard. *War and Politics.* New York: Macmillan, 1973.

Bui Diem, with David Chanoff. *In the Jaws of History.* Boston: Houghton Mifflin, 1987.

Buttinger, Joseph. *Vietnam: A Dragon Embattled:* Vol. 1, *From Colonialism to the Vietminh;* Vol. 2, *Vietnam at War.* New York: Praeger, 1967.

Charlton, Michael, and Anthony Moncrieff. *Many Reasons Why: The American Involvement in Vietnam.* New York: Hill and Wang, 1978.

Clark, Keith C., and Laurence J. Legere. *The President and the Management of National Security.* New York: Praeger, 1969.

Clarke, Jeffrey J. *The Final Years.* Washington, D.C.: Center for Military History, 1988.

Clodfelter, Mark. *The Limits of Airpower.* New York: Free Press, 1989.

Colby, William. *Lost Victory.* Chicago: Contemporary Books, 1989.

Colby, William, and Peter Forbath. *Honorable Men: My Life in the CIA.* New York: Simon and Schuster, 1978.

Cooper, Chester L. *The Lost Crusade: America in Vietnam.* New York: Dodd, Mead, 1970.

Epstein, Edward Jay. *News from Nowhere.* New York: Random House, 1973.

Esper, George, and the Associated Press. *The Eyewitness History of the Vietnam War, 1961–1975*. New York: Villard Books, 1983.

Fallaci, Oriana. *Interview with History*. Boston: Houghton Mifflin, 1976.

Fitzgerald, Frances. *Fire in the Lake: The Vietnamese and the Americans in Vietnam*. Boston: Little, Brown, 1972.

Gavin, James M. *War and Peace in the Space Age*. New York: Harper, 1958.

Gelb, Leslie, and Richard Betts. *The Irony of Vietnam: The System Worked*. Washington, D.C.: Brookings, 1979.

Vo Nguyen Giap. *People's War, People's Army: The Viet Cong Insurrection Manual for Underdeveloped Countries*. New York: Praeger, 1964.

Gibbons, William. *The U.S. Government and the Vietnam War, Part II, 1961–1964*. 3 vols. Princeton, N.J.: Princeton University Press, 1986–89.

Goulding, Phil G. *Confirm or Deny*. New York: Harper & Row, 1970.

Graff, Henry. *The Tuesday Cabinet: Deliberation and Decision on Peace and War Under Lyndon B. Johnson*. Englewood Cliffs, N.J.: Prentice-Hall, 1970.

Halberstam, David. *The Making of a Quagmire*. New York: Random House, 1965.

———. *The Best and the Brightest*. New York: Random House, 1972.

Hammer, Ellen J. *The Struggle for Indochina*. Stanford, Calif.: Stanford University Press, 1954.

Herr, Michael. *Dispatches*. New York: Alfred A. Knopf, 1977.

Hewes, James E., Jr. *From Root to McNamara: Army Organization and Administration, 1900–1963*. Washington, D.C.: Center for Military History, 1975.

Hilsman, Roger. *To Move a Nation*. New York: Doubleday, 1967.

Hoopes, Townsend. *The Limits of Intervention: An Inside Account of How the Johnson Policy of Escalation in Vietnam Was Reversed*. New York: David McKay, 1969.

Isaacson, Walter, and Evan Thomas. *The Wise Men*. New York: Simon and Schuster, 1986.

Johnson, Lyndon Baines. *The Vantage Point: Perspectives of the Presidency, 1963–1969*. New York: Holt, Rinehart and Winston, 1971.

Just, Ward. *Military Men*. New York: Alfred A. Knopf, 1970.

Karnow, Stanley. *Vietnam: A History*. New York: Viking, 1983.

Kattenburg, Paul M. *The Vietnam Trauma in American Foreign Policy*. New Brunswick, N.J.: Transaction, 1980.

Kaufmann, William W. *The McNamara Strategy*. New York: Harper & Row, 1964.

Kearns, Doris. *Lyndon Johnson and the American Dream*. New York: Harper & Row, 1976.

Kinnard, Douglas. *The War Managers*. Hanover, N.H.: University Press of New England, 1977.

————. *The Secretary of Defense*. Lexington, Ky.: University Press of Kentucky, 1980.

————. *President Eisenhower and Strategy Management*. McLean, Va.: Brassey's (US), 1989.

Kissinger, Henry. *White House Years*. Boston: Little, Brown, 1979.

Knightley, Phillip. *The First Casualty: From the Crimea to Vietnam—The War Correspondent as Hero, Propagandist, and Myth Maker*. New York: Harcourt Brace Jovanovich, 1975.

Kolko, Gabriel. *Anatomy of a War: Vietnam, the United States, and the Modern Historical Experience*. New York: Pantheon, 1986.

Komer, R.W. *Bureaucracy Does Its Thing: Institutional Constraints on U.S.-G.V.N. Performance in Vietnam*. Santa Monica, Calif.: Rand Corp., 1972.

Korb, Lawrence J. *The Joint Chiefs of Staff: The First Twenty-five Years*. Bloomington: Indiana University Press, 1976.

Krepinevich, Andrew F., Jr. *The Army and Vietnam*. Baltimore: The Johns Hopkins University Press, 1986.

Nguyen Cao Ky. *Twenty Years and Twenty Days*. New York: Stein and Day, 1976.

Lacouture, Jean. *Vietnam: Between Two Truces*. New York: Random House, 1966.

LaFeber, Walter. *America, Russia and the Cold War, 1945–1975*. New York: Wiley, 1976.

Lansdale, Edward Geary. *In the Midst of Wars: An American Mission to Southeast Asia*. New York: Harper & Row, 1972.

Lodge, Henry Cabot. *The Storm Has Many Eyes: A Personal Narrative*. New York: W.W. Norton, 1973.

Lyon, Peter. *Eisenhower: Portrait of the Hero*. Boston: Little, Brown, 1974.

McNamara, Robert S. *The Essence of Security: Reflections in Office*. New York: Harper & Row, 1968.

Mecklin, John. *Mission in Torment: An Intimate Account of the U.S. Role in Vietnam*. New York: Doubleday, 1965.

Mueller, John E. *War Presidents and Public Opinion*. New York: University Press of America, 1985.

Mylander, Maureen. *The Generals*. New York: Dial Press, 1974.

Nixon, Richard. *The Memoirs of Richard Nixon*. New York: Grosset & Dunlap, 1978.

————. *No More Vietnams*. New York: Arbor House, 1985.

Oberdorfer, Don. *Tet!* New York: Doubleday, 1971.

O'Neill, Robert J. *General Giap*. New York: Praeger, 1969.

Patti, Archimedes L.A. *Why Viet Nam?* Berkeley: University of California Press, 1980.

Perry, Mark. *Four Stars*. New York: Houghton Mifflin, 1989.

Pfeffer, Richard M. *No More Vietnams?* New York: Harper & Row, 1968.

Pike, Douglas. *Viet Cong*. Cambridge, Mass.: M.I.T. Press, 1966.

———. *Vietnam and the Soviet Union*. Boulder, Colo.: Westview Press, 1987.

Rostow, W.W. *The Diffusion of Power*. New York: Macmillan, 1972.

Rusk, Richard. *As I Saw It*. New York: W.W. Norton, 1990.

Schandler, Herbert Y. *The Unmaking of a President: Lyndon Johnson and Vietnam*. Princeton, N.J.: Princeton University Press, 1977.

Schilling, Warner R., Paul Y. Hammond, and Glen H. Snyder. *Strategy, Politics, and Defense Budgets*. New York: Columbia University Press, 1962.

Schlesinger, Arthur M., Jr. *A Thousand Days*. Boston: Houghton Mifflin, 1965.

Shaplen, Robert. *The Lost Revolution*. New York: Harper & Row, 1965.

———. *The Road from War: Vietnam 1965–1971*. New York: Harper & Row, 1971.

Sheehan, Neil. *A Bright Shining Lie*. New York: Random House, 1988.

Small, Melvin. *Johnson, Nixon and the Doves*. New Brunswick, N.J.: Rutgers University Press, 1988.

Smith, R.B. *An International History of the Vietnam War*. 2 vols. New York: St. Martin's Press, 1983–85.

Pham Von Son, ed. *The Viet Cong "Tet" Offensive (1968)*. Saigon: Printing and Publications Center (A.G./Joint General Staff) RVNAF, 1969.

Sorensen, Theodore C. *Kennedy*. New York: Harper & Row, 1965.

Spector, Ronald H. *Advice and Support: The Early Years*. Washington, D.C.: Center for Military History, 1983.

Stanton, Shelby L. *The Rise and Fall of an American Army: U.S. Ground Forces in Vietnam 1965–1973*. Novato, Calif.: Presidio Press, 1985.

Truong Nhu Tang. *A Vietcong Memoir*. New York: Harcourt Brace Jovanovich, 1985.

Taylor, John. *General Maxwell Taylor*. New York: Doubleday, 1989.

Taylor, Maxwell D. *Precarious Security*. New York: W.W. Norton, 1976.

———. *Swords and Plowshares*. New York: W.W. Norton, 1972.

———. *The Uncertain Trumpet*. New York: Harper, 1959.

Thompson, James Clay. *Rolling Thunder*. Chapel Hill: University Press of North Carolina, 1980.

Trewhitt, Henry L. *McNamara*. New York: Harper & Row, 1971.

Sun-Tzu, *The Art of War*. Samuel B. Griffith, translator. New York: Oxford University Press, 1963.

Walt, Lewis W. *Strange War, Strange Strategy: A General's Report on Vietnam*. New York: Funk & Wagnalls, 1970.

Westmoreland, William C. *A Soldier Reports*. New York: Doubleday, 1976.

———, and U.S. Grant Sharp. *Report on the War in Vietnam*. Washington, D.C.: U.S. Government Printing Office, 1969.

D. NEWSPAPERS AND ARTICLES

The *New York Times Index* was examined for relevant entries from May 1918, when Taylor entered West Point, through 1980.

Articles by and about Taylor are numerous, and most are contained in his papers at NDUL by year *1932* (2), *1939* (2), *1944* (1), *1946* (1), *1949* (2), *1951* (1), *1952* (2), *1953* (8), *1954* (2), *1955* (18), *1956* (15), *1957* (9), *1958* (9), *1959* (9), *1960* (2), *1961* (12), *1962* (11), *1963* (5), *1964* (20), *1965* (7), *1966* (9), *1967* (7), *1968* (1), *1969* (1), *1970* (1), *1971* (2), *1972* (2), *1973* (1). In addition, numerous op-ed articles by Taylor, not systematically filed, in the *Washington Post,* generally from the mid-1970s through the mid-1980s.

Index

WEST HILLS COLLEGE
LEMOORE LIBRARY/LRC

The Author

Douglas Kinnard graduated from West Point in 1944. He was in combat during World War II in Europe, as well as during the Korean War and two tours in Vietnam. The third general in his West Point class, he retired in 1970 to pursue an academic career and joined the Princeton department of politics, from which he received a Ph.D. in 1973. Most of his teaching career has been at the University of Vermont, from which he is professor emeritus. He is now on the faculty of the National Defense University, Washington, D.C. This book is his fifth.

LEMOORE STACKS
31965000066719
959.7043 KINN

DATE DUE

GAYLORD | | PRINTED IN U.S.A.

WEST HILLS COLLEGE
LEMOORE LIBRARY/LRC